Fed
Contracting
Made Easy

2nd edition

Federal Contracting Made Easy

2nd edition

Scott A. Stanberry

MANAGEMENTCONCEPTS

MANAGEMENTCONCEPTS

8230 Leesburg Pike, Suite 800
Vienna, VA 22182
(703) 790-9595
Fax: (703) 790-1371
www.managementconcepts.com

Printed in the United States of America

Library of Congress Cataloging-in-Publication Data

Stanberry, Scott A.
    Federal contracting made easy / Scott A. Stanberry.—2nd ed.
        p. cm.
    Includes index.
    ISBN 1-56726-150-7—ISBN 1-56726-158-2 (pbk.)
    1. Public contracts—United States. 2. Government purchasing—Law and legislation—United States. I. Title.

KF850.S73 2004
346.7302'3—dc22   2004042634

BERRY'S WORLD cartoons reprinted by permission of Newspaper Enterprise Association, Inc.

Glasbergen cartoons reprinted by permission of Randy Glasbergen.

About the Author

Scott A. Stanberry has been working with government contractors since 1992. He specializes in providing auditing and accounting services for commercial clients with federal government contracts and in assisting government agencies in the administration of federal contracts. Scott is a certified public accountant and is highly experienced in the application and interpretation of the Federal Acquisition Regulation.

The tragedy of life is not that it ends so soon,
but that we wait so long to begin it.

—Richard L. Evans

When the first edition of this book was published, a family friend jokingly referred to the words in the title, *Federal Contracting* and *Easy*, as an oxymoron. We all know what an oxymoron is: two or more words strung together that seem to contradict one another, like "jumbo shrimp." Even the immortal William Shakespeare used an oxymoron when he wrote, "Parting is such sweet sorrow."

As demonstrated in the first edition, I do not believe that *Federal Contracting* and *Easy* need to be an oxymoron. This updated edition expands on my philosophy.

Best wishes and happy contracting!

Scott Stanberry
July 2004

Contents at a Glance

Table of Contents

Part 3: How to Find Government Contracting Opportunities

Part 4: How the Government Issues Procurement Opportunities

Preface

© 1999 Randy Glasbergen.
www.glasbergen.com

SUZY'S LEMONADE INC.

GLASBERGEN

**"I can offer you a great benefits package:
liberal use of the company bike, paid nap time,
free cootie insurance, and a pension at age 10."**

Did you ever run a lemonade stand as a kid? Ever sit by the side of the road for hour after hour in the hot sun, waiting for someone—the mailman, the obnoxious neighbor kid, anyone—to walk by? Or maybe, as you got older, you decided to open a bicycle repair shop in your garage, dreaming of owning a bicycle empire, only to find that your business was still essentially sitting by the side of the road, waiting for customers?

That's the story of thousands of businesses that fail each year: a good idea or product, but no knowledge of how to run a business or attract customers.

This book was written to help you attract and make the most of the biggest customer of all: the U.S. government. The federal government spends more than $200 billion on supplies and services each year. Look at it this way: Every 20 seconds of every working day, the federal government awards a contract with an average value of $465,000. That's a lot of lemonade! What's more, every major federal agency and department is required by law to provide free assistance to businesses interested in bidding on federal work. So whether you're an entrepreneur interested in breaking into the federal market, or a mid- to large-sized company seeking to maximize your use of (and financial return on) subcontractors, this book tells you what you need to know.

What's the downside to government business? Marketing to the federal government is like trying to learn the rules to your kid's video games. The characters all have incomprehensible names, some players seem to have secret powers, and any second, somebody can throw a bomb that completely knocks you off the screen. How can you win if you're not the 11-year-old king of the arcade with a never-ending roll of quarters and the insider knowledge that comes from devoting yourself to the game 16 hours a day?

That's why I've written this book: to help you decode all the confusing rules, get to know the other players, understand the obstacles thrown in your path, and maybe even acquire some secret powers of your own. This book spells out everything you need to know to succeed in the federal marketplace—from the people who oversee the contracting process, to the regulations that govern contracting, to the types of contracts that are awarded. You'll get the inside scoop on government contracting—all from one source. You don't have to go to the library or wait on terminal hold for the right government employee to promise to send you the right publication.

All you need to know is inside this book and you can refer to these pages again and again, as your business grows and you go after greater government opportunities. And while much of this book deals with small business programs and services, it also contains a substantial amount of information that applies to all types of companies. Even if you or your staff are familiar with some pieces of the federal contracting puzzle, there may be areas where you could use some explanation or insight. Of particular interest to current contractors, this book offers specific suggestions on how mid- to large-sized companies can take advantage of some of those small business programs through subcontracting—something virtually every government contractor too big to qualify as a small business does on a regular basis. In short, if you're currently working for a business (large or small) or thinking of starting your own, this book is for you!

One word of caution: Government regulations and procedures do not make for keep-you-up-all-night, can't-put-it-down reading. Wading through some of this information may take patience and persistence but, just like that 11-year-old who suffers through hours of frustration to learn the video game, you'll find rewards at the end of the process. You can make good money—even big money—doing business with the federal government. Contracting with the government can make you king of the arcade and give you the biggest lemonade stand on the block!

PART

1

What Is Federal Government Contracting?

If you can dream it, you can do it.

—Walt Disney

How Does Federal Government Contracting Work?

What's in this chapter?

- The big picture
- Top buyers
- Future of federal contracting
- Can you sell to the federal government?
- Should you sell to the federal government?

Our federal government (a.k.a. Uncle Sam) uses a specific process to acquire the supplies and services needed to run its operations or fulfill its mission requirements. It enters into contracts with American citizens like you to acquire supplies and services needed to support government programs and services. Each year (actually, fiscal year, which begins on October 1 and ends on September 30), the federal government spends billions of dollars buying from nonfederal sources, or "commercial contractors."

Generally we only hear about government purchases for multimillion-dollar aircraft or those famous $1,000 toilet seats and $500 hammers. But are you aware that there are currently over 300,000 government contractors, receiving more than $200 billion worth of contracts each year—$40 billion of which goes to small businesses? In addition, the government either initiates or modifies over 350,000 contracts each year, two-thirds of which it grants to contractors outside the Washington, D.C., area. The key to sharing in these contracting opportunities is to understand how the federal government does business. This chapter describes what federal government contracting is all about.

THE BIG PICTURE

The United States government is by far the largest consumer of supplies and services in the world. No other nation, or corporation for that matter, can begin to match its purchasing power. In fact, every 20 seconds of each working day, the federal government awards a contract with an average value of $465,000.

The government purchases every type of supply and service, ranging from high-technology—like homeland security programs, missiles, ships, aircraft, vehicles, and telecommunication systems—to more mundane items like office furniture, repair and maintenance services, shoes, computers, food, janitorial services, video equipment, paper, hand tools, carpeting, accounting services, and real estate. You name it and the government probably buys it! And the government must tell us what, from where, and from whom it buys its products and services.

Because the government's needs vary, from those that individuals and small, singly owned enterprises can provide to those requiring the resources of large corporations, everyone has a potential share. In fact, it is no exaggeration to suggest that a small business can probably provide a service or create a product for nearly every federal agency. Furthermore, a business can supply the government with its products or services from wherever it customarily operates. In other words, contractors are not restricted to selling to federal agencies in their communities. For example, a contractor in Memphis, Tennessee, can supply the Naval Surface Warfare Center in Dahlgren, Virginia, just as easily as a contractor operating from Dahlgren. Anyone looking for more customers or thinking about starting a new business should consider the federal government as a prospect.

The federal government also has a policy of giving small business concerns maximum practical opportunities to participate in federal contracting. (See Chapter 4 of this book for information on what constitutes a small business in the eyes of the government.) The government offers a variety of programs and services that assist small businesses in doing just that, including credit assistance, procurement opportunities, technical assistance, management assistance, and grants. These programs and services have created and sustained thousands of small business firms, generating many millions of jobs in the process. As a result, many of these small businesses have grown into large businesses.

I have personally seen firms go from zero to $50 million or more in federal business in less than five years. No other industry provides more opportunities for small businesses than government contracting. Yet only one percent of the 22 million small businesses in the United States participates in federal contracting.

Why doesn't everyone contract with the government? Contracting with the government can be cumbersome, with its regulations, rules, laws, bureaucracy, and red tape. The primary purpose of these detailed rules and regulations is to ensure that the government spends public funds— our tax dollars—wisely. To be successful as a government contractor, you must understand these rules and regulations (see Chapter 2).

Although government contractors use many of the same business practices as commercial contractors, a number of characteristics clearly differentiate the two. To begin with, the federal government operates in a
market termed "monopsonistic," one in which there is only one buyer
and many sellers or suppliers. As a result of its sovereignty, the government has certain unusual powers and immunities that differ significantly from those of more typical buyers. For example, congressional mandate, rather than state law, controls federal policy.

Significant differences include:

Government Contracting	Commercial Contracting
General:	
Federal policy establishes formal competition criteria for purchases or procurements.	Company determines competition criteria.
Congress appropriates all available funds.	Many sources provide funds.
Laws, directives, policies, and procedural regulations define procurement actions.	Company determines procurement actions within legal boundaries.
Profit Margins:	
The government may negotiate a separate profit/fee.	Contractor builds profit into "total price."
The government may apply profit ceilings to certain contracts. (Profit/fee on federal contracts rarely exceeds 6%.)	Contractors rarely use profit ceilings. (Profit/fee on commercial contracts is often as high as 10–20% of the total contract price.)
Contract Clauses:	
Federal contracts contain extensive clauses, many of which are "take-it-or-leave-it."	Standard commercial code and those clauses agreed to by the parties regulate performance.

Contract Termination:

The government may terminate a contract for failure to make progress.	Termination is normally not available to commercial contractors.
The government may terminate a contract for its convenience.	Commercial regulations (such as the Uniform Commercial Code) ensure adequate performance.

Social and Economic Policies (such as a policy requiring contractors to maintain a drug-free workplace):

Federal contracts must incorporate these policies.	Social pressures typically dictate company policies; however, some polices are required by law.
The government may use incentive contracts.	Commercial contractors rarely use incentive contracts.
Federal law prohibits gratuities (e.g., tips).	Company policy determines gratuities.
The government may penalize contractors for noncompliance.	Penalties are illegal in commercial contracts.

Government business varies vastly, depending on the product or service you're selling. For example, selling copiers has little in common with selling jet engines. In addition, contracting with the Department of Defense (DOD) differs from contracting with civilian federal agencies. You need to determine which federal agencies purchase your supplies and services and what solicitation procedures those agencies use to acquire them. Part III of this book touches on a number of methods for soliciting and marketing to the various federal agencies.

It is not so much that doing business with the federal government is difficult; it's just different. Instead of selling directly to decision makers, as in the private (or commercial) world, government contractors must patiently wade through the government procurement process, which makes the sale more complex and longer to complete. If you learn the system and are patient and persistent, you can make good—even big— money doing business with the federal government.

Uncle Sam Can Be a Tough Sell; Small Tech Firms Seeking Government Contracts Won't Find It Easy

Ellen McCarthy, Washington Post

John D. Cohen figured in 1988 that he could make a business of helping state and local governments buy technology systems. With almost two decades of law enforcement and security experience on his résumé, Cohen thought he had the contacts that would help him succeed.

"One of the things that makes us different is that we understand the way government operates," said Cohen, who has been a senior investigator for the House Judiciary Committee and an adviser to the White House drug control policy director. "We selectively targeted people we knew were progressive in the way they thought about government. We wanted to work with the chiefs, work with the leadership, not get stuck in that mid-management level."

Last year his company, PSComm LLC, broke even. This year, the 46-employee firm expects to earn about $ 300,000 on $5 million in revenue, the first year since 1999 that it has earned a profit, said Cohen, the company's president and CEO.

PSComm appears to be on its way to becoming a success story among the growing wave of companies trying to cash in on government technology spending. But others may not be so fortunate.

Like former dot-com employees flocking to the stability of old-economy industries, many small technology firms are looking to Uncle Sam to increase their revenue streams. Seminars and workshops that aim to teach local entrepreneurs how to break into the government contracting industry have been jamming business calendars in the Washington region, particularly in the past nine months. And some of the seminars themselves have been jammed.

The Northern Virginia Technology Council's first procurement seminar on Nov. 1, for example, was attended by 750 people, prompting the organization to continue the series. Since then, the series has attracted an average of 175 to 200 people at a time, about 25 percent more than other seminars.

Although there is no doubt that contracting opportunities exist for small companies — many federal agencies allot certain portions of their budgets for small businesses — industry experts say some firms are much better positioned than others to cash in.

"It all depends, and it depends on the company's approach to the market. It's one thing to have a very small start-up with interesting technology, but if they don't know how to approach the market, it's going to be tough," said Ray Bjorklund, vice president of consulting services at Federal Sources Inc. "They can try to walk into a government office and say, 'I've got this great product you need,' and they may meet an engineer on the other side of the door that is enamored with it, but that doesn't mean the agency is going to buy."

Kevin Plexico, executive vice president at Input, a market research firm, said companies that don't have long-standing government connections, as PSComm does, will often need to establish relationships with bigger contractors rather than try to sell directly to the government.

"It can be a difficult hill to climb when you're just getting started," Plexico said. "And you're at a disadvantage in the market if you don't have those relationships."

That's a sentiment with which Rob Daly, co-founder and president of Number Six Software Inc. of Rosslyn, would agree. He said the changing commercial climate and his company's proximity to government agencies prompted an increased focus on the federal sector. The 50-person firm has landed some subcontracts, but Daly said government sales presented different challenges than commercial sales.

"The hardest thing is just getting people to know you're there. I don't know if we're just exploring the wrong avenues, but to compensate for that we're partnering with other companies," said Daly.

Cigital Inc., a 70-person Dulles firm that provides software security products, also began targeting the federal government after Sept. 11. Jeffery Payne, chief executive, said the company began to focus more on government clients because commercial spending had slowed and federal security needs seemed to be increasing.

Payne said that selling to the government is more difficult than selling to other industries because of the structured procurement procedures and the length of time it can take for a contract to be completed.

"There are going to be a lot of very unhappy people who try to sell to the federal government and have no success. You don't just show up and have the government hand you money," Payne said. "It's like expanding into a foreign country. You have to find people who live there, people [who] know the culture, understand the way it works."

Bjorklund said firms that specialize in a certain field are going to be much more attractive than those that try to sell general information technology consulting services.

"If there is a domain-savvy or technology-savvy kind of company that knows how to really do a job in a special way, that methodology may be something that the government is interested in," Bjorklund said.

While competition has increased, market researcher Plexico said he believes there is still potential for small companies with innovative technologies to be successful in the federal marketplace. The challenge for each company is to set itself apart from the rest.

"There is a lot of noise. Everybody is showing up saying that they've got the solutions for every agency's problems," said Payne. "It's kind of like the noise in the dot-com days, when you didn't know who was real and who wasn't."

June 14, 2002

TOP BUYERS

During FY2002, the federal government purchased $250 billion worth of supplies and services. The following table shows the major federal agencies and categories in federal procurement.

Federal Agency	FY2002 Expenditures ($ billion)
Department of Defense	
Air Force	$ 43.0
Navy	$ 41.5
Army	$ 39.5
Defense Logistics Agency (DLA)	$ 13.1
Other DOD	$ 17.3
Non-Defense (Civilian)	
Department of Energy (DOE)	$ 19.0
General Services Administration (GSA)	$ 12.4
National Aeronautics and Space Administration (NASA)	$ 11.5
Department of Health and Human Services (HHS)	$ 5.4
Department of Veterans Affairs (VA)	$ 4.6
Department of Justice (DOJ)	$ 4.1
Department of Transportation (DOT)	$ 3.5
Department of Agriculture (DOA)	$ 3.4
Department of Treasury (USTREAS)	$ 3.3
Department of Interior (DOI)	$ 2.2
Other Civilian	$ 11.0
By Product or Service Category	
Supplies and equipment	$ 84.3
Other services	$ 78.9
Research and development (R&D)	$ 31.3
Construction	$ 17.5
ADP equipment and services	$ 16.7
Real property-purchase/lease	$ 3.2
Architect-engineering	$ 3.0

The value of federal contracts awarded, by state (top 10) during FY2002, in billions of dollars, is as follows:

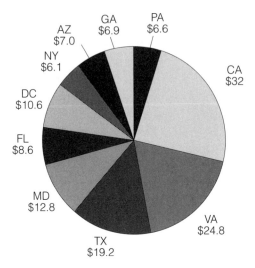

For more details on government purchases, see www.FPDS.gov.

FUTURE OF FEDERAL CONTRACTING

You hear it more and more every day: The federal government is too big and bureaucratic. Both Republicans and Democrats are pushing for a smaller bureaucracy, with all but the most essential government functions (such as national security) being contracted out to private industry. In fact, Congress is currently working on legislation that would force all federal agencies to downsize or eliminate functions that compete with the private sector.

Current projections estimate that the number of nonpostal government employees will shrink from 1.9 million to 500,000 within the next dozen years. These jobs will not go away; they will be contracted out to private industry. The belief is that the competitive forces of the commercial marketplace will produce better supplies or services at cheaper prices. There has never been a better time to look for contracting opportunities with the federal government.

CAN YOU SELL TO THE FEDERAL GOVERNMENT?

To be eligible for federal contracts, contractors must furnish proof that they are both "responsive" (usually in reference to a specific proposal) and "responsible," that they comply with many of the government's socioeconomic goals, and that they offer prices that are fair and reasonable. In general, the government requires the following information from a potential contractor:

- Is the contractor eligible, under existing laws and regulations, to do business with the government?

- Does the contractor have adequate financial resources to do the job?

- Does the contractor have a good performance record?

- Does the contractor's record demonstrate ethics and integrity?

- Does the contractor have the necessary skills to perform the job, or can it acquire them?

- Does the contractor have the necessary facilities and production capacity to deliver its products or services?

- Can the contractor meet the performance schedule (or delivery schedule), given other commitments?

The government uses this information and documentation to determine if potential contractors are eligible for federal contracts.

SHOULD YOU SELL TO THE FEDERAL GOVERNMENT?

Once you understand the contracting process, the next step is to decide whether you should sell your supplies or services to the federal government.

Advantages

There are tremendous advantages to working with the federal government:

■ The government purchases practically every type of supply and service.

■ The government currently has more than 2,500 buying offices (or "contracting activities") located throughout the United States.

■ Each major federal agency and department must provide free assistance to contractors.

■ In some cases, the government provides financial assistance, such as progress payments (payments made to a contractor based on a percentage of costs incurred by the contractor as work progresses under the contract). The government, more specifically, the Small Business Administration (SBA), will also arrange or guarantee loans to contractors to ensure their ability to perform the requirements of the contract.

■ The government has "preference programs" to encourage small business participation in federal contracting.

■ During FY2004, the government had an annual budget of more than $2.2 trillion.

■ The government mandates "full and open competition." In other words, a contractor can compete for federal contracts without having to belong to an exclusive club.

■ Generally, contractors do not need a massive product distribution system or a substantial advertising budget.

■ Numerous regulations governing federal contracting ensure fair play by both the government and the contractor. (These regulations do, however, create a certain amount of red tape.)

■ If you perform the work required by the contract, you will get paid. Checks cut by the federal government never bounce.

■ Federal programs often lead to business with other federal agencies as well as state and local governments. If you do business with the General Services Administration (GSA), for example, you often will get additional business with other agencies and departments.

■ Many government contracts run for a base year with up to seven option years. So if you live up to expectations you can expect to get your contract renewed.

■ Average government orders (or contracts) tend to be larger than commercial orders—$10 to $100 million is not uncommon.

■ Government business may complement your commercial business. For example, it is common for contractors to sell a product to the government and then sell additional versions of the product to government vendors who are required (or choose) to be compatible with its requirements.

■ In spite of legal changes in recent years, the government awards about 45 to 50% of its contracts to sole-source providers. A sole-source award is a contract that a federal agency awards after soliciting and negotiating with only one source. Therefore, contractors may be able to locate and bid on federal contracts that have limited competition.

■ Contracting with the government is patriotic.

With all these advantages, what businessperson wouldn't want to contract with the government? But as with any type of business, there are disadvantages to working with the government.

Disadvantages

The disadvantages of contracting with the government include:

■ Government red tape can produce volumes of paperwork. For example, contractors must fill out numerous federal forms, and even not knowing which one to do next, or to whom to send it, can be a major obstacle to your success. The best way to keep current with these federal forms is to use the General Services Administration's website at:

WWW.GSA.GOV/forms/

This book will also help you untangle the red tape.

■ To be successful in government contracting, you must learn how the government operates. This includes learning the clauses, terms, conditions, proper terminology, and methodology.

■ Once you sign a federal contract, you are locked into performing according to the terms of that contract. (The only exception is for a contract under $25,000, which may be canceled by a contractor at any time before performance begins.)

■ The requirements and specifications for government contracts tend to be much more stringent than for commercial contracts.

■ For many contracts, the government requires a company to establish a detailed quality control program (see Chapter 17 for contractor inspection requirements).

■ Government contracting can be very competitive—and seemingly unfair if competitors have established a personal relationship with that particular procurement office.

■ Certain common practices in commercial business are illegal in government contracting, such as entertaining federal personnel and helping the government define its needs. (See Chapter 15.)

■ Your company personnel may be unfamiliar with federal contracting regulations.

These disadvantages are not intended to discourage you from seeking to do business with the government. On the contrary, if prospective contractors can become aware of and obtain the necessary information before embarking on government business, the chances of success—in terms of both profit and efficiency—are greatly enhanced. If you can avoid learning through trial and error, everyone comes out ahead!

■   ■   ■

This book will help you learn how to do business with the federal government and take advantage of the business opportunities the government offers. The decision to plow through the red tape and jump through the government's hoops is up to you.

■   ■   ■

2 The Rules of the Game

Berry's World

Bureaucrat studying
a foreign language

What's in this chapter?

- Constitutional authority
- Congressional responsibilities
- Central Contractor Registration
- Federal Acquisition Regulation
- Federal Acquisition Streamlining Act
- Cost Accounting Standards
- Defense Contract Audit Agency
- General Accounting Office
- Federal Acquisition Reform Act
- Competition in Contracting Act
- Walsh-Healey Public Contracts Act
- Buy American Act
- Truth in Negotiations Act
- Service Contract Act
- Freedom of Information Act

Understanding the opportunities the federal government has to offer is one thing; it is quite another to understand the federal contracting rules and regulations. This can be quite an intimidating task because these rules and regulations are extremely difficult to understand. A contractor would find navigation through the government's market almost impossible without a reasonable level of knowledge about its requirements. And, while the government doesn't intend to put anyone out of business, it nevertheless expects a contractor to know and understand the technical and administrative requirements of the signed contract.

In other words, the government will not rescue a company from the consequences of a bad business decision. In addition, the government will unsympathetically penalize a company for violating a procurement regulation or failing to fulfill a contractual term or condition as a result of ignorance or misinterpretation of the requirements. Far too many contractors watch their profits on a government contract drastically shrink or totally disappear because they overlooked, misunderstood, or just plain ignored the applicable regulations. This chapter will guide you through the maze of federal contracting regulations and offer suggestions on how to handle these rules and regulations.

CONSTITUTIONAL AUTHORITY

The U.S. Constitution gives the federal government the legal authority to enter into contracts with private citizens and nongovernment organizations. This is the case even though the Constitution does not contain any language that specifically authorizes such actions. The authority derives from a statement in the Preamble that says that the federal government shall "provide for the common defense, promote the general welfare, and secure the blessings of liberty."

For a contract to become the legal obligation of the federal government, however, the contract must be based on statutory authority. In fact, the federal government may actually avoid liability for a contract that is unsupported by a legally enacted provision.

CONGRESSIONAL RESPONSIBILITIES

The U.S. Congress is responsible for passing the laws that regulate federal contracting. Currently, more than 4,000 of those laws are in effect. In addition, numerous bills pending in Congress could affect how the government exercises its contracting functions.

Congress is also responsible for drafting and passing the laws and statutes that establish the various federal agencies and the specific programs proposed by those federal agencies. These laws and statutes are called "authorization acts."

Congress derives its powers from Article I, Section 8, of the Constitution—General Powers of Congress, which states that Congress shall:

1. . . . lay and collect taxes, duties, imports and excises, to pay the debts and provide for the common defense and general welfare of the United States;

12. . . . raise and support Armies;

13. . . . provide and maintain a Navy;

14. . . . make rules for the government and regulation of the land and naval forces;

18. . . . make all laws which shall be necessary and proper for carrying into execution the foregoing powers, and all other powers vested by the Constitution in the Government of the United States, or in any Department or Officer thereof.

Why are these regulations so confusing? Is the government trying to hide something from us? I keep thinking about a political advertisement I saw a while back that said "there's got to be something in the water" over there in Washington, D.C. The government is notorious for binding its affairs with red tape, and federal contracting regulations certainly entail their fair share.

Well, believe it or not, these regulations are complicated for a reason, and it's not because the government is hiding something. Although the Constitution gives the federal government the power to contract for supplies and services, it also mandates that "no money shall be drawn from the Treasury, but in Consequence of Appropriations made by law. . . ." Therefore, the government can only purchase those supplies and services that Congress votes to fund. Sounds simple enough.

However, in approving funds, Congress often places restrictions and conditions on the money for various programs and socioeconomic goals. It's those restrictions and conditions that create many of the contradictions, exceptions, and loopholes in the contracting regulations. For example, suppose a senator includes a new code of contractor ethics in an agency or appropriations bill. If Congress approves this appropriations bill and the President signs it, the regulation becomes applicable to all future agency bills. Regulation writers, therefore, must prepare a new regulation that accurately reflects this change.

Congress also passes laws that affect government contracts. If Congress passes a law that restricts the purchase of products from Iraq, regulation writers must write a regulation to reflect this law. The gradual pile-up of these laws and restrictions over the years has created a contracting process that is convoluted, confusing, and inefficient.

Funding Requirements

Congress supports each federal agency and its programs by putting into law an appropriations act. The appropriations act provides the funds with which that federal agency functions. Congress derives the authority to enact appropriations acts from Article I, Section 9, of the Constitution, which states, "no money shall be drawn from the Treasury, but in consequence of appropriations made by law. . . ." This basically means that Congress must approve any funds used to purchase supplies or services.

Each appropriations act specifies the time period for which the funds are available for use by the agency. The appropriation can be for a single year, for multiple years, or unrestricted. Most appropriations are awarded for a single year. This approach requires federal agencies to return annually to Congress to justify the budgets for their operations and programs. Multiple-year appropriations generally apply to major multiple-year programs and projects, such as research and development projects. Federal agencies prefer multiple-year appropriations because they tend to provide significant savings to both the government and contractors. However, for the savings to be realistic, the multiyear program requirements must remain stable and predictable, and the requesting agency must ask for enough money to carry out the contract. Once Congress approves the funds, they are available for use by the federal agencies.

Budget Process

The budget process is long and tedious. Each fiscal year (October 1 to September 30), federal agencies are required to submit budgets to Congress detailing their operation costs for the upcoming year. The preparation of these proposed budgets usually takes federal agencies several years to complete. Once a federal agency completes its budget, it submits that budget to the President through the Office of Management and Budget (OMB). OMB holds hearings on the proposed budget and makes recommendations to the federal agency. Upon agreement between the parties, OMB passes the budget on to Congress.

Once Congress receives the proposed budget, it is forwarded to the Congressional Budget Office (CBO) and the individual budget committees for in-depth review. During this review process, the CBO and the committees within Congress set targets and ceilings for the various federal functions or programs. The budget is then dissected by the CBO and sent to various House and Senate authorization and appropriation committees. These committees and their subcommittees hold hearings on the proposed programs and draft legislation.

This draft legislation then moves on to the House and Senate for debate and approval. Only after both legislative bodies approve the final budget is it returned to the President for signature. If this process is not completed by the start of the government's fiscal year (October 1), the agency is in jeopardy of being shut down because of inadequate funding.

CENTRAL CONTRACTOR REGISTRATION

The Central Contractor Registration (CCR) is a central database and application suite, managed by the Defense Logistics Agency (DLA), that records, validates, and distributes specific data about government and commercial trading partners (or contractors). All prospective federal contractors must be registered in the CCR before the government awards any contract, basic agreement, basic ordering agreement, or blanket purchase agreement. Contractors are required to register in the database only once, with subsequent annual updates or renewals.

The CCR:

■ Provides worldwide visibility of sources to government buyers and finance officers to streamline contract awards and payments.

■ Increases efficiency and lowers costs by simplifying and streamlining the procurement process.

■ Allows trading partners (or contractors) to avoid registering with multiple procurement offices.

■ Reduces errors and saves time by creating an accurate record of data, or a trading partner profile (TPP), for each business. (A TPP is information about a company that wants to do business with the government.)

■ Provides banking information to the Defense Finance and Accounting Service (DFAS), which enables trading partners to be paid via electronic funds transfer. (Electronic funds transfer is the method of forwarding and receiving payments electronically using routing numbers that include bank identification and checking account information.)

To register for the CCR, you must contact Dun & Bradstreet to obtain a DUNS (Data Universal Numbering System) number, which is a unique, nine-character company identification number. For assistance contact:

Dun & Bradstreet
103 JFK Parkway
Short Hills, NJ 07078
Phone (800) 234-3867

WWW.DNB.COM

After getting your DUNS number, you will need the following information to register:

■ Taxpayer identification number or Social Security number.

■ Legal business name.

■ Business address.

■ Corporate status.

■ North American Industry Classification System (NAICS) codes (see Chapter 4).

■ Banking and electronic funds transfer information.

■ CAGE code: A Commercial and Government Entity (CAGE) code is a five-character (alphanumeric) identifier automatically generated by the Defense Logistics Information Service (DLIS) after your registration information has been entered into the CCR. If you already have a CAGE code, DLIS will validate it during this process; a new one will not be generated. To find your current CAGE code, call DLIS at (888) 352-9333. The CAGE code supports a variety of mechanized systems throughout the government, such as those for a facility clearance, a pre-award survey, automated bidders lists, pay processes, and supply sources. Some prime contractors may require their subcontractors to have CAGE codes.

To register on CCR (you must have your DUNS number to register), visit the following website:

WWW.CCR.GOV

CCR standardizes the method by which contractors register to do business with the federal government. Contractors must ensure the accuracy of their data and are the only ones authorized to change their data. The government uses the CCR data internally to expedite information exchange among various federal agencies looking for business sources.

FEDERAL ACQUISITION REGULATION

The Federal Acquisition Regulation (FAR) is the body of regulations governing federal acquisitions. It contains uniform policies and procedures governing acquisitions (including acquisitions for services and construction), whether the government obtains these through purchase or lease and regardless of whether the supplies or services already exist or whether they must be developed. In laymen's terms, the FAR contains "the rules of the game." Each federal agency is required to adhere to rules of the FAR when acquiring supplies and services with congressionally appropriated funds.

The FAR is jointly issued and maintained by the General Services Administration (GSA), the Department of Defense (DOD), and the National Aeronautics and Space Administration (NASA). Currently, the FAR includes more than 1,600 pages divided into 53 parts, each dealing with a separate aspect of the procurement process. If you plan to contract with the federal government, the FAR will serve as your "bible."

FAR Numbering System

Each of the 53 parts of the FAR addresses a separate aspect of procurement. The first six parts address general contracting matters, and the next six address acquisition planning. Part 13 describes simplified acqui-

sition procedures (see Chapter 10), and Parts 14 through 17 address procurement procedures for contracts over $100,000 (see Part IV). Parts 19
through 26 include procedures and regulations affecting small and small
disadvantaged businesses (see Chapter 5). The remaining sections address
such matters as labor laws, contract cost principles, contract administration, and standard clauses. The FAR also contains sample forms.

Each part is further subdivided into sections and paragraphs according to
the numbering system shown below.

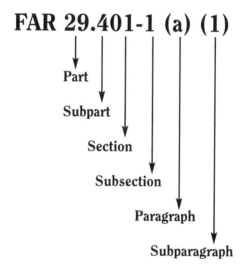

As an example, here's the current outline for Part 29:

PART 29   **TAXES**

SUBPART 29.4   **CONTRACT CLAUSES**

29.401   **DOMESTIC CONTRACTS**

29.401-1   **Indefinite-delivery contracts for leased equipment.**

29.401-2   **Construction contracts performed in North Carolina.**

29.401-3   **Federal, State, and local taxes.**

29.401-4   **New Mexico gross receipts and compensating tax.**

PART 6—COMPETITION REQUIREMENTS

[¶ 29,700]

6.000 Scope of part.

This part prescribes policies and procedures to promote full and open competition in the acquisition process and to provide for full and open competition, full and open competition after exclusion of sources, other than full and open competition, and competition advocates. As used in this part, full and open competition is the process by which all responsible offerors are allowed to compete. This part does not deal with the results of competition (e.g., adequate price competition), which are addressed in other parts (e.g., Part 15). [FAC 84-5, 50 FR 1729, 1/11/85, effective 4/1/85]

[¶ 29,701]

6.001 Applicability.

This part applies to all acquisitions except—

(a) Contracts awarded using the simplified acquisition procedures of part 13 (but see 13.501 for requirements pertaining to sole source acquisitions of commercial items under subpart 13.5);

(b) Contracts awarded using contracting procedures (other than those addressed in this part) that are expressly authorized by statute;

(c) Contract modifications, including the exercise of priced options that were evaluated as part of the initial competition (see 17.207(f)), that are within the scope and under the terms of an existing contract;

(d) Orders placed under requirements contracts or definite-quantity contracts;

(e) Orders placed under indefinite-quantity contracts that were entered into pursuant to this part when—

(1) The contract was awarded under Subpart 6.1 or 6.2 and all responsible sources were realistically permitted to compete for the requirements contained in the order; or

(2) The contract was awarded under Subpart 6.3 and the required justification and approval adequately covers the requirements contained in the order; or

(f) Orders placed against task order and delivery order contracts entered into pursuant to subpart 16.5. [FAC 84-5, 50 FR 1729, 1/11/85, effective 4/1/85; FAC 84-13, 50 FR 52431, 12/23/85, effective 2/3/86; FAC 90-3, 55 FR 52790, 12/21/90, effective 1/22/91; FAC 90-29, 60 FR 34732, 7/3/95, effective 7/3/95; FAC 90-33, 60 FR 49706, 9/26/95, effective 10/1/95; FAC 90-45, Final rule, 62 FR 224, 1/2/97, effective 1/1/97, corrected 62 FR 10709, 3/10/97; FAC 97-3, 62 FR 64912, 12/9/97, effective 2/9/98]

[¶ 29,702]

6.002 Limitations.

No agency shall contract for supplies or services from another agency for the purpose of avoiding the requirements of this part. [FAC 84-5, 50 FR 1729, 1/11/85, effective 4/1/85]

[¶ 29,703]

6.003 Definitions.

"Full and open competition," when used with respect to a contract action, means that all responsible sources are permitted to compete.

"Procuring activity," as used in this part, means a component of an executive agency having a significant acquisition function and designated as such by the head of the agency. Unless agency regulations specify otherwise, the term "procuring activity" shall be synonymous with "contracting activity" as defined in Subpart 2.1.

"Sole source acquisition" means a contract for the purchase of supplies or services that is entered into or proposed to be entered into by an agency after soliciting and negotiating with only one source.

"Unique and innovative concept," when used relative to an unsolicited research proposal, means that, in the opinion and to the knowledge of the Government evaluator, the meritorious proposal is the product of original thinking submitted in confidence by one source; contains new novel or changed concepts, approaches, or methods; was not submitted previously by another; and, is not otherwise available within the Federal Gov-

Sample Page of Federal Acquisition Regulation

Suppose you want to locate information on time-and-materials contracts. The first step is to determine which part of the FAR would likely contain this information.

Federal Acquisition Regulation
by Part

Part 1 Federal Acquisition Regulation System
Part 2 Definitions of Words and Terms
Part 3 Improper Business Practices
Part 4 Administrative Matters
Part 5 Publicizing Contract Action
Part 6 Competition Requirements
Part 7 Acquisition Planning
Part 8 Required Sources of Supplies/Services
Part 9 Contractor Qualifications
Part 10 Market Research
Part 11 Describing Agency Needs
Part 12 Acquisition of Commercial Items
Part 13 Simplified Acquisition Procedures
Part 14 Sealed Bidding
Part 15 Contracting by Negotiation
Part 16 Types of Contracts
Part 17 Special Contracting Methods
Part 18 [Reserved]
Part 19 Small Business Programs
Part 20 [Reserved]
Part 21 [Reserved]
Part 22 Labor Laws to Acquisitions
Part 23 Occupational Safety
Part 24 Privacy Protection
Part 25 Foreign Acquisition
Part 26 Other Socioeconomic Programs
Part 27 Patents, Data, and Copyrights
Part 28 Bonds and Insurance
Part 29 Taxes
Part 30 Cost Accounting Standards
Part 31 Contract Cost Principles
Part 32 Contract Financing
Part 33 Protests, Disputes, and Appeals
Part 34 Major System Acquisition

Part 35 R&D Contracting
Part 36 Construction Contracts
Part 37 Service Contracting
Part 38 Federal Supply Schedules
Part 39 Acquisition Resources
Part 40 [Reserved]
Part 41 Acquisition of Utility Services
Part 42 Contract Administration
Part 43 Contract Modifications
Part 44 Subcontracting Policies
Part 45 Government Property
Part 46 Quality Assurance
Part 47 Transportation
Part 48 Value Engineering
Part 49 Termination of Contracts
Part 50 Extraordinary Contractual Actions
Part 51 Use of Government Sources
Part 52 Solicitation Provisions/Contract Clauses
Part 53 Forms

After examining this list, the best place to start would be Part 16—Types
of Contracts. The next step would be to examine the subparts within this
part. Part 16 currently consists of the following subparts:

Subpart 16.1 Selecting Contract Types
Subpart 16.2 Fixed-Price Contracts
Subpart 16.3 Cost-Reimbursement Contracts
Subpart 16.4 Incentive Contracts
Subpart 16.5 Indefinite-Delivery Contracts
Subpart 16.6 Time-and-Materials, Labor-Hour, and Letter Contracts
Subpart 16.7 Agreements

In this example, the most obvious choice would be Subpart 16.6. Finally,
go to Section 16.601 to find the required information. Once you get the
hang of this numbering system, you will be able locate information in the
FAR easily.

Federal Acquisition Circulars

Amendments or changes to the FAR are issued in Federal Acquisition Circulars (FACs). GSA, DOD, and NASA are responsible for issuing these circulars. In laymen's terms, FACs are updates to the FAR. These changes are typically the result of congressional actions or presidential orders. FACs are published daily in the *Federal Register*. (The *Federal Register* is a daily newspaper issued by the government to inform the public of congressional and federal enactments.) Each FAC is issued sequentially, using the following numbering system:

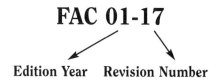

FAC 01-17

Edition Year   Revision Number

The first two digits in the FAC identify the FAR edition. This particular FAC amends the 2001 edition of the FAR. The final two digits in the FAC represent the revision number. This is the 17th revision to the 2001 edition of the FAR. (FAC 01-17 revises the definition of contract bundling to expressly include multiple award contract vehicles.) The best way to keep current with these FACs is to access the FAR at:

WWW.ARNET.GOV/far

Agency Supplements

Each federal agency is authorized by Congress to issue its own supplement to the FAR. These supplements contain policies and procedures that apply only to that particular agency. For example, the Department of Defense FAR Supplement (DFARS) provides contracting personnel detailed procedures for acquiring military-specific items or equipment. The rules and regulations included in these supplements cannot contradict FAR provisions; they can only provide additional guidance for dealing with a particular agency.

A federal agency can deviate from the FAR only by a congressional order. For instance, the FAA was permitted to deviate from the FAR for the purpose of creating a simplified Acquisition Management System (AMS) to help speed up its acquisition process.

Currently more than 20 federal agencies issue supplements to the FAR. These supplements include:

■ Department of Defense FAR Supplement (DFARS)

■ Department of Health and Human Services Acquisition Regulation (HHSAR)

■ Department of Agriculture Acquisition Regulation (AGAR)

■ General Services Administration Acquisition Regulation (GSAR)

■ Agency for International Development FAR Supplement (AIDAR)

■ Veterans Administration FAR Supplement (VAAR)

■ Department of Energy Acquisition Regulation (DEAR)

■ Department of Transportation Acquisition Regulation (TAR)

■ Department of Commerce Acquisition Regulation (CAR).

You can find a complete listing of these supplements in Title 48 of the Code of Federal Regulations (CFR). The CFR is available online at:

WWW.GPOACCESS.GOV/cfr/index.html

Potential contractors must follow the rules of the FAR or risk being eliminated from consideration. Although some contractors feel that the FAR does not allow enough latitude, contracting officers must adhere to the regulations protecting the expenditure of public funds. Contractors should always have a current copy of the FAR. However, because the FAR is updated throughout the year, you need to ensure that your copy remains current. The best way to obtain and maintain a current version of the FAR (including each agency's FAR supplements) is to get a FAR subscription from:

Superintendent of Documents
Government Printing Office
Washington, DC 20402-9371
Phone (202) 512-1800

The FAR is also available online at:

WWW.ARNET.GOV/far

FEDERAL ACQUISITION STREAMLINING ACT

Congress enacted the Federal Acquisition Streamlining Act (FASA) of 1994 to simplify and streamline the federal acquisition process. It was passed in response to calls for government downsizing and the recognition that red tape had caused the acquisition process to become convoluted and inefficient. FASA directs federal agencies to maximize the use of commercial buying practices, as opposed to government-specific buying practices. By using commercial buying practices, the contracting parties are able to avoid federal specifications and standards, which tend to prolong the procurement process and create red tape.

For example, if a contracting activity in DOD wants to purchase an all-terrain boot, it must seek commercial sources before issuing a solicitation for a military-specific boot. FASA also requires the government to accept the terms and conditions offered in the private sector, unless the government can negotiate better terms and conditions through commitment guarantees, purchasing compliance, or volume purchases.

Other significant provisions of FASA include:

■ A requirement that contracts between $2,500 and $100,000 must be reserved for small businesses or individuals, unless a contracting officer cannot obtain at least two offers with competitive market prices.

(More than 90% of annual federal procurement transactions are under $100,000.)

■ A micropurchase threshold of $2,500 (see Chapter 10). Purchases that are valued at less than the micropurchase threshold are not subject to the small business set-aside requirements or the Buy American Act, and the government can purchase these goods and services without obtaining competitive quotations, if the prices are reasonable.

■ A requirement for prompt notice of award. For invitations for bids (IFBs) and requests for proposals (RFPs), federal agencies must notify losing offerors in writing, within three days of award (see Part IV).

COST ACCOUNTING STANDARDS

Cost accounting standards (CAS) are accounting policies that contractors and subcontractors are required to abide by on selected large-dollar value contracts. (The FAR specifies exemptions for commercial companies not doing large dollar volume business.) The purpose of these standards is to provide uniformity and consistency in estimating, accumulating, and reporting costs in connection with the pricing and administration of negotiated procurements (see Part V). Cost accounting standards are established by the Cost Accounting Standards Board (CASB) and incorporated in Part 30 of the FAR.

By following cost accounting procedures, contractors are able to keep track of costs that apply to each contract or major task they undertake. This is not the same as financial accounting, which is the accumulation of information that enables contractors to know how much total cost they incur and profit they make during a particular period of time. Financial accounting alone does not tell a contractor what each individual job costs and the profit or loss on that particular job. (See the Appendix of the FAR for a complete listing of the cost accounting standards.)

DEFENSE CONTRACT AUDIT AGENCY

The Defense Contract Audit Agency (DCAA) performs contract audit functions required by DOD and many civilian agencies. These audits generally include the examination of records, documents, and other data relating to claimed performance costs; cost and pricing data used to support contract pricing; and any cost, funding, or performance reports required under the contract. Virtually all federal contracts are subject to audit; however, because audits require significant time and expense to perform, they are typically not used for small purchases (under $100,000) or contracts awarded under sealed bidding procedures (see Chapters 10 and 11).

Currently, DCAA consists of approximately 4,000 people located at more than 300 field audit offices throughout the United States and Europe. In addition to performing contract audits, DCAA assists federal agencies in reviewing and evaluating:

■ Contractor efficiency

■ Contractor internal control systems

■ Contractor accounting system suitability

■ Contractor performance.

DCAA is probably the best known and most influential (or feared) of the government audit agencies because of its reputation for being an aggressive defender of the taxpayers' money. DCAA's website is:

WWW.DCAA.MIL

GENERAL ACCOUNTING OFFICE

The General Accounting Office (GAO) is the investigative arm of Congress. GAO has broad authority to oversee federal programs and operations and to review government contracts to ensure that appropriated funds are spent in accordance with the laws enacted by Congress. In addition, GAO gets involved with:

■ Contract award disputes or protests

■ Defective cost and pricing data

■ Investigations requested by a member of Congress

■ Compliance issues surrounding cost accounting standards

■ Fraud allegations.

GAO's findings and recommendations are published as reports to congressional members or delivered as testimony to congressional committees. GAO's website is:

WWW.GAO.GOV

FEDERAL ACQUISITION REFORM ACT

The Federal Acquisition Reform Act (FARA) of 1996 (also called the Clinger-Cohen Act) expands on the Federal Acquisition Streamlining Act of 1994. FARA reinforces the commercial buying preference and limits the number of regulatory FAR clauses that apply to simplified acquisitions (see Chapter 4). In addition, this act significantly changed protest and claim procedures by expanding the use of alternative dispute resolution (ADR) for disagreements between the government and private industry. Protests are written objections by interested parties to a solicitation, proposed award, or award of a contract (see Chapter 12). ADR simplifies and expedites methods to resolve disputes (see Chapter 17).

COMPETITION IN CONTRACTING ACT

The Competition in Contracting Act (CICA) of 1984 is the basic law governing contract formation. It explicitly requires the government to use "full and open competition" in purchasing supplies and services. This means that all responsible sources must be allowed an opportunity to compete for government contracts. Government procurement officials (or contracting officers) do not have the luxury of buying from sources based on past good business relations.

In addition, procurement officials cannot restrict their sources to suppliers known for quality products and on-time delivery. This regulation is in marked contrast to the selection criteria of commercial and private sector businesses, which return to favorite vendors repeatedly rather than risk disappointment by using a vendor with which they have no business experience.

CICA specifies seven exceptions to the "full and open competition" requirement. These exceptions come into play if:

■ Only one responsible source (or vendor) is available, and no other supplies or services will satisfy the agency's requirements.

■ An unusual and compelling urgency (such as a war) exists.

■ Vital supplies or facilities are needed for national emergencies.

■ An international agreement between the United States and a foreign government regulates the conditions of a contract.

■ A statutory requirement (such as the Small Business Act) calls for an exception.

■ Disclosure of the government's needs would threaten national security.

■ The contracting officer determines that "full and open competition" contradicts the public's best interest.

In addition, the government does not need to obtain full and open competition for purchases under the simplified acquisition threshold (SAT). The SAT refers to the $100,000 limit applied to simplified acquisition procedures (see Chapter 10). Different rules on competition also apply for small businesses eligible to participate in the 8(a) program (see Chapter 5).

WALSH-HEALEY PUBLIC CONTRACTS ACT

To qualify for a federal contract for materials, supplies, articles, and equipment exceeding $10,000, a contractor must comply with the Walsh-Healey Public Contracts Act. This law requires the government to purchase or procure such items from either a "manufacturer" or a "regular dealer":

■ A manufacturer is a company that owns, operates, or maintains a factory or similar establishment that produces materials, supplies, articles, or equipment.

■ A regular dealer is a company that owns, operates, or maintains a store, warehouse, or other type of establishment in which it regularly maintains a stock of materials, supplies, articles, or equipment.

This law is designed to prevent "bid brokering," which is the practice of buying items and then reselling them to the government without the reseller adding value to the items. For example, if a contractor purchased a surveillance camera from another contractor, it would not be eligible to resell the camera to the government, unless the contractor adds value to it or the contractor is a regular dealer of surveillance equipment.

Contracts for the following items are exempt from this act:

■ Agricultural or farm products, including dairy, livestock, and nursery products

■ Public utility services

■ Supplies manufactured outside the United States, Puerto Rico, or the Virgin Islands

■ Newspapers, magazines, or periodicals

■ Any item authorized by the express language of a statute.

An agency head may also ask the Secretary of Labor to exempt specific contracts or classes of contracts from the inclusion or application of one or more of the act's stipulations.

BUY AMERICAN ACT

The Buy American Act of 1933 requires the federal government to buy domestic articles, materials, and supplies for public use. An article, material, or supply is considered domestic if:

■ It is an unmanufactured end product mined or produced in the United States.

■ It is an end product that is manufactured in the United States (i.e., if the costs of its components mined, produced, or manufactured in the United States exceed 50% of the cost of its components).

The primary purpose of this act is to discourage the government from buying foreign products. However, there are five exceptions to the Buy American Act:

■ Items to be used outside the United States.

■ Domestic items that are unreasonably priced. (Unless an agency determines otherwise, the offered price of a domestic item is considered unreasonable when the lowest acceptable domestic offer exceeds the lowest acceptable foreign offer by more than 6% if the domestic offer is from a large business, or more than 12% if the domestic offer is from a small business.)

■ Situations in which compliance with the Buy American Act would not be in the government's best interest.

■ Items that are not mined, produced, or manufactured in the United States in sufficient and reasonably available commercial quantities.

■ Items purchased specifically for commissary resale.

The Buy American Act does not apply to purchases under the micropurchase threshold of $2,500.

DOD and NASA have determined that it is inconsistent with the public interest to apply the restrictions of the Buy American Act to their acquisitions of certain supplies mined, produced, or manufactured in certain foreign countries. Detailed procedures for implementing these determinations are delineated in specific agencies' FAR supplements.

TRUTH IN NEGOTIATIONS ACT

The Truth in Negotiations Act (TINA) was enacted by Congress to protect the government from unscrupulous contractors who falsify their cost proposals with erroneous information. TINA requires contractors and subcontractors to submit cost or pricing data to support their proposals (see Part IV). Cost and pricing data include information and facts available to the contractor as of the date of agreement on the contract price. These facts should include information that prudent buyers and sellers would reasonably expect to affect price negotiations. TINA does not apply to competitive procurements or noncompetitive procurements under $550,000 (unless the contracting officer determines that it is necessary).

As a contractor, you must provide factual (not judgmental or subjective) cost and pricing data, and you must be able to support those data. Cost and pricing data are more than historical accounting data; they are the facts and information that reasonably can be expected to contribute to the soundness of estimates of future costs and to the validity of determinations of costs already incurred. Examples of cost and pricing data include:

- Vendor quotations

- Unit cost trends

- Information on management decisions that could have a bearing on costs (such as changes in production methods)

- Lease or buy decisions

- Data supporting projections of business prospects and objectives and related operational costs

- Estimated resources to attain business goals.

The requirements of TINA generally apply to contracts for amounts greater than $550,000. However, the contracting officer may require cost and pricing data for negotiated contract actions that are more than $100,000. You are exempt from providing cost and pricing data if:

- The cost or pricing data are at or below the simplified acquisition threshold (see Chapter 10)

- The contracting officer determines that the agreed-upon prices are based on adequate price competition

- The contracting officer determines that prices agreed upon are based on prices set by law or regulation

- A contract or subcontract for commercial items is being acquired

- A waiver has been granted.

The head of a contracting activity may, without the power of delegation, waive the requirement for submission of cost and pricing data in exceptional cases. The authorization for the waiver and the supporting rationale must be in writing. For example, if a contractor furnished cost or pricing data on previous production buys and the head of the contracting activity determines that such data are sufficient when combined with updated information, the contracting officer may grant a waiver.

If a contract is subject to TINA, the contractor and subcontractor must also certify, to the best of their knowledge and belief, that the data provided are current, accurate, and complete. If the cost and pricing data are not certified, the government can institute a defective pricing claim and the contract can be reduced. If the defective pricing claim was willful, severe civil and criminal penalties may be imposed. Many contracts require the following certification:

Certificate of Current Cost or Pricing Data

This is to certify that, to the best of my knowledge and belief, the cost or pricing data (as defined in section 15.801 of the Federal Acquisition Regulation [FAR] and required under FAR subsection 15.804-2) submitted, either actually or by specific identification in writing, to the contracting officer or to the contracting officer's representative in support of [Identify the proposal, quotation, request for price adjustment, or other submission involved, giving the appropriate identifying number (e.g., Solicitation No._____)] are accurate, complete, and current as of _____. This certification includes the cost or pricing data supporting any advance agreements and forward pricing rate agreements between the offeror and the government that are part of the proposal.

SERVICE CONTRACT ACT

The Service Contract Act (SCA) was enacted in 1965 to ensure that government contractors compensate their employees fairly and properly. It generally applies to federal contracts and subcontracts for services (performed in the United States) that are over $2,500. These service contracts must contain mandatory provisions regarding minimum wages and fringe benefits, safe and sanitary working conditions, notification to employees of the minimum allowable compensation, and equivalent employee classifications and wage rates.

The following types of services are generally covered by the SCA:

■ Parking, taxicab, and ambulance services

■ Packing and storage

■ Janitorial, housekeeping, and guard services

■ Food service and lodging

■ Laundry services

■ Repair and maintenance services

■ Data collection, processing, and analysis services.

The SCA does not apply to:

■ Contracts for construction or repair of public buildings, including painting and decorating

■ Contracts subject to the Walsh-Healey Public Contracts Act

■ Contracts for transporting freight or personnel

■ Contracts subject to the Communications Act of 1934 (radio, telephone, cable, etc.)

■ Contracts for public utility services

■ Any employment contract providing for direct services to a federal agency by an individual or individuals

■ Contracts for operating postal contract stations for the U.S. Postal Service.

The U.S. Department of Labor defines the prevailing wage rates and fringe benefits by locality. The minimum wage requirement is specified in the Fair

Labor Standards Act. All federal contracts are subject to this minimum wage. For more information on the Service Contract Act, see FAR 22.10.

FREEDOM OF INFORMATION ACT

The Freedom of Information Act (FOIA) is less a regulation to follow than it is an opportunity for contractors to get valuable information. Contractors are encouraged to use FOIA when they conduct market research. FOIA is particularly useful in obtaining information on federal agency buying trends and past contractual data. Even competitor proposals can be obtained under FOIA.

FOIA was enacted into law on July 4, 1967, to give the public access to information that the federal government assembled, created, and maintained. This act significantly changed the government's information disclosure policy. Before the enactment of FOIA, the individual bore the burden to establish the right to examine government records or documents. No statutory guidelines or procedures existed to help individuals seeking federal information. In addition, no remedies (judicial or otherwise) were available for those denied access.

With the passage of FOIA, the burden of proof shifted from the individual to the government. The "right to know" doctrine replaced the "need to know" standard. Therefore, individuals who seek federal information no longer must show a need for the requested information. The government must now justify the need for secrecy. FOIA further requires federal agencies to provide the fullest possible disclosure of information to the public, and it provides administrative and judicial remedies for individuals who are unjustly denied access to federal records.

FOIA applies to documents or records held by federal agencies in the government's executive branch. The executive branch includes cabinet departments, military departments, government corporations, government-controlled corporations, and independent regulatory agencies. FOIA does not apply to federally elected officials, including the President, Vice President, senators, and members of Congress.

Each federal agency must have FOIA request and response procedures. All changes to established agency regulations must be published in the *Federal Register*. Any citizen may request any record in the possession of a federal agency that is not exempt under the provisions of FOIA. These exemptions include:

■ Matters specifically required by executive order to be kept secret in the interest of national defense or foreign policy

■ Matters related solely to the internal personnel rules and practices of a federal agency

■ Matters specifically exempt from disclosure by statute

■ Trade secrets and commercial or financial information received by the government in confidence

■ Internal memoranda related to the decision-making process of the federal agency

■ Personnel or medical files

■ Investigative records compiled for law enforcement purposes

■ Examination, operation, or condition reports prepared by a federal agency responsible for the regulation or supervision of financial institutions

■ Geological data and information (such as maps).

In addition to these exemptions, there are other, common sense, reasons for which the government would reject a FOIA request, such as the agency does not hold the requested record or the requested record does not exist. In general, however, if you request information that does not fall under one of the exemptions listed above, you are entitled to it. Potential contractors should have no reservations about referencing FOIA for fear of being blackballed; negotiation with FOIA is an accepted part of the procurement process. Actually exhibiting an understanding of FOIA indicates a contractor's knowledge of the contracting process.

The first step in making a request under FOIA is to identify the federal agency that has the information. If you are unsure which agency has the information you seek, consult a government directory, such as the United States Government Manual. This manual (available through the Government Printing Office at 202-512-1800) lists all federal agencies, a description of their functions, and their addresses.

Each federal agency must institute FOIA implementation procedures or instructions. These procedures are contained in their respective FAR supplements. In addition, each federal agency has a FOIA officer, whose function is to ensure that vendors (or contractors) obtain the legitimate information they seek. The best way to get in touch with an agency FOIA center or officer is to contact the Federal Information Center at:

WWW.INFO.GOV

If you prefer, you can call the Federal Information Center at: (800) FED-INFO.

Your FOIA request should be in writing and addressed to the agency's FOIA officer. If you plan to mail your FOIA request, be sure to mark the envelope "Freedom of Information Act Request" on the bottom left-hand corner to expedite the process. In your letter, identify the documents or records you need and state that your request is being made under the Freedom of Information Act.

When you make a request under FOIA, try to be as precise as possible. If you don't know the title of the document, describe what you seek as accurately as possible. For example, a prospective contractor might say, "I would like the names of those small businesses that were awarded contracts within the past six months for 5 x 12 white envelopes." Put your telephone number on your request, so the agency employee can call you with questions about the requested information.

Sample FOIA Request

Date

FOIA Officer
Name of Agency
Address

RE: Freedom of Information Act Request

Dear [Name of FOIA Officer]:

XYZ Corporation is hereby requesting under the Freedom of Information Act a copy of the winning technical proposal for Solicitation No._____. In addition, please forward the following information:

- Incumbent's name and address;
- Contract number; and
- Subsequent contract amendments.

If you deny all or any part of this request, please cite each specific exemption you think justifies your refusal to release the information and notify me of appeal procedures available under the law. In addition, if there are any fees ([optional] greater than $30) for copying or searching for the records, please let me know before you fill my request.

As prescribed under 5 U.S.C. Section 552, XYZ Corporation anticipates response within 10 working days upon receipt of this request. Portions of this request may be forwarded as you locate the documents; a complete package does not have to be forwarded at once.

If you have any questions please feel free to call me at (800) 867-5309. Thank you for your cooperation.

Sincerely,

Joe Smith
President

Federal agencies typically charge you for the costs associated with obtaining and reproducing the FOIA information (usually between $10 to $30). If you request a small amount of information that is easy to obtain, the agency may provide it for free. Federal agencies must respond to a FOIA request within 10 working days of receiving it. If an agency needs more time, it must acknowledge receipt of the request within 10 days and attempt to fulfill the request within 10 additional working days. The total response time of a federal agency should not exceed 20 working days.

Any FOIA request denial may be appealed to the U.S. District Court. Keep in mind that government records are public property and you have the right to this public information. For more detailed information on the Freedom of Information Act, obtain a publication called *Your Right to Federal Records* by calling the Consumer Information Center at (888) 878-3256.

■   ■   ■

The government needs extensive rules and regulations because of its dual role in the marketplace. The government's contracting capacity establishes it as a vast business organization, purchasing a wide variety of supplies and services from every segment of the private sector. At the same time, it is a political entity that must establish policies and procedures that not only represent good business judgment but also are fair to all concerned.

The government constantly balances these concerns as it establishes procurement policies and processes. However, a contractor should not look at these unique requirements as insurmountable barriers to the economically rewarding experience of doing business with the government. Just keep in mind that the government can be a good customer only when a contractor understands the rules and regulations as well as the specific actions that are required.

■   ■   ■

The Key Players

3

© 1999 Randy Glasbergen.

"I'm paid $4,000,000 a year. You're paid $40,000. The only difference is a few zeros. Everyone knows that zero equals nothing. So what's the problem?"

What's in this chapter?

- Head of agency
- Contracting officer
- Competition advocates
- Small business specialists
- Requirements personnel

With the federal government having more than 1.9 million (nonpostal) employees and more than 2,500 contracting activities (or buying offices) located throughout the United States, it is essential for a contractor to be familiar with its "key players." This chapter lists many of the government's key players and describes their main functions.

HEAD OF AGENCY

The head of agency (or agency head) has the responsibility and authority to contract for supplies and services needed to run an agency's mission requirements. The agency head also establishes "contracting activities" and delegates the duties of these activities to authorized representatives. An authorized representative is any person or persons (other than the contracting officer) authorized to manage an agency's contracting functions.

Each agency head (or designee) must establish and maintain a procurement career management program and a system for selecting, appointing, and terminating contracting officers. The contracting officer is the only federal employee authorized to bind the government to a contract over $2,500. These selections and appointments must be consistent with the Office of Federal Procurement Policy's standards for skill-based training in performing contracting and purchasing duties.

In selecting a contracting officer, the appointing official considers the complexity and dollar value of the acquisitions to be assigned and the candidate's experience, training, education, business acumen, judgment, character, and reputation. For example, the appointing official will want to know if the candidate has:

■ Experience in government contracting and administration, commercial purchasing, or related fields

■ Education or special training in business administration, law, accounting, engineering, or related fields

■ Knowledge of acquisition policies and procedures

■ Specialized knowledge in the particular assigned field of contracting

■ Satisfactory completion of the acquisition training courses.

CONTRACTING OFFICER

A contracting officer (CO) enters into, administers, or terminates contracts and makes related determinations and findings. The contracting officer is the only person who can bind the government to a contract that is greater than $2,500. Further, the contracting officer's name and agency/department must be typed, stamped, or printed on the contract. There are currently more than 28,000 contracting officers in the government (three-quarters of whom work at the Defense Department).

A contracting officer is issued a Certificate of Appointment, Standard Form 1402, when he or she is appointed by the head of agency. This certificate is also referred to as a "warrant." Each Certificate of Appointment identifies the contracting officer, the federal agency for which he or she works, and any limitations on his or her authority. A contracting officer may bind the government only to the extent of the authority delegated to him or her. For example, the Certificate of Appointment might limit a contracting officer's purchasing authority to supplies and services that are less than $200,000. If you have any doubts about a contracting officer's authority, ask to see his or her warrant.

Contracting officers ensure performance of all necessary actions for effective contracting, ensure compliance with the terms of the contract, and safeguard the interests of the United States in its contractual relationships. If the contracting officer is unable to ensure that all requirements of law, executive orders, regulations, and all other applicable procedures, including clearances and approvals, have been met, he or she is prohibited from executing the contract. For example, the contracting officer ensures that:

■ Sufficient funds are available for the obligation

■ The price paid by the government is "fair and reasonable"

Certificate of Appointment

Under authority vested in the undersigned and in conformance with Subpart 1.6 of the Federal Acquisition Regulation

Scott Stanberry

is appointed

Contracting Officer

for the

United States of America

Subject to the limitations contained in the Federal Acquisition Regulation and to the following:

Unless sooner terminated, this appointment is effective as long as the appointee is assigned to:

Contracts Division
(Organization)
General Services Administration
(Agency/Department)

_____
(Signature and Title)
Head of Contracting Activity

10/15/06
(Date)

GSA-115
(No.)

STANDARD FORM 1402 (10-83)
Prescribed by GSA
FAR (48 CFR). 53.201-1

NSN7540-01-152-5815
1402-101

Sample Certificate of Appointment

■ The contractor receives impartial, fair, and equitable treatment

■ The contract meets the requirements of the applicable laws and regulations.

Because the contracting officer is the only government official with this authority, he or she is always under intense scrutiny from both contractors and government personnel. The contracting officer often requests the help of specialists in audit, law, engineering, transportation, and other fields when making these determinations. In addition, the contracting officer uses the Federal Acquisition Regulation (FAR) for guidance. The FAR is written specifically for the contracting officer, and it offers hundreds of options to consider.

The term "contracting officer" typically includes other authorized representatives. For example, a termination contracting officer is authorized only to settle terminated contracts. The contracting officer may delegate duties and authority to other authorized representatives or maintain full responsibility for all these areas.

Procurement Contracting Officer

The procuring contracting officer (PCO) is responsible for issuing solicitations, accepting bids, and making the original award of the contract. If you have a problem with a solicitation before award, the PCO is the person to call. By law, the PCO's name and phone number must be on the cover of the solicitation and in the FedBizOpps synopsis. FedBizOpps is the single government point-of-entry on the Internet for federal government procurement opportunities over $25,000 (see Chapter 8).

Administrative Contracting Officer

The contracting officer may delegate administrative responsibility for your contract to the administrative contracting officer (ACO). These administrative functions typically include monitoring the contractor's performance, inspecting and accepting the contractor's supplies and services, and ensuring that the contractor is properly paid.

Administrative contracting officers are stationed around the country to keep a close eye on contractors' performance. This allows the CO to concentrate on awarding new contracts. The CO still has the final authority on issues that have a significant impact on the contract.

Termination Contracting Officer

For companies contracting with the government, the possibility that the contract may be terminated is a fact of life. A contracting activity typically uses a termination contracting officer (TCO) to settle contracts terminated for the government's convenience or because of the contractor's default (see Chapter 17). When this occurs, the TCO follows the uniform policies and procedures on contract terminations in FAR Part 49, Termination of Contracts.

When a contracting officer terminates a contract, the settlement process is turned over to the TCO. The TCO then orders the contractor to stop work on the contract and to submit a settlement proposal (supported by appropriate schedules). A settlement proposal details the proposed charges (or expenses) for work done to date, for which the contractor is seeking reimbursement. The TCO also monitors the contractor during the settlement process to protect the government's interests. If any significant matters come up during this settlement process, the TCO informs the contracting officer.

Once the contractor completes the settlement proposal, the TCO (with the help of government auditors) examines the proposal to verify its accuracy. If the TCO agrees with the settlement proposal, he or she signs the agreement and binds the government. If the TCO and the contractor disagree, however, they negotiate a settlement agreement. The TCO may approve the settlement proposal without the contracting officer's approval.

Contracting Officer's Representative

Most federal agencies allow the contracting officer to appoint a contracting officer's representative (COR). Some agencies refer to this person as the contracting officer's technical representative (COTR). These representatives assist the contracting officer in ensuring that the contractor's performance proceeds in accordance with the terms and conditions of the contract. CORs typically provide technical advice and guidance regarding the contract's specifications and statements of work. They also perform the contract's inspections, acceptance, and quality assurance functions.

The COR also keeps the contracting officer updated on the contract's status or progress. For example, the COR reports to the contracting officer any unusual circumstances involving the contract, such as late deliveries or security violations. The COR also assesses whether the contractor has assigned adequate personnel to perform the contract's requirements.

The contracting officer appoints a COR to a contract or program in writing. This appointment letter must state the COR's duties and authority, along with any limitations placed on that authority. The contracting officer may appoint as many CORs as necessary to adequately perform the requirements of the contract or program. CORs cannot give direction or instructions that exceed their appointment authority. Only the contracting officer handles any changes involving unit cost, total cost or price, quantity, quality, or delivery schedule.

COMPETITION ADVOCATES

The Competition in Contracting Act of 1984 requires each federal agency and procuring activity to appoint a competition advocate, who is responsible for promoting full and open competition. The competition advocate promotes full and open competition by challenging barriers to competition, such as unnecessarily restrictive statements of work, unnecessarily detailed specifications, and unnecessarily burdensome contract clauses.

Competition advocates also review the agency's contracting operations to ensure that all appropriate actions are being taken to encourage competition and the acquisition of commercial items. For example, a competition advocate might examine all purchase transactions expected to exceed $100,000 that a contracting officer proposes to conduct without full and open competition. The competition advocate must report its findings to the contracting agency's senior procurement executive.

The competition advocate is a member of the contracting activity's head (or executive) staff. However, the competition advocate may hold no duties or responsibilities that would conflict with his or her primary responsibilities. To help the competition advocate carry out his or her responsibilities, the contracting activity's head provides him or her a staff and allows him or her to use the contracting activity's specialists in contract administration, technical operation, supply management, and engineering.

Competition advocates are always looking for ways to increase competition. Therefore, if you find that a solicitation contains unnecessary restrictions or limitations, first contact the contracting officer listed on the solicitation and discuss your concerns with him or her. If you are not satisfied with the contracting officer's response, contact the competition advocate.

SMALL BUSINESS SPECIALISTS

Each major federal agency and department has an Office of Small and Disadvantaged Business Utilization, with at least one small business specialist (see Chapter 9). These specialists, also referred to as Small and Disadvantaged Business Utilization Specialists (SADBUS), assist and counsel small businesses on any problems in understanding procurement regulations and practices, determining the appropriate buying offices for their products or services, or acquiring data on current or future procurements.

Small business specialists ensure that their departments or contracting activities award a fair portion of their contracts to small businesses. The Small Business Act of 1953 requires each federal agency to establish goals for contract awards to small businesses. For example, the Department of

Defense currently has an agency goal of awarding 5% of its federal contracts to small businesses owned by women (see Chapter 4). The small business specialist analyzes the contracting activity's actual contract awards to small businesses using these agency goals. These findings are reported to the head of the contracting activity. A small business specialist can also introduce you to the actual customer (or contracting personnel) who will purchase your supplies and services.

Finally, small business specialists review all purchase transactions over the simplified acquisition threshold of $100,000 to determine if they can be performed by a small business. If such purchase transactions are identified, the small business specialist may recommend to the contracting officer that the purchase be "set aside" for small businesses.

Small business specialists are an invaluable resource. For a current list of small and disadvantaged business utilization offices, visit the following website:

WWW.ACQ.OSD.MIL/sadbu/

The Government Printing Office also has a publication called *Small Business Specialists,* which lists the DOD small and disadvantaged business utilization offices by state, including their addresses, telephone numbers, and contacts. For information about this publication, contact:

Superintendent of Documents
Government Printing Office
Washington, DC 20402-9371
(202) 512-1800

REQUIREMENTS PERSONNEL

The government personnel responsible for determining which products and services a federal agency needs to run its operations are referred to as "requirements personnel" or "users," but there is no universal title for these individuals. The following illustration should help clarify which government personnel would be considered requirements personnel.

Each contracting activity in the Defense Advanced Research Projects Agency (DARPA) must submit an annual budget for the supplies and services it will need to run its research projects. DARPA is the central research and development organization for DOD. It manages and directs selected basic and applied research and development projects for DOD.

DARPA requires two separate groups to prepare budget requests. The first group consists of the agency's program managers (or head scientists), who prepare budgets for the supplies and services they will need to run their research projects or programs during the upcoming fiscal year. The second group consists of the agency's logistics managers, who purchase commonly used supplies and services (such as pens, computers, and office furniture). Each logistics manager prepares a budget for the supplies and services that will be needed during the upcoming fiscal year.

These completed budgets are submitted to a contracting officer for approval. Once they are approved, the contracting officer sends the budgets to DARPA's budget office, where they are grouped together with the budgets of other contracting officers to establish the total budget of the contracting activity.

In this example, there are two types of requirements personnel: the program managers (or head scientists) and the logistics managers. If you want to market your supplies or services to DARPA, you need to find out which program or logistics managers typically purchase your supplies or services. The best way to get in touch with a contracting activity's requirements personnel is to have the small business specialist set up an appointment for you.

The government encourages prospective contractors to contact requirements personnel directly because it enables both parties to gain valuable information about the other. First, requirements personnel find out which supplies and services are available to fulfill their needs. Second, the contractor finds out which types of supplies and services the contracting activity typically purchases. However, requirements personnel are prohibited from discussing upcoming solicitations during these exchanges.

Having a meeting with an agency's requirements personnel is a great way to learn about a contracting activity's current and future needs. I can't think of a better way to get a head start on your competition.

■   ■   ■

These key players are not the only government personnel you will run into—just the ones that seem to pop up most frequently. The trick to being a successful contractor is to know who the "key players" are and to focus your attention and efforts on them.

■   ■   ■

PART 2

How Your Business Size Offers Opportunity

I find the harder I work, the more luck I seem to have.

—Thomas Jefferson

By now you know that the federal government has an enormous impact on business. But you may not know that the government provides a variety of programs and services to assist small businesses, including procurement opportunities, technical assistance, management assistance, and financial assistance. In fact, the policy of the United States government is to give small businesses the maximum practical opportunity to participate in federal contracting, and Congress has enacted numerous laws and regulations that promote the participation of small businesses in the federal contracting process.

What's more, mid- to large-sized companies can benefit from these small business programs by providing subcontracting opportunities to businesses that meet the government's criteria on their contracts.

Opportunities for Small Businesses/ Independent Contractors

© 1999 Randy Glasbergen.

"We're the only company in the world that sells organic cookies made with goat urine, but the government isn't trying to break up *our* monopoly."

What's in this chapter?

- Small Business Act
- Governmentwide goals
- North American Industry Classification System
- Size certification
- Small business affiliates
- Certificate of competency
- Small business set-asides

Everyone knows that there is a big size difference between a major corporation like Microsoft and a Mom-and-Pop convenience store on your
street corner. But how do you determine your actual business size? Is
yours a small business and, if so, what happens when your business
grows? When does your business cease to be small? These are very important questions because many of the government's programs and services
are targeted toward small businesses specifically.

Did You Know That . . .

According to the Small Business Administration (see www.sba.gov):

- More than 22.9 million small businesses are operating in the United
  States?

- New business formation reached a record high in 1996?

- Thirty-five percent of federal contracts go to small businesses each
  year?

- During FY2002, the government issued more than $53 billion worth of
  federal contracts to small businesses?

Small businesses . . .

- Create three out of every four new jobs

- Produce 39% of the gross national product

- Represent 99.7% of all employees

- Provide 55% of innovations

- Account for 52% of the private sector output

- Represent 97% of all U.S. exporters

- Account for 39.1% of jobs in high-technology sectors

- Provide 47% of all sales in the country

- Employ 50.1% of the workforce

- Provide 67% of workers with their first jobs.

As you can see, the federal government offers tremendous opportunities for individuals looking to start new businesses or increase the size of their existing businesses. This chapter will help you determine your business size and will discuss some of the advantages of being a small business or independent contractor.

SMALL BUSINESS ACT

In the mid-1900s, the government began to recognize a problem with its procurement process. It seemed that a few large companies dominated some industries almost to the point of monopolization, and smaller companies were unable to compete for federal contracts. As a result, Congress passed the Small Business Act of 1953.

The Small Business Act requires the government to award a "fair proportion" of its federal contracts to small businesses. It also requires the government to provide small and small disadvantaged businesses with the maximum practical opportunity to participate in federal contracting (see Chapter 5). To help ensure that these requirements are met, this act established the Small Business Administration (SBA) to offer financial, technical, and management assistance to small businesses. The agency accomplishes this goal by providing small businesses with a wide variety of programs and services.

GOVERNMENTWIDE GOALS

Congress establishes governmentwide goals for awards of contracts and subcontracts to small businesses. These goals are generally stated as percentages of the procurement dollars spent by the government each year.

Congress established the following governmentwide goals for FY2003: 23% of all federal contracts should go to small businesses, 5% of all federal contracts should go to small "disadvantaged" businesses (SDBs), 5% of all federal contracts should go to small women-owned businesses (WOBs), 3% of all federal contracts should go to small HUBZone businesses, and 3% of all federal contracts should go to small disabled veteran-owned businesses. Federal contract awards to small, disadvantaged, women-owned, HUBZone, and disabled veteran-owned businesses all count toward the 23% goal for all small businesses. (See www.sba.gov for more details.)

SBA negotiates with each federal agency to determine an estimate for contract awards to small businesses. These estimates may be higher or lower than the governmentwide goals, depending on the types of supplies and services purchased by a particular federal agency. For example, a federal agency with a $40 million annual budget might have the following agency goals:

Awards to SDBs: 6% x $40,000,000 = $2,400,000

Awards to small WOBs: 4% x $40,000,000 = $1,600,000

                                                 $4,000,000

Awards to small businesses: 15% x $40,000,000 = $6,000,000

Total small business awards 25% $10,000,000

SBA then compares each agency's estimates against its actual results to determine its success in meeting its goals. Federal agencies pay close attention to these results because they are given to Congress for review. Agency goals provide two primary advantages for small businesses. First, they ensure that each federal agency has plans for awarding federal contracts to small businesses. Second, the goals give federal agencies a baseline against which to measure their progress yearly. If, six months into the year, a federal agency notices that it has awarded only 2% of its contracts to small disadvantaged businesses, government policy mandates that it concentrate in this area over the following six months.

NORTH AMERICAN INDUSTRY CLASSIFICATION SYSTEM

SBA has taken the lead in defining what constitutes a small business in the eyes of the government. SBA issues a body of definitions called "size standards" classified on an industry-by-industry basis. Size standards are defined by number of employees, average annual sales, assets (for financial and insurance organizations), or total electric output (for utility firms).

SBA uses the North American Industry Classification System (NAICS, pronounced "nakes") to identify the various types of industries and establishments. On April 9, 1997, NAICS officially replaced the U.S. Standard Industrial Classification (SIC) system.

Why Switch from SIC to NAICS?

For more than 60 years, the Standard Industrial Classification (SIC) system served as the structure for the collection, aggregation, presentation, and analysis of the U.S. economy. It was developed in the 1930s, at a time when manufacturing dominated the U.S. economic scene. However, today's services-centered economy has rendered the classification structure of the SIC system obsolete, as the SIC often failed to adequately account for new and emerging service industries.

Enter NAICS! NAICS focuses on how products and services are created as opposed to the SIC system, which focuses on what is produced. This "process"-oriented classification methodology yields industrial groupings that are more homogenous, and thus better suited for economic analysis. For example, under the SIC system the category of food services was classified as retail trade, where it accounted for over one-third of that sector's employment. Consequently, retail trade represents a smaller share of the economy under NAICS than under the SIC.

Retail Trade, March 2002

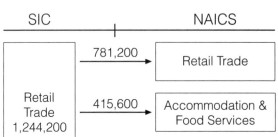

NAICS groups the economy into 20 broad sectors, up from the 10 divisions of the SIC system.

Code	NAICS Sectors	\<Previous> SIC Divisions
11	Agriculture, Forestry, and Fishing,	Agriculture, Forestry, and Fishing
21	Mining	Mining
23	Construction	Construction
31-33	Manufacturing	Manufacturing
22	Utilities	Transportation, Communications, and
48-49	Transportation and Warehousing	Public Utilities
42	Wholesale Trade	Wholesale Trade
44-45	Retail Trade	Retail Trade
72	Accommodation and Food Services	
52	Finance and Insurance	Finance, Insurance, and Real Estate
53	Real Estate and Rental and Leasing	

51	Information Services	
54	Professional, Scientific, and Technical Services	
56	Administrative Support/ Waste Mgmt Services	
61	Educational Services	
62	Health Care and Social Assistance	
71	Arts, Entertainment, and Recreation	
81	Other Services	
92	Public Administration	Public Administration
55	Management of Companies	(Parts of all divisions)

The shift to NAICS means a break in historical time series. SIC and NAICS industry groupings are not directly comparable since the code changes for NAICS have split some SIC groups.

NAICS industries are identified by a six-digit code, in contrast to the four-digit SIC code. This six-digit hierarchical structure allows for greater coding flexibility.

XX	Industry Sector (31-33 = Manufacturing)
XXX	Industry Subsector (321 = Wood Product Manufacturing)
XXXX	Industry Group (3219 = Other Wood Product Manufacturing)
XXXXX	Industry (32191 = Millwork)
XXXXXX	Country—U.S., Canadian, or Mexican (321911 = Wood Window/Door Manufacturing)

The NAICS coding system was developed to focus on the identification of new and emerging industries and high technology industries. Currently, NAICS has identified over 350 new industries, including pet supply stores, casinos, interior design services, convenience stores, and HMO medical centers.

In developing NAICS, the United States, Canada, and Mexico agreed that the 5-digit codes would represent the level at which the system is comparable among the three countries. The sixth digit allows for each of the countries to have additional detail (i.e., subdivisions of a 5-digit category). In cases where the United States did not choose to create additional detail, the 5- and 6-digit categories within U.S. NAICS are the same, and the 6-digit U.S. NAICS code ends in zero.

Comparison of SIC to NAICS Code

SIC	NAICS
4-Digit Industry Code	6-Digit Industry Code
1,005 Industry Codes	1,170 Industry Codes
10 Major Divisions	21 Sectors
Industry classifications based on their primary type of activity	Industry classifications based on production processes they use

SBA Size Standards

Suppose SBA is issuing a small business solicitation for construction services and you want to determine whether your firm is eligible to bid on the contract. As a general construction contractor, your NAICS code is "236210."

23	⟶ Construction
236	⟶ Construction of Buildings
2362	⟶ Nonresidential Building Construction
23621	⟶ Industrial Building Construction
236210	⟶ Industrial Building Construction

The following website allows you to search SBA's size standard by NAICS:

https://eweb1.sba.gov/naics/dsp_naicssearch2.cfm

In this case, any company independently owned and operated with $28.5 million or less in average revenues over the past three years could submit a bid. SBA makes these size determinations annually.

The amount of average gross revenue over a three-year period usually determines size. For example, an accounting services firm is considered to be a small business if it has less than $7 million in average gross revenue. Certain service industries have a higher maximum, ranging up to $23 million. For example, engineering services on military equipment, NAICS number 541330, has a small business size standard of $23 million.

Occasionally, the number of employees is used as a size standard. A regular dealer or wholesale trader is considered a small business if it has fewer than 100 employees (500 for government contracting) averaged over 12 months of the year. Manufacturers in certain industries can have up to 1,500 employees and still be considered small businesses. For example, an aircraft manufacturer, NAICS number 336411, has a small business size standard of 1,500 employees. A company that has more than one business line can possibly qualify as a small business when proposing for a particular requirement and not qualify when pursuing another.

You probably think that these classifications are too high for most small businesses—and you're probably right. The government's aim is to let small businesses grow into thriving medium-sized businesses before taking away the small business benefits or perks. The government wants to make sure that a small business is self-sufficient before it graduates from the small business program.

SBA also establishes small business size standards for federal programs and services. For example, SBA will establish small business size standards for financial assistance loans, bond guarantees, 8(a) program participation, registration on the Procurement Marketing and Access Network (Pro-Net), and participation in the Small Business Innovative

Research (SBIR) program. For more information about these size standards, contact:

Small Business Administration
Size Standard Division
(202) 205-6618

or visit the following website:

WWW.SBA.GOV/size/indexsize.html

SIZE CERTIFICATION

Each offeror must certify that it is a small business. The contracting officer then opts to accept this certification or request that SBA formally determine the company's size. Unsuccessful offerors can also compel the contracting officer to make a formal size determination by submitting a timely protest. A protest is a written objection by an interested party to a solicitation, proposed award, or award of a contract. Interested parties typically include actual or prospective offerors whose direct economic interests would be affected by the award of a contract or by the failure to award a contract.

An unsuccessful offeror could protest the winning contractor on several grounds. For example, an unsuccessful offeror would have a valid complaint if the small business:

- Is affiliated with or controlled by a large business

- Has an agreement with a large business to be purchased

- Is really a large business when the time period and methodology for measuring annual receipts are properly considered.

If a company's owners intentionally misrepresent the company's size on a federal procurement, they may be subject to fines and/or imprisonment. The Small Business Act allows for fines of up to $500,000 and imprisonment for up to ten years, in addition to administrative remedies, such as suspension and debarment.

Protests must be submitted to the contracting officer within five working days of notification of the announced winner or ten working days of being notified of the competitive range. If the protest is not made in that time period, SBA's findings will apply only to future procurements.

SMALL BUSINESS AFFILIATES

The most significant stumbling block for determining whether or not you qualify as a small business is the concept of affiliates. Business concerns, organizations, or individuals are considered to be affiliates of each other if, directly or indirectly, either one has the power to control the other, or a third party controls or has the power to control both. Affiliates must combine their respective incomes and employees when determining their status as a small or large business. SBA's rule for affiliation is that "size determinations shall include the applicant concern and all its domestic and foreign affiliates."

Most business owners think of affiliates as divisions or subsidiaries, but SBA looks at an affiliation in terms of substance, rather than mere form. SBA looks at who has the control. If a company can directly or indirectly control (or has the power to control) another company, the two are considered to be affiliates and SBA will treat them as one company. Whether the controlling company exercises its power is of no consequence, as long as the ability to control is present.

CERTIFICATE OF COMPETENCY

SBA also manages the Certificate of Competency (COC) program. This program's primary purpose is to assist small businesses in obtaining federal contracts for which they were determined to be the lowest responsive and responsible bidder. If your business is the low bidder on a federal contract and the contracting officer questions your ability to perform the contract, you may apply to SBA for a COC. The COC applies to all federal acquisitions. It does not, however, extend to questions concerning regulatory requirements that other federal agencies impose and enforce.

Here's how the program works:

1. Upon determining and documenting that an apparently successful small business offeror lacks certain elements of responsibility, the contracting officer withholds the contract award for a period of 15 business days (or longer if SBA and the contracting officer agree) following receipt of the documentation that was used to arrive at the nonresponsibility determination and refers the matter to the appropriate SBA regional office. The elements of responsibility include, but are not limited to, capability, competency, capacity, credit, integrity, perseverance, tenacity, and limitations on subcontracting.

2. SBA informs the small business that it has been determined to be nonresponsible and offers the business an opportunity to apply for a COC.

3. Once SBA receives a complete and acceptable COC application, an authorized SBA representative visits the small business and reviews the areas of nonresponsibility cited by the contracting officer. SBA also performs an on-site survey of the firm's facilities, management, performance record, and production capacity in relationship to the contract in question. The authorized SBA representative then sends his or her findings to the SBA regional director.

4. The regional director decides whether or not to issue a COC.

5. If the regional director decides to issue a COC, the contracting officer generally awards the contract to the small business. If the contracting officer disagrees with the determination, he or she appeals the case to SBA headquarters in Washington, D.C. However, the contracting officer may not appeal the regional director's decision if the award is valued at $100,000 or less.

SMALL BUSINESS SET-ASIDES

Small business set-asides are solicitations that are reserved exclusively for small business participation. The purpose of these set-asides is to ensure that a fair proportion of the government's acquisitions or procurements go to small and small disadvantaged business concerns. The contracting officer reviews acquisitions to determine if they can be set aside for small business. Federal agencies also may establish threshold levels for this review depending on their needs. All solicitations involving set-asides must specify the applicable small business size standard and product classification. Small business set-asides may be conducted using simplified acquisition procedures, sealed bidding, or negotiated procurement procedures.

Rule of Two

The "rule of two" states that procurements or purchases (other than purchases made using federal supply schedules—see Chapter 7) that have an anticipated dollar value exceeding $2,500 must be set aside exclusively for small business participation if the contracting officer determines that there is a reasonable expectation that:

■ Offers will be received from at least two responsible small business concerns.

■ Awards will be made at fair market prices.

If the contracting officer receives no acceptable offers, the set-aside requirement may be withdrawn and the procurement may be resolicited on an unrestricted basis.

Don't confuse small business set-asides with simplified acquisition procedures (see Chapter 10). The main difference between small business set-asides and simplified acquisition procedures is that set-asides typically are used for purchases that are greater than $100,000. The following example should clarify this difference.

Suppose a major computer manufacturer and a regular dealer work together to sell computers to the government. The manufacturer is considered a large business and the regular dealer, a small business. A firm qualifies as a regular dealer if:

■ It regularly maintains a stock of supplies (computers, in this case) for which it claims to be a dealer.

■ The stock maintained is true inventory from which sales are made.

■ The supplies stocked are of the same general character as those to be supplied under the contract.

■ Sales to the public are made regularly in the usual course of business.

■ Sales are made regularly from stock on a recurring basis.

■ The business is established and ongoing.

Assume that a contracting officer plans to make two separate purchases using small business set-aside procedures. The first purchase is for 20 computers with an anticipated dollar value of $80,000. This purchase would fall under simplified acquisition procedures because it is below the simplified acquisition threshold of $100,000. Under these procedures, a small business regular dealer may furnish any domestically manufactured product, regardless of the manufacturing company's size. In this example, then, the regular dealer would be eligible for this solicitation.

The second purchase is for 40 laser printers with an anticipated dollar value of $200,000. When a small business set-aside is greater than the simplified acquisition threshold, the regular dealer and the manufacturer must both qualify as small businesses. In the example, then, the regular dealer would not be eligible for the solicitation because the manufacturer is a large business.

Partial Set-asides

Partial set-asides enable the contracting officer to set aside a portion of a contract for small businesses. A contracting officer may use partial set-asides when:

- A total set-aside is not appropriate. (For example, suppose the Defense Advanced Research Projects Agency is issuing a research and development contract to study the atmosphere on Mars. Because this contract requires sophisticated equipment, it cannot be performed exclusively by a small business. Therefore, the contracting officer decided to set aside the reporting requirements of the study for a small business.)

- The procurement can be split into two or more economic production runs or reasonable lots.

- One or more small business concerns are expected to have the technical competence and production capacity to satisfy the set-aside portion of the requirement at a fair market price.

- More than one large and one small business are expected to submit bids.

To set aside a portion of an acquisition, the contracting officer divides the requirement into a set-aside portion and a non-set-aside portion. The non-set-aside portion is awarded using normal contracting procedures. To be eligible for the set-aside portion of the procurement, a small business, along with other businesses, submits a bid or proposal on the non-set-aside portion. Once all the awards have been made on the non-set-aside portion of the contract, the contracting officer negotiates the set-aside portion with the eligible small business concerns. The contracting officer typically awards the set-aside portion to the small business that submitted the lowest responsive bid or offer. Partial small business set-asides may be conducted using sealed bidding or negotiated procurement procedures.

Very Small Business Set-asides

The Very Small Business (VSB) set-aside program is an extension of the small business set-aside program administered by SBA. The purpose of the program is to improve access to federal contracting opportunities for firms that are substantially below SBA's small business size standards by reserving certain procurements for competition among such VSB concerns. To be eligible, a firm must have 15 or fewer employees as well as average annual receipts that do not exceed $1 million.

The pilot program is currently limited to VSB concerns whose business headquarters are located within the geographic areas of the following 10 SBA district offices:

- Albuquerque, New Mexico

- Boston, Massachusetts

- Columbus, Ohio

- Detroit, Michigan

- El Paso, Texas

- Los Angeles, California

- Louisville, Kentucky

- New Orleans, Louisiana

- Philadelphia, Pennsylvania

- Santa Ana, California.

Under the program, acquisitions greater than $2,500 (the micropurchase threshold—see Chapter 10) but less than $50,000 are to be reserved for VSBs, provided that two or more VSBs are eligible to compete. Therefore, acquisitions for supplies (valued between $2,500 and $50,000) will be set-aside for VSBs by the contracting officer if the buying activity is in one of the participating SBA districts and two or more VSBs headquartered within that SBA district are expected to submit competitive offers.

Acquisitions for services or construction (valued between $2,500 and $50,000), on the other hand, will be reserved for VSBs by the contracting officer if the requirement will be performed within one of the participating SBA districts and two or more VSBs headquartered within that SBA district are expected to submit competitive offers.

For more information on the VSB Set-Aside Pilot Program, visit the following website:

WWW.SBA.GOV/gc/indexprograms-vsb.html

Class Set-asides

Class set-asides are particular classes of products and services reserved for small businesses. Each procurement office can determine which supplies and services to set aside. For example, a procurement office might decide to create a class set-aside for stationery supplies. Accordingly, only small businesses can bid on pencil sharpener procurements for that particular procurement office.

■ ■ ■

The Small Business Act requires the government to award a fair share of its contracts to small businesses. To be successful in federal contracting, you must ensure that your business size standard accurately reflects your company's business size. For more detailed information on small business size standards, size status, and size protests, visit SBA's website at:

WWW.SBA.GOV/size

or consult a size determination specialist in one of SBA's six Offices of Government Contracting.

■ ■ ■

5 Small Business Preference Programs

© 1997 Randy Glasbergen. www.glasbergen.com

GLASBERGEN

"You and Steve were both qualified for the promotion, but Steve's shirts are whiter and brighter and smell springtime fresh."

What's in this chapter?

- Definition of small disadvantaged businesses
- Evaluation preference for SDBs
- 8(a) business development program
- Status of preference programs
- Women-owned small businesses
- Veterans business outreach program
- Labor surplus area set-asides
- SBA HUBZone empowerment contracting program
- Small business competitiveness demonstration program
- Small business innovative research program

The federal government gives preference to certain kinds of businesses in awarding federal contracts. These preference programs ensure that every U.S. citizen has an opportunity to participate in government contracting. Because these are preference programs, however, they are always under intense scrutiny. This chapter describes some common preference programs and offers insight into what the future holds for these programs.

DEFINITION OF SMALL DISADVANTAGED BUSINESSES

To qualify as a small disadvantaged business (SDB), a firm must be a small business that is at least 51% owned by persons belonging to a socially and economically disadvantaged group. Socially disadvantaged individuals are those who have been subjected to racial or ethnic prejudice or cultural bias based on their identity as a member of a group without regard to their individual qualities. Examples of these disadvantaged groups include:

- Asian Americans

- Black Americans

- Hispanic Americans

- Native Americans.

Economically disadvantaged individuals are socially disadvantaged individuals whose ability to compete in the free enterprise system has been impaired as a result of diminished capital and credit opportunities, compared to others in the same or similar line of business and competitive market area who are not socially disadvantaged. In determining the degree of economic disadvantage, the government considers the following:

- Personal financial condition of the disadvantaged individual

- Business financial condition

■ Access to credit and capital

■ Comparisons with other businesses in the same or similar lines of business.

Handicapped individuals and women are not presumed to be socially and economically disadvantaged. See FAR 19.001 for a more detailed definition of small disadvantaged business concerns.

EVALUATION PREFERENCE FOR SDBs

The Federal Acquisition Streamlining Act of 1994 allows federal agencies to use an "evaluation preference" when evaluating offers received from SDBs on unrestricted solicitations. This evaluation preference allows an SDB to receive a contract even if its bid is higher than its competitors, up to a limit of 10% of the proposed contract price. The primary purpose of this evaluation preference is to help attain the governmentwide goal of awarding 5% of its contract dollars to SDBs (see Chapter 4). SDB set-asides are still subject to the rule of two.

To be eligible for a price evaluation preference, an offeror must submit a certification, obtained within the past three years, that one or more socially disadvantaged persons own and control the business. Businesses owned by individuals who are not members of the statutorily presumed groups can qualify as SDBs by submitting evidence demonstrating their social and economic disadvantage.

The evaluation preference may not be used if the acquisition is:

■ 100% set aside for SDBs.

■ Partially or totally set aside for small businesses.

■ Made pursuant to the 8(a) program or the Labor Surplus Area Program (these programs are discussed later in this chapter).

■ Under the simplified acquisition threshold of $100,000.

- Under the U.S. Trade Agreement Act and other agreements with foreign governments.

- Made in a designated industry group. The four designated industry groups are: construction, architect and engineering services, non-nuclear ship repair, and refuse system and related services (see Small Business Competitiveness Demonstration Program later in this chapter).

The following example clarifies how this evaluation preference works. Assume that the Department of Defense plans to award a contract that has an evaluation preference of 10% for SDBs. Also assume that two businesses are competing for this contract, one of which is an SDB. These firms make the following bids for this contract:

> Regular business bid $ 475,000
> SDB bid $ 500,000

Assuming the contract will be awarded on price-related factors alone, which contractor do you think would win? Let's do the math:

> SDB bid $500,000
>   × 10% SDB evaluation preference
> Evaluation preference
> adjustment $50,000

The evaluation preference gives the SDB the following bid price:

> SDB bid $500,000
> Evaluation preference   ($50,000)
> SDB bid (after evaluation preference) $450,000
>
> Regular business bid $475,000

In this example, the SDB would win the contract because its bid is $25,000 lower than that of the regular business.

8(a) BUSINESS DEVELOPMENT PROGRAM

The 8(a) Business Development Program fosters business ownership by individuals who are socially and economically disadvantaged, and promotes the competitive viability of such firms by providing management, contract, financial, and technical assistance. The program is named for the section of the Small Business Act from which it derives its authority (see Chapter 4). The program channels noncompetitive (sole-source) federal contracts to small businesses that are owned and controlled by eligible disadvantaged persons to help them become self-sufficient and competitive.

SBA is responsible for awarding these noncompetitive contracts to eligible program participants. More than 4,000 companies are currently in this program.

8(a) Qualifications

A small business qualifies for the 8(a) program if it is at least 51% owned by one or more socially and economically disadvantaged individuals. Individuals who are not black, Hispanic, Native American, or of any other group presumed to be socially disadvantaged may qualify for the 8(a) program by establishing social disadvantage based on a "preponderance of evidence" instead of the more stringent "clear and convincing evidence" standard.

Applicants also must have been in operation for at least two full years, as evidenced by business income tax returns for each of the two previous tax years that show operating revenues in the primary industry in which the applicant firm seeks 8(a) program certification. You can obtain a waiver of this two-year business requirement if you meet all of the following five conditions:

■ The individual or individuals upon whom eligibility is based must have substantial business management experience.

- The applicant firm must demonstrate the technical experience to carry out its business plan with a substantial likelihood for success.

- The applicant firm must have adequate capital to sustain its operations and carry out its business plan.

- The applicant firm must have a record of successful performance on contracts from governmental or nongovernmental sources in its primary industry category.

- The applicant firm must have, or must be able to demonstrate that it has, the ability to obtain the personnel, facilities, equipment, and any other requirements needed to perform in a timely manner on contracts if it is admitted to the 8(a) program.

Eligibility Constraints

The conditions governing the definition of socially and economically disadvantaged individuals impose constraints on the way in which an 8(a) business organization is structured and operated. Transactions that would be routinely permissible for a non-8(a) venture could jeopardize an 8(a) contractor's continued program participation. If your enterprise is to maintain its program eligibility, you need to be aware of these constraints.

For example, if a business is organized as a corporation, it must comply with the unconditional ownership requirement, as evidenced by at least 51% ownership of each class of voting stock by socially and economically disadvantaged individuals. The business must maintain this level of ownership throughout its participation in the program or risk losing its eligibility.

The 8(a) program can be a powerful tool for assisting disadvantaged individuals and their companies in the government marketplace. A thorough understanding of the program's qualifications and requirements can help 8(a) contractors avoid situations that could jeopardize their continued program eligibility.

Program Participation and Duration

Program participation is divided into two stages: the developmental stage and the transitional stage. The developmental stage lasts for four years and the transitional stage lasts for five years. The developmental stage helps 8(a)-certified firms overcome their economic disadvantage through business development assistance. During the developmental stage, SBA wants participants to achieve the following objectives:

■ Maintain an existing business base

■ Develop and implement a marketing strategy to facilitate the achievement of non-8(a) revenues, as established in the business plan.

During the transitional stage, participants attempt to overcome the remaining elements of economic disadvantage and prepare to leave the 8(a) program. During the transitional phase, targeted non-8(a) support levels are based on the length of time a company has been in the program. For example:

Transitional Stage Year	Non-8(a) Revenue/ Total Revenue
1	15–25%
2	25–35%
3	35–45%
4	45–55%
5	55–75%

If your company is to survive or prosper, you should try to develop an "exit strategy" from the 8(a) program as soon as possible. That strategy might include developing a mix of government and commercial contracts and establishing long-term business partnerships or relationships with major prime contractors.

Here's an example of how the 8(a) Business Development Program works. Typically, three parties are involved in the 8(a) program process. These include:

■ The federal agency that awards the contract

■ SBA, which receives the contract (in government contracting terminology, the party that receives the contract is referred to as the prime contractor)

■ The 8(a) firm that performs the contract (in this scenario, the 8(a) firm would be considered the subcontractor).

For this example, the General Services Administration (GSA) plans to award a contract for security services. This contract is for two years at an estimated contract value of $200,000 per year. After reviewing the plans for this contract, the job's contracting officer decides that this contract would be perfect for an 8(a) firm, so the contracting officer contacts SBA and tells them about it. Contracting officers always look for opportunities for 8(a) firms to ensure that they meet their agencies' goals.

SBA then looks for a qualified 8(a) firm to perform the contract's requirements. SBA typically selects several 8(a) firms and requests that they submit competitive bids for the work. The contract will then be awarded to the 8(a) firm with the lowest bid (there are no negotiations).

Once SBA selects a qualified 8(a) firm to perform the contract, it negotiates a price for the contract with the contracting officer. When these negotiations are complete, the contracting officer will mail the solicitation to the 8(a) firm and award the contract to SBA. SBA then awards a subcontract to the 8(a) firm, and the 8(a) firm begins work on the contract.

During performance of the contract, the 8(a) firm deals directly with the federal agency that awarded the contract. Payments are also made directly from the federal agency to the 8(a) firm. SBA has very little involvement once the contract is awarded.

Other Assistance

Financial assistance in the form of loans and advance payments is also available to 8(a) program participants. In addition, contractors can receive a wide range of management assistance, including pamphlets, individual counseling, and seminars.

Reporting Requirements

SBA annually reviews 8(a) firms for compliance with eligibility requirements. As part of the annual review, each participant firm submits the following items to the servicing SBA district office:

- Certification that the company meets the 8(a) program eligibility requirements

- Certification that no changes that could adversely affect the participant's program eligibility have been made

- Personal financial information for each disadvantaged owner

- Record of all payments, compensation, and distributions (including loans, advances, salaries, and dividends) made by the participant to each of its owners, officers, and directors, or to any person or entity affiliated with such individuals

- IRS Form 4506, Request for Copy or Transcript of Tax Form

- Other information SBA deems necessary.

If a participant fails to provide this information for the annual review, SBA may initiate termination proceedings.

How to Apply for 8(a) Status

Any individual or business has the right to apply for Section 8(a) assistance, whether or not it appears to be eligible. You may get an application from:

SBA Washington District Office
1110 Vermont Avenue, NW, Suite 900
Washington, D.C. 20005
(202) 606-4000

WWW.SBA.GOV

Once you complete your application for admission, you will need to file it at the SBA field office that serves your company's principal place of business. (SBA has more than 100 field offices.) Your principal place of business is the location of your books and records and the office at which the individuals who manage the company's day-to-day operations work.

Once your application is submitted, the regional Division of Program Certification and Eligibility (DPCE) has 15 days to review the application for completeness. If the application is incomplete, you will have 15 days to provide the additional information and resubmit it to DPCE. If DPCE determines the application is complete, it provides a final decision regarding 8(a) program eligibility within 90 days of SBA's determination that the application is complete.

If DPCE declines your application, you can request that SBA reconsider it. During the reconsideration process, you may submit additional or revised information. If your application is declined after reconsideration, a new application will be accepted 12 months from the date of the reconsideration decision.

SDB Program/8(a) Program Comparison

The purpose of the SDB program is to encourage minority-owned businesses, including contractors that were 8(a) certified, to seek federal contracts. The SDB program, therefore, provides an alternative to SBA's 8(a) program for small minority-owned businesses seeking to participate in the economic mainstream. Here are a few characteristics that differentiate the two programs:

■ The eligibility requirements for the SDB program are less stringent than for the 8(a) program.

■ SDBs may compete directly for any federal contracts for which they are qualified; 8(a) firms, on the other hand, rely on SBA to identify and approve sole-source contract awards.

■ An 8(a) firm must be certified by SBA to receive an 8(a) contract, while an SDB may self-certify that it meets the definition of an SDB.

STATUS OF PREFERENCE PROGRAMS

Preference (or affirmative action) programs are always under intense scrutiny and change with the nation's moods or political views. Are they fair? Do they do enough to help disadvantaged U.S. citizens? Are they constitutional? Is there a way to make everyone happy? What does the future hold for these preference programs? These are some questions that affirmative action programs evoke, and unfortunately there really isn't a definitive answer to any of them. However, if there is an indication of what the future holds for these preference programs, it would have to be the Supreme Court case of *Adarand Constructors, Inc. v. Pena.*

On June 12, 1995, the Supreme Court made a decision that had a profound impact on affirmative action programs. The case of *Adarand Constructors, Inc. v. Pena* involved a Department of Transportation (DOT) contract clause that rewarded the prime contractor on the job for exceeding an SDB subcontracting goal. This contract clause was stated as follows:

> Monetary compensation is offered for awarding subcontracts to small business concerns owned and controlled by socially and economically disadvantaged individuals. . . .Compensation is provided to the Contractor to locate, train, utilize, assist, and develop SDBs to become fully qualified contractors in the transportation facilities construction field. The contractor shall also provide direct assistance to disadvantaged subcontractors in acquiring the necessary bonding, obtaining price quotations, analyzing plans and specifications, and planning and management of the work. . . .The Contractor will become eligible to receive payment under this provision when the dollar amount. . . of the DBE subcontract(s) awarded exceeds [10 % for Colorado] of the original [prime] contract award.

In other words, the government would pay a prime contractor a 1.5% bonus if it awarded more than 10% of its subcontracts to SDBs.

Adarand Constructors, Inc. (owned by a white male), submitted the low bid for a guardrail subcontract. The prime contractor (Mountain Gravel) awarded the guardrail subcontract to the second lowest bidder, a certified SDB, to collect the contract bonus. Adarand filed suit against the government, claiming that it violated the 14th Amendment of the Constitution, which guarantees "every citizen equal protection under the law." Adarand claimed that, because the contract was awarded on class-based, noncompetitive grounds, the company did not receive equal protection under the law. All the lower courts ruled against Adarand's lawsuit, and the case was sent to the Supreme Court.

The Supreme Court found DOT's subcontractor clause to be neither constitutional nor unconstitutional. Rather, it used the case to set a standard of review that the courts must follow when evaluating such preferences. The Supreme Court "altered the playing field in some important respects," holding that "all racial classifications, imposed by whatever federal, state, or local governmental actor, must be analyzed by a reviewing court under strict scrutiny." In other words, preferences or programs based on racial classifications are constitutional only if they are narrowly tailored measures that further compelling governmental interests.

Although the Supreme Court raised the bar that affirmative action programs must clear, the strict scrutiny standard does not necessarily spell the end of preference programs. Seven justices expressed continued support for affirmative action, and the Supreme Court emphasized that the government is not disqualified from acting in response to the lingering effects of racial discrimination. The SBA interprets these guidelines by limiting the credits offered to SDBs bidding in industries that show the ongoing effects of discrimination.

WOMEN-OWNED SMALL BUSINESSES

Women-owned small businesses (WOSBs) are businesses that are at least 51% owned and controlled by one or more women who are U.S. citizens. The government offers WOSBs many outreach programs and services that provide counseling and assistance.

However, women as a group are not considered socially or economically disadvantaged and their businesses are, therefore, treated like any other small business—although the government has established a goal of awarding WOSBs 5% of the total value of contracts each year.

If the WOSB owner (or owners) happens to be socially or economically disadvantaged, the business will qualify for all three business categories: small business, small disadvantaged business, and small women-owned business. Federal agencies look for firms with this particular combination because contracts awarded to these firms can be applied to all of their small business goals.

Here are a few of the incredible statistics SBA has gathered on women business owners:

■ Women create new businesses and new jobs at twice the national rate.

- Seventy-five percent of new businesses started by women succeed, compared to only 25% of those started by men.

- More than one-third of all businesses are now owned by women.

- Over the last 15 years, the number of women-owned businesses has nearly doubled.

VETERANS BUSINESS OUTREACH PROGRAM

The Veterans Business Outreach Program (VBOP) provides entrepreneurial development services such as business training, counseling, and mentoring to eligible veterans owning or considering starting a small business. A veteran is a person who served in the active military, naval, or air service, and who was honorably discharged. Similar to women-owned businesses, veterans as a group are not depicted as socially or economically disadvantaged and are therefore treated like any other small business. Federal agencies are, however, responsible for ensuring that veterans receive fair consideration in agency purchases or procurements. Congress has established a governmentwide goal of awarding 3% of all federal contracts to disabled veteran-owned small businesses.

LABOR SURPLUS AREA SET-ASIDES

The Labor Surplus Area Program restricts competition to businesses that agree to perform most (at least half) of the contract work in areas that have higher than average unemployment, even if their headquarters are not located in the designated areas. This program directs government contract dollars into areas of severe economic need. Labor surplus area set-asides are applied only when enough qualified businesses are expected to bid, so that SBA can award contracts at fair and reasonable prices. The government also encourages contractors to place subcontracts with businesses located in labor surplus areas.

The U.S. Department of Labor defines and classifies labor surplus areas. It puts out this information in a monthly publication called *Area Trends in Employment and Unemployment,* which is available from the U.S. Government Printing Office.

SBA HUBZONE EMPOWERMENT CONTRACTING PROGRAM

This program encourages economic development in historically under-utilized business zones (HUBZones) by establishing preferences for awarding federal contracts to small business concerns located in such areas. A HUBZone is an area with an unemployment rate that is at least 140% of the state's average or an average household income of no more than 80% of the nonmetropolitan state median. The HUBZone Empowerment Contracting Program was enacted into law as part of the Small Business Reauthorization Act of 1997.

Under this statute, SBA:

■ Determines whether or not individual businesses qualify as HUBZone small business concerns that are eligible to receive HUBZone contracts

■ Maintains a listing of qualified HUBZone small business concerns for use by acquisition agencies in awarding contracts under the program

■ Adjudicates protests of eligibility to receive HUBZone contracts

■ Reports to Congress the degree to which the HUBZone Empowerment Contracting Program has yielded increased employment opportunities and investment in HUBZones.

All federal agencies participate in the HUBZone program. Currently, Congress has established a governmentwide goal of awarding 3% of all federal contracts to small HUBZone businesses (see Chapter 4).

Program Benefits

Contracting officers must set aside acquisitions over $100,000 for HUBZone small business concerns if two or more HUBZone small businesses make offers and if the award is at a fair market price. HUBZone awards take precedence over small business set-asides. In addition, contracting officers may award sole-source contracts to HUBZone small business concerns if only one HUBZone small business satisfies the contract requirements. In these cases, the contract must be greater than $100,000 but less than $3 million ($5 million for manufacturing contracts), and the award must be at a fair market price.

Small business concerns located in HUBZone areas receive a 10% price evaluation preference in full and open competition procurements. This 10% evaluation preference works just like the SDB evaluation preference. The price offered by a HUBZone small business is considered to be lower than the price offered by a non-HUBZone firm, as long as the HUBZone business's price is not more than 10% of the price offered by the otherwise lowest responsive offeror. This evaluation preference may not be used when:

- Price is not a selection factor (as in architectural-engineering contracts)

- The successful offeror is a non-HUBZone small business

- The application of the preference is inconsistent with a treaty or Memorandum of Understanding with a foreign government.

Another significant provision of this program is that a firm that is both a HUBZone small business concern and an SDB can receive both the HUBZone evaluation preference and the SDB price evaluation adjustment. For example, suppose Sandy's Editorial Services is located in a HUBZone area and is owned by a socially and economically disadvantaged individual. Sandy Spellman, the owner, is looking to bid on a Department of Agriculture (DOA) contract for editing services. DOA received the following bids for this contract:

| Sandy's Editorial Services | $300,000 |
| Editorial Services, Inc. | $250,000 |

This solicitation is subject to full and open competition, and Editorial Services is not eligible for any preferences. This solicitation also allows for an evaluation preference of 10% for SDBs and a HUBZone preference of 10%. Therefore, the final bids will be:

Sandy's original bid price	$300,000
SDB evaluation preference (300,000 x 10%)	(30,000)
HUBZone preference (300,000 x 10%)	(30,000)
Sandy's bid price (after preferences)	$240,000
Editorial Services, Inc., bid price	$250,000

Assuming the contract will be awarded on price-related factors alone, Sandy's Editorial Services would win the contract because its recalculated bid is $10,000 lower than Editorial Services' bid.

Qualifications

To qualify for this program, a firm must be located within a designated HUBZone area. Metropolitan areas can qualify based on census tract criteria. Nonmetropolitan counties must meet a specific income or unemployment test. Lands within the external boundaries of an Indian reservation also qualify. In addition, the firm must be a small business that is owned and controlled by U.S. citizens and at least 35% of its employees must reside in a HUBZone. Small business concerns must be certified by SBA as meeting the HUBZone requirements.

The Bureau of the Census estimates that approximately 9,000 census tracts (out of 61,000) and 900 nonmetropolitan counties (out of 3,000) are HUBZones, and SBA estimates that approximately 30,000 firms will apply to become certified HUBZone small business concerns. The following website provides more information on the HUBZone Empowerment Contracting Program:

WWW.SBA.GOV/hubzone

SMALL BUSINESS COMPETITIVENESS DEMONSTRATION PROGRAM

The Small Business Competitiveness Demonstration Program Act of 1988 established this program in response to the concern that a disproportionately large number of contracts in certain industries were being set aside for small businesses. At the same time, this program recognizes that opportunities for small businesses were unavailable in other industries in which small business participation rates were historically low. This program has three primary objectives:

■ To test whether small businesses (with significant federal contracting experience) in certain industry groups can compete successfully with larger businesses for federal contracts on an unrestricted basis

■ To measure whether targeted goals can expand federal contract opportunities for small businesses in categories in which small businesses have been historically underrepresented

■ To determine if the expanded use of full and open competition would adversely affect small business participation in certain industry groups.

This program suspends the use of small business set-asides in four designated industry groups:

■ Construction (under NAICS codes that constitute Major Groups/Subsectors 236, 237, and 238)

■ Refuse systems and related services

■ Architectural and engineering services (including surveying and mapping)

■ Non-nuclear ship repair (including overhauls and conversions performed on non-nuclear propelled and nonpropelled ships under NAICS code 336611).

The following federal agencies participate in the program:

■ Department of Agriculture

■ Department of Defense (except the Defense Mapping Agency)

■ Department of Energy

■ Department of Health and Human Services

■ Department of Interior

■ Department of Transportation

■ Department of Veterans Affairs

■ Environmental Protection Agency

■ General Services Administration

■ National Aeronautics and Space Administration.

Under the program, small business set-asides generally were eliminated for individual federal procurements with an anticipated award value of more than $25,000 in the four designated industry groups. However, contracts could be awarded in each of the designated industry group categories under Section 8(a) of the Small Business Act. This program provides a floor of protection for small businesses by requiring participating agencies to conduct quarterly reviews based on the previous four quarters

of experience and to reinstitute small business set-asides for any designated industry group that did not achieve a 40% small business award
goal. In addition, SBA reinstitutes set-asides for any individual Product
and Service Code (PSC) or NAICS code in any of the designated industry
groups if the small business participation rate for that code fell below
35% during the previous complete four-quarter period.

Federal agencies must reinstitute set-asides to maintain these goals and
to return to full and open competition once these goals are attained.
Modifications to agency solicitation practices (either reinstituting small
business set-asides or reestablishing full and open competition) must be
made no later than the beginning of the fiscal quarter following completion of the review.

For example, assume that for a program that requires a 40% small business participation rate, DOT had the following participation rates during
each quarter of FY2005 for construction groups 236, 237, and 238.

Construction—Major Groups/Subsectors

	236	**237**	**238**
Participation Rates:			
1st Qtr	39%	20%	31%
2nd Qtr	40%	29%	39%
3rd Qtr	40%	28%	43%
4th Qtr	41%	30%	45%
Total for FY2005	40%	28%	42%

In this example, major group 236 achieved a 40% participation rate.
Major groups 237 and 238, on the other hand, varied between falling

below and exceeding the participation goal of 40%. DOT reviewed these participation rates at the beginning of the first quarter of 2006. Based on the review, DOT reinstituted set-asides in Group 237 to raise the participation rate. The set-asides were not reinstituted in major group 238 because it achieved the program participation rate for the year.

Emerging Small Business Concerns

The Small Business Competitiveness Demonstration Program also measures the extent to which contract awards are being made to a new category of small businesses called emerging small businesses (ESBs). An ESB must be no greater than 50% of the applicable small business size standard. For example, a manufacturer of office furniture, NAICS code number 337214, has a small business size standard of 500 employees. Therefore, a firm must have 250 or fewer employees to be eligible as an ESB.

The four designated industry groups reserve all acquisitions that have an estimated value of $25,000 or less for ESBs, if the contracting officer determines that there is a reasonable expectation of obtaining offers from two or more responsible ESBs that will be competitive in terms of market price, quality, and delivery. This program also requires ESBs to receive 15% of the dollar value of contracts awarded in each designated industry group.

Targeted Industry Categories

Finally, the Small Business Competitiveness Demonstration Program requires each participating agency, in consultation with SBA, to designate 10 targeted industry categories for enhanced small business participation. A federal agency expands its small business participation in these targeted industry categories through the continued use of set-aside procedures, increased management attention, and specifically tailored acquisition procedures. These targeted industry categories represent supplies and services that are bought by a federal agency that has a small business participation rate below the agencywide goals. For example, NASA selected the following targeted industry categories during FY2002:

NAICS Code	Industry Category
334111	Electronic Computer Manufacturing
334418	Printed Circuit Assembly Manufacturing
334613	Magnetic and Optical Recording Media Manufacturing
334119	Other Computer Peripheral Equipment Manufacturing
33422	Radio and Television Broadcasting and Wireless Communication Equipment Manufacturing
336415	Guided Missile and Space Vehicle Propulsion Unit and Propulsion Unit Parts Manufacturing
336419	Other Guided Missile and Space Vehicle Parts and Auxiliary Equipment Manufacturing
334511	Search, Detection, Navigation, Guidance, Aeronautical, and Nautical Systems Manufacturing
333314	Optical Instrument and Lens Manufacturing
541511	Custom Computer Programming Services
541512	Computer Systems Design Services
51421	Data Processing Services
541519	Other Computer Related Services

Each participating agency's targeted industry categories are listed in its FAR supplement. In addition, each agency's small business specialist can provide you with a list of its targeted industry categories.

SMALL BUSINESS INNOVATIVE RESEARCH PROGRAM

An individual or firm can become involved with federal research and development projects in two ways:

■ By responding to a Small Business Innovation Research (SBIR) solicitation of a federal agency

■ By initiating an unsolicited proposal (see Chapter 13).

Agencies award SBIR contracts for the development of new ideas and approaches for meeting current federal needs, not for performing routine services. The government also has a research and development program, called the Small Business Technology Transfer Research (STTR) program, which works almost exactly like the SBIR program. For our purposes, these programs are treated as if they were the same.

The SBIR program is a highly competitive, three-phase award system that provides qualified small businesses with opportunities to propose innovative ideas that meet the federal government's specific research and development needs. This program is designed to:

■ Encourage small business participation in government research programs

■ Foster and encourage participation by minority and disadvantaged persons in technological innovations

■ Stimulate technological innovations

■ Provide incentives for converting research results into commercial applications.

Since its enactment in 1982, as part of the Small Business Innovation Development Act, SBIR has helped thousands of small businesses to compete for federal research and development (R&D) awards. The Internet was created and developed with funding from a government program similar to SBIR. During FY2002, the government spent more than $1.5 billion on research and development projects under this program. This program is a major channel for obtaining research funding!

Participating Agencies

All federal agencies that fund more than $100 million in external research and development projects must participate in the SBIR program. These federal agencies currently include:

- Department of Agriculture — (202) 401-4002

- Department of Commerce — (301) 713-3565

- Department of Defense — (703) 526-4162

- Department of Education — (202) 219-2004

- Department of Energy — (301) 903-5867

- Department of Health and Human Services — (301) 206-9385

- Department of Transportation — (617) 494-2051

- Environmental Protection Agency — (202) 260-7899

- National Aeronautics and Space Administration — (202) 488-2931

- National Science Foundation — (703) 306-1391

Every year, the participating federal agencies assemble solicitations that briefly describe the topics they are interested in. Most federal agencies also allow potential contractors to propose subjects not included in their solicitation packages. Each participating agency receives and competitively evaluates proposals submitted in direct response to its SBIR solicitations.

SBIR Qualifications

A small business must meet certain eligibility criteria to participate in the SBIR program:

■ The business must be American-owned and independently operated.

■ The business must be for-profit.

■ The principal researcher must be employed by the business.

■ The company size is limited to 500 employees.

■ The principal place of business must be located in the United States.

For most contractors, eligibility isn't a problem. Your primary challenge will be to communicate your idea and why it should be funded in 25 pages or less. Obviously, a well-written proposal is critical for success in this program. Because only a small fraction of R&D funding actually results in a commercial product, the evaluators look for convincing arguments that describe the innovation, its use to the federal agency, its commercial potential, and the proposer's qualifications. Only after the prospective contractor establishes its technical competence and the value of its idea will the evaluators consider the cost proposal.

R & D Brochure

If your firm is interested primarily in obtaining R&D contracts, you should consider preparing an R&D brochure describing your organization and its capabilities. Obtaining an R&D contract requires marketing to the technical personnel of the appropriate contracting (or purchasing) activity. Experienced firms report that a well-thought-out brochure quickly establishes their basic qualifications and fields of endeavor. At a minimum, an R&D brochure should identify work you have done or are doing, the type of work for which you are qualified, and the names and qualifications of primary technical personnel on your staff. When you contact a government contracting activity, you should present your brochure to both the contracting and technical personnel.

The Three-Phase Program

Phase I is the start-up phase. Phase I awards are generally in the neighborhood of $100,000 for approximately six months. This phase is intended to determine the scientific or technical merit and feasibility of the ideas submitted.

Phase II is the performance phase. During this time, the R&D work is performed and the developer evaluates commercialization potential. Only Phase I award winners are considered for Phase II. Roughly 50% of the Phase I award winners go on to Phase II. Awards of up to $750,000, for as long as two years, allow contractors to expand Phase I results. Phase II R&D projects result in a well-defined deliverable product or process. Phase I and II contracts may include a profit/fee.

Phase III is the period during which Phase II innovation moves from the laboratory into the marketplace. No SBIR funds support this phase. The small business must find funding in the private sector, or federal agencies may award non-SBIR-funded follow-on contracts for products or processes that meet the mission needs of those agencies.

Work for all phases of this program must be performed in the United States.

More than 35,000 SBIR awards have been made to date, and the General Accounting Office (GAO) estimates that more than one-quarter of the awards have produced commercial products or services.

SBA's Role

SBA plays an important role as the coordinating agency for the SBIR program. It directs each participating agency's implementation of the SBIR program, reviews agency progress, and reports annually to Congress on the program's operation. Use it as your point of contact and information source.

SBA is also the information link to the SBIR program. SBA collects solicitation information from all participating agencies and publishes it in a presolicitation announcement. Presolicitation announcements are published periodically throughout the year because each federal agency solicits proposals at different times. The presolicitation announcement is a single source for the topics and anticipated release and closing dates for each agency's solicitations. Each presolicitation announcement includes the agency's address and telephone number for requesting SBIR solicitations. In addition, the presolicitation announcement includes the names and telephone numbers of each agency's contact for SBIR-related inquiries. Presolicitation announcements are only available on the Internet, at the following website:

WWW.SBA.GOV/sbir/

SBA also publishes the *SBIR Proposal Preparation Handbook,* which is available on the Internet at the same site.

For more information on the SBIR program, contact:

U.S. Small Business Administration Office of Technology
409 Third Street, SW
Washington, DC 20416
(202) 205-6450

■   ■   ■

These programs give small businesses a chance to compete with large firms for government contracts. The qualifications and restrictions of some of these programs require a little work to understand, but the effort certainly pays off in government assistance and procurement preferences.

■   ■   ■

6 Subcontracting Opportunities

© Randy Glasbergen, 1996

GLASBERGEN

"It is important to learn from your mistakes, Bob...but let's try not to learn quite so much."

What's in this chapter?

- Selecting a subcontractor
- Awarding the subcontract
- DOD Mentor-Protégé Program

When a company enters into a contract to perform work for a customer (or the government), and another firm provides a portion of the goods or services necessary to fulfill the contract, the company is said to be "subcontracting" part of its contractual requirements. The company's contract with the government is usually referred to as the prime contract, and the company's contracts with its suppliers are referred to as subcontracts. The subcontractor does not have a direct contractual relationship with the government. Some examples of major prime contractors include Lockheed Martin, Northrop Grumman, Cisco, General Dynamics, and Westinghouse.

For many small businesses, subcontracting to a prime contractor is the most effective way to share in the federal marketplace. The Small Business Administration (SBA) develops and promotes subcontracting opportunities for small businesses by referring small contractors to prime contractors (see Chapter 9). The market for subcontract work is nearly as large as the basic government market for contracting. During FY2002, for example, Department of Defense prime contractors awarded more than $75.5 billion in subcontracts; $25.7 billion (or 34%) of this was awarded to small businesses.

Another good reason to look for subcontracting opportunities is to take advantage of contracts that are available only through prime contractors. For example, because most construction projects are awarded as "turnkey" contracts, an air conditioning contractor would be unable to perform all the work required to build an office building. A turnkey contract is a contract that places the responsibility for completion completely on the winning contractor or prime contractor. Therefore, if the air conditioning firm wanted to be part of this building project, it would need to subcontract with the prime contractor that receives the contract.

Why would a prime contractor want to subcontract? Besides the obvious reason that few companies are able to offer a full spectrum of supplies and services, prime contractors are responsible for developing plans and goals for subcontracting with qualified small, small disadvantaged, and women-owned small business concerns. Accordingly, prime contractors are required to submit a subcontracting plan for contract awards valued at over $500,000 ($1,000,000 for construction).

Each subcontracting plan includes separate percentage goals for awarding subcontracts to small, small disadvantaged, and women-owned small business concerns, as well as a statement of the total dollars planned to be subcontracted. In addition, the subcontracting plan includes a description of the principal types of supplies and services to be subcontracted and a description of the method that will be used to identify potential sources.

SBA reviews and monitors these subcontracting plans. If a prime contractor fails to submit a small business subcontracting plan or fails to negotiate an acceptable plan, it becomes ineligible for the contract. The government can also assess "liquidated damages" to those prime contractors that fail to make a good faith effort to meet subcontracting goals for small businesses, small disadvantaged businesses, and women-owned businesses.

This requirement forces federal contracting dollars to flow down to small business concerns. The contracting officer may also encourage increased subcontracting opportunities in negotiated acquisitions by providing monetary incentives to prime contractors, such as award fees. The amount of the incentive is negotiated and depends on the prime contractor's use of small, small disadvantaged, and women-owned small business concerns, the technical assistance and outreach programs it intends to provide, and the geographic location of the subcontractor in relation to the prime contractor.

When significant subcontracting opportunities exist, the contracting officer may publish in FedBizOpps the names and addresses of prospective offerors (see Chapter 8). In addition, the contracting officer synopsizes in FedBizOpps contract awards exceeding $25,000 that are likely to result in the award of subcontracts. Prime contractors and subcontractors are also encouraged to publicize subcontracting opportunities in FedBizOpps.

SELECTING A SUBCONTRACTOR

A prime contractor will consider a number of factors when selecting a subcontractor, including the:

■ Degree to which the company's products or services fit the requirements of the contract.

■ Degree to which a mutually agreeable deal can be struck between the parties.

■ Size and socioeconomic status of the firm. (Subcontract awards to small, small disadvantaged, and women-owned small business concerns help the government and the prime contractor meet their award goals to small businesses.)

■ Company's asking price for its goods or services.

■ Technical superiority of the company's goods or services.

Perhaps the most important consideration in a subcontracting relationship is that the terms and conditions in the prime contractor's agreement with the government generally flow down to the subcontractor. In other words, the subcontractor is equally bound to comply with the applicable acquisition rules and regulations. The solicitation enumerates the terms and conditions, and the potential subcontractor should understand their significance before entering into any agreement. Subcontracting to a prime contractor is a great way for a small business to gain experience in government contracting.

AWARDING THE SUBCONTRACT

Companies may negotiate and sign a subcontract agreement at any point during the procurement process. It is generally advantageous to the prime contractor if the agreement is signed prior to award, because the agreement locks in the subcontractor's terms and pricing. It also allows the prime contractor to calculate the total amount of risk it is taking on. Agreements signed prior to award tend to be less advantageous for the subcontractor because the subcontractor must devote resources to negotiating a subcontract that may, in fact, never be executed.

It is generally advantageous to the subcontractor if the subcontract is signed following award because the subcontractor has been part of the solicitation offering and therefore is in a better position to negotiate price. This situation makes signing a subcontract less advantageous for a prime contractor because the prime has no idea how much risk it will ultimately have to assume.

Most federal agencies publish a list of businesses that received contracts over $500,000 ($1 million for construction) and are subject to subcontracting goals. The Department of Defense (DOD) maintains an online subcontracting directory at:

WWW.ACQ.OSD.MIL/sadbu/publications/subdir/

The directory lists DOD prime contractors alphabetically, including their addresses, telephone numbers, contacts, and the products or services purchased. SBA also has an online subcontracting directory at:

WWW.SBA.GOV/GC/sbsd.html

DOD MENTOR-PROTÉGÉ PROGRAM

The purpose of the DOD Mentor-Protégé Program is to provide incentives to major DOD contractors to assist small disadvantaged businesses (SDBs) and qualified organizations that employ severely disabled persons in enhancing their capabilities for performing DOD contracts and subcontracts. Through such assistance, the program attempts to increase the participation of SDBs in DOD contracting.

The program also encourages SDBs and DOD prime contractors to establish long-term business relationships free from government interference and regulation. Any prime contractor with an active subcontracting plan negotiated with DOD can participate as a mentor. In addition to DOD, many federal agencies have their own mentor-protégé programs (e.g., DOE, EPA, NASA).

Contracting officers may encourage mentors (prime contractors) to participate in the program by providing such incentives as cost reimbursement, credit toward SDB subcontracting goals, or a combination of both. Mentors are also encouraged to strengthen and expand their own capabilities throughout their program participation.

Protégé Qualifications

To qualify as a protégé, a firm must be a small disadvantaged business concern, as defined by section 8(d)(3)(C) of the Small Business Act. Any firm that is not an 8(a)-certified firm but seeks eligibility as a small disadvantaged business for participation as a protégé under this program must be certified by SBA. Self-certifications are insufficient.

To qualify, contact your local SBA District Office for an application package at:

WWW.SBA.GOV

Submit the completed application to SBA's Assistant Administrator for Small Disadvantaged Business Certification and Eligibility or to an approved private certifier, if directed by SBA.

Finding a Mentor

You can identify a mentor in *Subcontracting Opportunities with Department of Defense (DOD) Major Prime Contractors*. This publication lists most major DOD prime contractors that have negotiated subcontracting plans, including the names and telephone numbers of the firms' small business liaison officers and the firms' primary products or service lines. You can download this publication at the following website:

WWW.ACQ.OSD.MIL/sadbu/publications/

As a prospective protégé, you will select a firm with the technical capabilities you seek and a similar business focus. Look for one that may afford you the best future partner for teaming relationships. Keep in mind that a mentor may want to establish a subcontracting relationship before negotiating a mentor-protégé agreement. Be prepared to market your firm's capabilities and address what you will be bringing to the table.

To participate in the program, the mentor and the protégé must formalize their relationship through a letter of intent and a mentor-protégé agreement. These documents set forth the duration of the mentor-protégé relationship and detail the developmental assistance being provided. Although DOD must approve these documents, it will have a limited oversight role during the program.

Mentor Responsibilities

The mentor can provide a broad array of assistance to the protégé, but the protégé must perform its own contracts and subcontracts. For example, a mentor may assist the protégé by sharing its management expertise, technical skills, and administrative support to enhance the protégé's competitiveness. DOD will not, however, give credit for or reimburse the mentor for any costs related to direct work the mentor performs on the protégé's contracts. The program aims to produce viable SDBs capable of performing contracts requiring high technology skills.

Visit the following website for more information about this program:

WWW.ACQ.OSD.MIL/sadbu/mentor_protege/

■   ■   ■

Both large and small companies can benefit from establishing subcontracting agreements. Mid- to large-sized companies can strengthen and expand their own capabilities while meeting their goals for providing opportunities for small, small disadvantaged, and women-owned small business concerns. As a result, federal contracting dollars flow down to small business concerns.

■   ■   ■

7 Federal Supply Schedules/GSA Schedules

What's in this chapter?

- Federal Supply Service
- Multiple award schedule
- Schedules e-Library
- Federal supply classification codes
- GSA Advantage
- *MarkeTips* magazine
- Problems with federal supply schedules

If you're in the business of manufacturing or selling commercial supplies and services, the Federal Supply Schedule program might be a good option for you. The primary objective of this program is to provide contracting activities (or buying offices) with a simplified process for acquiring commercial supplies and services at discounted prices. This procurement process allows agency buying offices to purchase needed supplies and services with shorter leadtimes, lower administrative costs, and reduced inventories. The program uses the buying power of the government to obtain volume discounts on its purchases.

Because this program uses a simplified process for acquiring supplies and services, only commercial items are solicited. Historically, this program has accounted for over 10% of all federal purchases or procurements, which adds up to over $26 billion worth of supplies and services each year. Federal supply schedules are currently the government's fastest growing procurement method, especially for services. However, there are also disadvantages to using federal supply schedules.

FEDERAL SUPPLY SERVICE

The Federal Supply Service (FSS), a division of the General Services Administration (GSA), manages and operates the Federal Supply Schedule program. Its primary responsibility is to negotiate indefinite-delivery/indefinite-quantity, no-guarantee-of-sale contracts with commercial firms to provide supplies and services at stated prices for specific periods of time (usually three years). (See Chapter 16.)

FSS currently negotiates schedule contracts for more than 40 different product groups, ranging from furniture and office supplies, to information technology, to financial services, to travel and transportation services. It awards contracts under negotiated procurement procedures (see Chapter 12). A contractor is eligible for the Federal Supply Schedule program only after FSS approves a schedule contract for its supplies or services.

Once FSS approves these schedule contracts, they are grouped together by classification code and published in a catalog or listing called a federal supply schedule (or GSA schedule). Each schedule covers a particular product or group of products, or a particular type of service. For example, federal supply schedule number 76, Publication Media, includes publications, encyclopedias, reference and instructional books and pamphlets, technical books, medical books, almanacs, geography books, and maps and atlases.

The federal supply schedule also contains the information necessary for ordering activities to place orders directly with vendors or contractors, including the covered supplies and services, the eligible contractors and their telephone numbers and addresses, schedule contract numbers, terms and conditions, prices, maximum and minimum order sizes, and ordering instructions. It is crucial for a contractor to get on a federal supply schedule that accurately reflects its supplies or services and to fill out the schedule requirements properly and competitively.

Federal supply schedules also identify specific federal agencies in designated geographic areas that must use the contracts as primary sources of supply. If an agency buying office requires a product or service not covered by a federal supply schedule, it can either do its own contracting or ask FSS to make a special purchase for the agency.

Federal supply schedules offer the following benefits:

■ They expose a contractor's supplies and services to a vast number of contracting activities or buying offices throughout the government for at least one year and, in some cases, up to five years.

■ Schedule holders are pre-approved to contract with federal agencies, so your company joins a list of "preferred vendors."

■ They enable the government to use its buying power to obtain volume discounts on purchases.

■ State and local governments can purchase from Schedule 70— Information Technology. In addition, certain prime contractors are eligible to purchase from federal supply schedules (see Part 51 of the FAR).

- Agency buying offices are not required to synopsize their orders in FedBizOpps (see Chapter 8). In addition, buying offices are not required to perform solicitation or procurement procedures for the federal supply schedule items because FSS has already determined the prices to be fair and reasonable (see Part IV).

- Agency buying offices are not required to follow small business set-aside requirements (see Chapter 4) when purchasing from a schedule. This permits large contractors, in theory, to compete with small businesses.

- When a schedule is mandatory, the federal agencies specified in the schedule must use it.

FSS may also authorize other federal agencies to award schedule contracts and publish schedules. For example, the Department of Veterans Affairs awards schedule contracts for certain medical items. The Department of Defense uses a similar system of schedule contracting for military items that are not part of the FSS program. In addition, approximately 25 states have their own versions of federal supply schedules.

MULTIPLE AWARD SCHEDULE

The most common federal supply schedule type is the multiple award schedule (MAS). A multiple award schedule is a list of contracts that the government establishes with more than one contractor for the same types of supplies and services. Each year, federal agencies spend billions of dollars through MASs, buying everything from desks and paperclips to computers and software. MAS contracts are awarded on a "variable" basis, meaning that contractors can respond to MAS solicitations at any time.

There are no government specifications for the items listed in an MAS schedule. All responsible contractors may submit offers in response to a solicitation for MAS contracts and, for the most part, the contractors do not participate in head-to-head competition, although agencies may hold competitions among schedule holders. Each contractor on the MAS submits a different price list for its supplies and services, and may offer specific options and features. An agency buying office selects the contractor that best meets its particular needs.

MAS contract holders must provide the government with prices/discounts that are at least as good as the prices they offer commercial clients. This negotiation objective is commonly known as "most favored customer" pricing. Moreover, contractors can offer additional discounts to make their schedule more competitive. Your MAS prices represent a "ceiling" price. Once a schedule price is approved, it can be changed only by GSA authorization.

The FSS contracting officer must follow negotiated procurement procedures when issuing MAS contracts. After the MAS contract is issued, the contractor prepares and distributes a catalog and/or price list to the various ordering offices. The agency buying office then uses these catalogs, along with an MAS, to purchase supplies and services. MAS holders must accept payment using the governmentwide purchase card (see Chapter 10).

Agency buying offices may not purchase a product or service from the open/commercial marketplace if it is available under an MAS. As a result, if a company has a schedule contract, it is likely to have a competitive advantage over contractors who do not participate in the MAS program.

MASs help agencies avoid cumbersome and costly traditional procurement procedures in their purchases of commercially available, common-use items and receive the benefit of the government's high-volume purchasing power.

SCHEDULES e-LIBRARY

The Schedules e-Library is GSA's official on-line source for Federal Supply Schedule information. The site contains basic ordering guidelines, complete schedule listings, the latest information on schedule program changes, and a search engine that allows you to search by keyword, schedule number, item number, contractor name, and contract number. It is updated daily to ensure access to the latest award information. For more information on Schedules e-Library, visit the following website:

WWW.GSAELIBRARY.GSA.GOV

FEDERAL SUPPLY CLASSIFICATION CODES

Buying offices use Federal Supply Classification (FSC) codes by buying offices to identify products and services. FSC codes currently consist of 78 groups, which are subdivided into 639 classes. Although contractors are not required to use FSC codes when registering to do business with the government, they are encouraged to include all the FSC codes that apply to their company's products and services because it helps buying offices identify a contractor's capabilities more accurately.

The FSC code uses a four-digit structure. The first two digits of the code number identify the group, such as:

Group	Title
70	Data Processing Equipment
71	Furniture
75	Office Supplies and Devices
81	Containers, Packaging, and Packing Supplies
85	Toiletries
91	Fuels, Lubricants, Oils, and Waxes
95	Metal Bars, Sheets, and Shapes

The last two digits of the code number identify the classes within each group. For example, group 71, Furniture, currently has the following classes:

FSC	Title
7125	Cabinets, Lockers, Bins, and Shelving
7105	Household Furniture
7195	Miscellaneous Furniture and Fixtures
7110	Office Furniture

Code numbers are assigned to make it possible to expand the number of groups and classes as it becomes necessary. For more information on FSC codes, visit:

WWW.DLIS.DLA.MIL/h2/

Getting Started

The following steps will help you get your supplies and services listed on a schedule with the Federal Supply Service:

1. Review the *FSS Contractor Guide* on the Internet at:

http://APPS.FSS.GSA.GOV/contractorguide/

2. Identify the federal supply schedule that covers your supplies or services. There are currently over 40 different federal supply schedules. For example:

FSS Schedule	Schedule I.D.
Financial and Business Solutions (FABS)	520
Office Furniture	71I
Leasing of Autos and Light Trucks	751
Professional Engineering Services (PES)	871
Environmental Services	899

Hardware and software schedules generally require the contractor to offer support, such as maintenance or repair service. Visit the following website for a complete listing of federal supply schedules:

WWW.GSAELIBRARY.GSA.GOV

Note: Each GSA schedule has a point of contact that can provide specific information about individual GSA schedule items.

3. Obtain a copy of a federal supply schedule solicitation for your particular supplies or services by searching:

WWW. FEDBIZOPPS.GOV

4. Obtain a Dun & Bradstreet (D&B) reference check. For more information on reference checks, call Dun & Bradstreet at (800) 234-3867, or apply at:

WWW.DNB.COM

5, Complete all information in the solicitation. Each solicitation has different requirements, so be sure to read it carefully.

6. Be prepared to offer a competitive price.

The GSA Vendor Support Center maintains a library of federal supply schedules and authorized contractor catalog price lists. It is also a receiving point for customer and vendor questions regarding FSS supplies and services. For more information on the GSA Vendor Support Center, visit:

http://VSC.GSA.GOV

or call (877) 495-4849

Now What?

You've just been awarded your first schedule contract. Congratulations! So now you're ready for all those orders to pour in. Unfortunately, having a schedule contract does not guarantee that you will receive government orders. It only indicates that you are an eligible contractor and that your supplies and services are reasonably priced. Therefore, while the ink is drying on your contract, you should immediately turn your attention to marketing your new award.

The first step in marketing your schedule contract is to develop your contract price list. A contract price list is a "catalog" that lists the items you have been awarded and identifies the terms and conditions of the contract (see clause I-FSS-600, Contract Price List, of your Multiple Award Schedule). Your price list is your initial "face" to the customer. When designing your price list, be sure to make it user-friendly. A one-page flyer covering only the required items specified in your contract usually is best.

Once your price list is completed, you will need to distribute it to potential customers. For many schedules, GSA provides a mailing list of customers who have expressed an interest in the products and services on a particular GSA schedule. Be sure to ask your Procurement Contracting Officer (PCO) if your schedule has a customer mailing list.

Although the government is moving toward a paperless environment, it's not there yet. Therefore, contractors should still take the time to mail a hard copy of their price list to prospective customers. Also, in your mailing be sure to include your company brochure and other literature about your products or services.

GSA Schedule
Price List
Contract #GS-35F-0213M

Products:

Part #	Product Description	GSA Price
DS01	GEMS	$80,607.00
PS01	mCAT!	$6,525.36
CA01	LaserCat 2003	$4,310.00

Software Maintenance:

Part #	SW Maintenance Description	GSA Price
DS01-2	GEMS Year 2	$9,521.24
DS01-3	GEMS Year 3	$17,258.47

Labor Rates:

Cat #	Labor Category	Year 1	Year 2	Year 3	Year 4	Year 5
L001	Program Manager	$116.03	$120.56	$126.33	$133.08	$138.63
L002	Senior Network Engineer	$85.68	$93.04	$95.57	$100.35	$106.37
L003	Software Engineer	$59.38	$62.27	$65.43	$68.65	$73.09
L004	Database Administrator	$54.38	$57.48	$62.45	$63.37	$66.54
L005	Financial Analyst	$54.38	$57.48	$62.45	$63.37	$66.54
L006	Network Engineer	$54.74	$58.48	$62.45	$63.37	$66.54
L007	Technical Writer	$51.06	$53.78	$55.21	$57.97	$61.35
L008	Administrative Support	$23.43	$25.55	$26.82	$28.13	$29.61

Buy Now Using GSA Advantage
For more information, contact: 800-555-3000 ext. 101 or email: GSA@baystate.com

GSA ADVANTAGE

Your price list also needs to be posted to GSA Advantage, an online shopping service or ordering system. GSA Advantage provides online access to several thousand contractors and millions of products and services. During FY2003, GSA Advantage did more than $113 million in online sales.

The government uses GSA Advantage to:

■ Search for items using keywords, part numbers, national stock numbers, supplier names, contract numbers, etc.

■ Compare features, prices, and delivery options

■ Configure products and add accessories

■ Place orders directly online

■ Review and choose delivery options

■ Select a convenient payment method

■ View order history.

Contractors use GSA Advantage to:

■ Research the competition

■ Check out the market

■ Sell to the federal marketplace.

To post a company catalog/profile/price list to GSA Advantage, go to http://VSC.GSA.GOV and click on the Schedule Input Program (SIP) User link. The Schedule Input Program also allows contractors to post product photos to GSA Advantage. It is the contractor's responsibility to keep its GSA Advantage catalog/profile information current, accurate, and complete.

GSA Advantage gives contractors an opportunity to put a controlled marketing spin on their products and services by linking their company website to their catalog/profile. Be sure to make your website "GSA-friendly." For example, put GSA's logo and your contract number on an easy-to-spot location on your website. Also, set up a separate e-mail account for GSA schedule inquiries only.

For more information on GSA Advantage, visit:

WWW.GSAADVANTAGE.GOV

MARKETIPS MAGAZINE

Another way to market your products and services to potential customers is to supply advertisements to *MarkeTips,* a bimonthly publication for GSA customers. Advertising space in *MarkeTips* is free of charge, and is offered on a first-come, first-served basis. Because of limited ad space, vendors are restricted to two ads per year, per GSA contract. *MarkeTips* is sent to over 110,000 federal and military subscribers worldwide and is available online at:

http://APPS.FSS.GSA.GOV/pub/marketips.cfm

Getting a GSA schedule is just the tip of the iceberg when it comes to generating sales through your schedule contract. You must still aggressively market to agency buying offices that could potentially purchase your supplies and services. Call the buying offices directly and tell them about your supplies and services or send them publications or brochures. Be sure to use GSA logos on all your marketing materials. Remember that each federal supply schedule will list many suppliers (unless you have a single award schedule), so you must find a way to get your supplies or services noticed!

PROBLEMS WITH FEDERAL SUPPLY SCHEDULES

You would think that federal supply schedules are a gold mine for many small- and medium-sized companies. However, selling or wholesaling common-use commercial supplies and services to the federal government is extremely competitive. In the face of this competition, companies mark up supplies and services that they sell to the government by only about 8 to 12%. These low markups put small businesses at a disadvantage because they are unable to maintain a large enough sales volume to be profitable.

Suppose that your small business is a regular dealer of Compaq equipment and your agreement with Compaq allows you to purchase computers for $1,000 each (this would be considered the unit price of the computer). After reading this book, you decide to apply to FSS to get your computer products on a federal supply schedule. You review the GSA Schedules e-Library on the Internet and determine that federal supply schedule number 70, Information Technology Equipment, Software, and Services, is appropriate for your computers.

Next, you obtain your Dun & Bradstreet (D&B) reference check and use FedBizOpps (see Chapter 8) to obtain the solicitation for federal supply schedule number 70. Finally, you complete the solicitation.

Assume that a contracting officer in the Department of Commerce plans to purchase 200 Compaq computers and has selected your federal supply schedule. The contracting officer making this purchase does not need to be concerned about the price of the computers because FSS has already determined that the price of the computers is fair and reasonable. Assuming you have a 10% markup, your total sales price for this order will be:

200 Compaq computers x $ 1,000 =	$ 200,000
Markup	x 10%
Total sales price	**$ 220,000**

You will earn a total gross profit (or margin) of $20,000 on this transaction. The next step is to apply your indirect costs against this sales transaction.

Indirect costs are expenses incurred by a contractor that cannot be attributed to any one particular contract. For example, an indirect cost would be the lighting in a manufacturing area that houses the work of several contracts. The lighting benefits all the contracts, but it cannot be specifically identified with a particular contract.

Indirect costs are classified further as either overhead (O/H) expenses or general and administrative (G&A) expenses.

O/H expense describes general costs, such as indirect labor, rent, supplies, insurance, and depreciation.

G&A expense is any management, financial, or other expense that is incurred by or allocated to a business unit and is for the general management and administration of the business unit as a whole.

The following breakdown shows the indirect costs and profit of this sales transaction.

Total gross profit (or margin)	**$ 20,000**
LESS:	
O/H expenses:	
Salaries	$ 3,500
Supplies	$ 750
Equipment rental	$ 500
Depreciation	$ 2,250
G&A expenses:	
Executive salaries	$ 4,000
Personnel costs	$ 1,500
Professional services	$ 1,750
Training costs	$ 1,250
Total (net) profit	**$ 4,500**

When you consider these indirect costs, you barely break even on this transaction. That's the main problem with serving as a small business regular dealer or wholesaler to the government. How can a small business survive with such a low markup on its sales? In addition, what happens to the small business if the government doesn't consistently buy its products or services?

The key to being a successful regular government dealer or wholesaler is to have a large sales volume. Because many indirect costs remain consistent, regardless of sales volume, a large sales volume allows a contractor to cover more indirect expenses, increasing total profit. These indirect costs are referred to as fixed costs.

For example, suppose Joe's Janitorial Services provides your office cleaning and maintenance services for $1,000 per month. This expense would be considered a fixed cost because it remains the same regardless of sales volume. If you increase product sales, you earn a greater total profit, because your fixed costs remain at $1,000 even though you take in more sales. Large businesses enjoy a tremendous advantage because they can maintain lower markups with larger sales volumes.

Another problem for small business regular dealers is that there is not much incentive for a large business or manufacturer to use a regular dealer to sell products to the government. Why would a large manufacturer need to use the services of a regular dealer, if the government ordering activities can contact the manufacturer directly? Think about it: If your company was a larger manufacturer, like Compaq, wouldn't you want to sell your products directly to the government, so you could charge a more competitive price?

■   ■   ■

The Federal Supply Schedule program is designed to closely mirror commercial buying practices. It provides government buying offices with millions of state-of-the-art, high-quality commercial products and related services at volume discount pricing on a direct-delivery basis. All government buying offices, large or small, even those in remote locations, receive the same services, convenience, and pricing.

This program also gives commercial contractors an excellent opportunity to increase market share while taking on only some of the red tape that usually accompanies government purchases. A company must have adequate cash flow, an effective delivery system, and an aggressive marketing plan to be successful in the Federal Supply Schedule program.

PART 3

How to Find Government Contracting Opportunities (Marketing)

Marketing isn't a science. It's persuasion.
And persuasion is an art.

—*Bill Bernbach*

8 How to Market to the Federal Government

© 1999 Randy Glasbergen.

GLASBERGEN

"The number one rule in sales is:
'Find Out What The Customer Wants'.
The customer wanted me to go away."

What's in this chapter?

- Finding markets for your supplies and services
- Using the Internet
- FedBizOpps
- *Federal Register*
- Federal agency acquisition forecasts
- Bidders lists
- Procurement Marketing and Access Network
- SUB-Net
- TECH-Net
- SBAExchange
- Federal Procurement Data System-NG
- Year-end procurements

You would think that marketing to the federal government would be an easy subject to write about. The government has more than 300,000 contractors, who receive more than $200 billion worth of contracts each year. But as I began asking successful contractors and government officials about marketing to the government, I was amazed at how little they actually knew about the subject. Don't get me wrong—they all had some good ideas, but in the end, they all seemed to conclude that who you know is the deciding factor in getting government contracts.

Now that's great, and I'm sure that to be successful in any business, who you know is very important. But my question is: Who is it that I should get to know, and how do I get to know them? And that question got me a lot of blank stares and answers like, "You've just got to find a way." So that's what Part III of this book is all about: learning how to market to the federal government.

Marketing to the government differs from marketing to other types of industries because the government purchases supplies and services with funds that are financed by the public (that is, tax dollars). This means that the government has a higher degree of accountability for the ways in which those funds are spent. (Parts IV and V of this book deal with how the government makes its purchasing decisions.) The government also must allow full and open competition for its purchases. This mandate ensures that each contractor can compete for federal contracts, without having to belong to an exclusive club.

The bottom line is that there really is no one way to market your supplies or services to the government because each federal agency makes acquisitions in a different way. But understanding some of the government's procurement methods (or sources) and some of the support services it offers to contractors can surely help. This chapter touches on a number of marketing methods. Although not all of these will work for your particular situation, you should be able to incorporate some of the ideas into your business marketing plans.

FINDING MARKETS FOR YOUR SUPPLIES AND SERVICES

One important thing to remember about government contracting is that you do not have to be located near a federal agency to compete for contracts. The government currently has more than 2,500 buying offices (or contracting activities), located throughout the United States. SBA has grouped these into 10 regions.

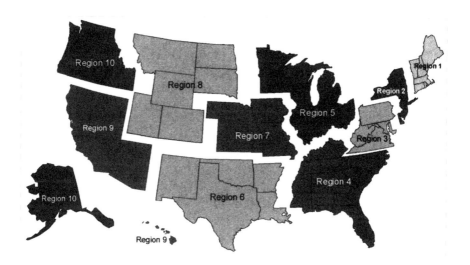

To market successfully in the large and diverse federal marketplace, a contractor must focus on a specific area that offers the greatest opportunity for success based on available resources. The following questions might help you decide which markets to concentrate on:

■ *Where is your business located?* Is it in a densely populated area like New York City or a rural area like Greenville, North Carolina? In a densely populated area, you can concentrate on using a business center that is close to your location because heavily populated areas tend to have larger government markets. On the other hand, in a rural area, you will probably use a business center that is farther away, because these areas have fewer government buying offices.

- *What is your business type?* If you are in a business that requires you to work at the job site, you should consider a smaller geographical area. For example, if you operate a construction company, the majority of your work will take place at the job site; therefore, it will be beneficial for you to work close to your home office.

- *How much experience do you have?* If yours is a relatively new business and you are still learning the ropes, you should probably look for opportunities near home. If you have been in business for many years and have a good share of the local market, you might consider expanding your market base.

At the outset, you should have a pretty good feel for how far your company can venture and still successfully perform a contract's requirements. Reaching out too far to perform government contracts could be a mistake that endangers your company's future business opportunities. Carefully identify the government market that you want to go after and stick to that plan. Once you determine your target markets, your next step is to locate opportunities for your supplies and services within those markets. The following website lists SBA offices by state:

WWW.SBA.GOV/regions/states.html

USING THE INTERNET

The federal government provides more and more Internet information every day. Whether you seek general information about a contracting activity or information about the Freedom of Information Act, you can look on the Internet. Each federal agency has its own web page, and one of the best ways to familiarize yourself with a federal agency is to browse its site. As you'll quickly notice, most federal government websites end in .GOV, an abbreviation for "government."

Finding an agency's website on the Internet is easy. Most agencies use their acronym names as their web addresses. To find the General Services Administration's website, for example, you would type:

WWW.GSA.GOV

If you wanted to go to the Department of Energy's website, you would type:

WWW.DOE.GOV

If an agency's web address doesn't agree with its acronym name, you can try to locate it using another agency's site (each agency's website allows you to transfer—or link—to other agencies' sites). For example, you can use GSA's website to link to the Department of Commerce's website and vice versa. The Internet provides unlimited marketing potential.

FEDBIZOPPS

FedBizOpps (FBO), formerly known as the Electronic Posting System (EPS), is the single government point-of-entry on the Internet for federal government procurement opportunities over $25,000. On January 4, 2002, FedBizOpps replaced the *Commerce Business Daily* (CBD) as the official source for procurement opportunities and information. Government buyers are able to publicize their business opportunities by posting information directly to FedBizOpps via the Internet, and contractors looking to do business with the government are able to search, monitor, and retrieve opportunities solicited by the entire federal contracting community.

FedBizOpps lists synopses/notices of proposed contract actions, contract solicitations, amendments/modifications, subcontracting leads, contract awards, and other business opportunities. While the General Services Administration (GSA) is responsible for the operation and maintenance of the website, the content of the notices is the sole responsibility of the federal agency/buying office that issues the notice.

The website is updated every business day, with approximately 500–1,000 new notices being posted on a daily basis. FedBizOpps currently supports more than 21,300 federal buyers in 95 federal agencies and hosts more than 380,000 solicitation documents. Over 95% of all federal opportunities are listed on FedBizOpps.

Getting Started

Let's assume you want to identify opportunities for Facilities Support Services (NAICS code 561210).

1. Go to WWW. FEDBIZOPPS.GOV

2. Locate the "Finding Business Opportunities" section of the web page (upper left side) and click on the GO icon. This will take you to the FBO Synopsis/Awards Search page. FBO search options include:

   ■ Full Text Search
   ■ Active or Archived Documents
   ■ Synopses or Awards
   ■ Solicitation/Award Number
   ■ Dates to Search (e.g., Last 3 Days, One Week)
   ■ Search by Place of Performance (Zip Code)
   ■ Search by Set-Aside Code
   ■ Search by Procurement Classification Code
   ■ Search by Agency.

   Note: The full text search can be used in a number of ways, including searches for NAICS codes, key words, and opportunities in your state.

   In this case, we are going to search by NAICS code 561210, using the full text search and a search by agency, Department of Agriculture (USDA). Once you have filled in the appropriate criteria, click on "Start Search" to execute the search.

3. Search results:

Search Results

Business Opportunities

Synopsis and Solicitation Grouped by Organization and Posted Date

Active Postings: 27/89099

July 21, 2003
Agency: Department of Agriculture
Office: Forest Service
Location: R-5 Northern Province Acquisitions, Yreka Office
➡ **Posted:** July 21, 2003   **Type: <u>Synopsis</u>**
Title: Z—USDA Forest Service, Region 5, Pacific Southwest, Grounds and Facilities Maintenance Services
SOL: Reference-Number-R5NP072103-GFM-TB

August 12, 2003
Agency: Department of Agriculture
Office: Forest Service
Location: R-5 Northern Province Acquisitions, Yreka Office
➡ **Posted:** August 12, 2003   **Type: <u>Solicitation</u>**
Title: Z—USDA Forest Service, Region 5, Pacific Southwest, Grounds and Facilities Maintenance Services
SOL: Reference-Number-R5NP072103-GFM-TB

To view the actual posting, click on the highlighted link (e.g., Synopsis). Clicking on "Synopsis" will bring you to the listing page for this solicitation. The listing page lists everything posted to a particular solicitation. In this case, a synopsis and solicitation have been posted. To view any of these postings, click on the highlighted link. A good idea might be to review the synopsis first, since it gives a basic description of the opportunity, along with point-of-contact information.

Z—USDA Forest Service, Region 5, Pacific Southwest, Grounds and Facilities Maintenance Services

General Information

Document Type:	Presolicitation Notice
Solicitation Number:	Reference-Number-R5NP072103-GFM-TB
Posted Date:	Jul 21, 2003
Original Response Date:	Sep 05, 2003
Current Response Date:	Sep 16, 2003
Original Archive Date:	Sep 27, 2003
Classification Code:	Z—Maintenance, repair, and alteration of real property

Contracting Office Address

Department of Agriculture, Forest Service, R-5 Northern Province Acquisitions, Yreka Office, 1312 Fairlane Road, Yreka, CA, 96097

Description

Region 5, USDA Forest Service intends to issue a solicitation for Grounds and Facilities Maintenance Services, pursuant to and in accordance with an Office of Manpower and Budget (OMB) Circular No. A-76, 'Performance of Commercial Activities'. The agency anticipates up to three (3) subsequent awards - one each for the Northern, Central and Southern California areas. The solicitation will be available on or around August 6, 2003 for electronic download only. The NAICS code for this acquisition is 561210. The small business size standard is $6.0 million.

Point of Contact

Doris Broussard, Contracting Officer, Phone 530-242-2219,
e-mail tbroussard@fs.fed.us

Place of Performance

Address: Region 5, USDA Forest Service

Register to Receive Notification

Government-wide Numbered Notes
You may return to Business Opportunities at:
- USDA FS listed by [Posted Date]
- USDA Agency-wide listed by [Posted Date]

Note: Many solicitations are reserved, or "set aside," for small businesses, minority-owned businesses, women-owned firms, and veteran-owned businesses and they are listed as such.

Be sure to click on the "Register to Receive Notification" box at the bottom of the synopsis and provide your e-mail address. This is a subscription to a mailing list for all future announcements on this particular solicitation.

Vendor Notification Service

By clicking on the Vender Notification Service (under Related Links on the right-hand side of the FedBizOpps homepage), vendors can register to receive procurement announcements/information by e-mail. Vendors can specify the notices they receive by solicitation number, selected organizations, and product service classification. To date, more than 140,000 vendors are registered to receive notification of business opportunities from FedBizOpps.

FedBizOpps also includes the capability to join and view a published list of vendors interested in a particular solicitation. This is useful for vendors who are interested in teaming on procurement opportunities. To register as an interested vendor for a particular solicitation, the "Register as Interested Vendor" button must be available on the listing page of the solicitation.

FedBizOpps was designed to broaden the federal marketplace and minimize the effort and cost associated with finding government business opportunities. Eventually, federal agencies/buying offices will use this site regularly to receive proposals electronically. FedBizOpps helps "level the playing field" for small businesses.

Business Solutions Awards—GSA
Online Business Intelligence

By Shane Harris, Government Executive

In January, the procurement world bid a solemn adieu to the trusted, true and utterly obsolete *Commerce Business Daily,* the government-printed newspaper that for 51 years had been companies' main source of information on what federal agencies were shopping for. In years past, prospective contractors had scoured the CBD, as it was commonly called, like unemployed workers searching the classified ads. Agencies posted their procurement notices in the publication faithfully.

But readership plummeted in recent years, from a high of 55,000 subscriptions in 1986 to 2,600 in 2001, as the government turned to the Web as a vehicle for advertising procurement opportunities. Vendors also used the Internet to hunt for new leads, or simply paid other companies to compile procurement notices for them. The Government Printing Office, which published the CBD, tried to revitalize it in 1996 by launching an online version called CBDNet. But that site didn't aggregate all procurement opportunities.

The time for change had arrived. On Jan. 4, as the CBD and CBDNet were officially terminated, the General Services Administration launched a new website called FedBizOpps.gov. It has quickly become the procurement source of record. Every agency is required to post procurement notices on the site.

FedBizOpps was recognized for acquisition excellence by this year's Business Solutions in the Public Interest Awards because of its simplicity. "One of the major reasons that we all thought it should be a winner," says Allan Burman, the former administrator of the Office of Federal Procurement Policy and one of this year's judges, "is the effort they made at simplifying how people get information from the government—putting it in one place and getting it electronically."

Until the launch of FedBizOpps, vendors had to spend hours looking for agencies' procurement announcements and solicitations. To do so online, they had to visit hundreds of individual agency websites. And many agencies didn't post their procurements online. Michael Sade, procurement chief at the Commerce Department and also one of this year's judges, says FedBizOpps saves time. That's especially helpful, he says, for small vendors, who have fewer resources to spend hunting in paper documents for new business opportunities.

Burman says judges admired FedBizOpps for its growth from humble beginnings at a single agency into a massive governmentwide project. NASA officials first came up with the idea of consolidating their own purchasing process online. The agency is one of the biggest single buyers in the government, with $10 billion in spending on prime contracts in fiscal 2001. But NASA officials realized the project was a huge undertaking, even for them. They needed help funding the site, so they joined forces with GSA, says David Drabkin, GSA's deputy associate administrator for acquisition policy. GSA's Office of Governmentwide Policy and the Federal Supply Service took over the project and guided the site into its current form.

In their pitch to judges, Burman says GSA officials predicted that FedBizOpps would have a wide-ranging effect on agencies' business, because it would be a highly reliable system that the whole government could use to simplify the procurement process. Officials said the site had already registered 180,000 vendors and incorporated 23 million documents in its first year of operation. In spring 2000, in preparation for the launch, GSA officials launched a training program and taught 2,000 procurement offices how to use FedBizOpps.

Companies that register at FedBiz Opps receive tailored e-mails about procurements announced in specific agencies or categories. They can search the site for solicitations by selecting from a list of agencies or entering a specific solicitation number. Notices are listed by the contracting agency and the date posted. Each notice presents a link to the full text of the solicitation. Users can search one or all agency solicitations for key words.

Sade says FedBizOpps also is a useful tool for procurement officials. They can search for information about acquisitions similar to theirs conducted at other agencies around the country.

Contracting officers can contact their colleagues, whose names are listed on the notices, to get their advice and discuss challenges in constructing their acquisition efforts.

Most often, Sade says, contracting officers just want to see a document to know how a particular procurement was structured in the past.

FedBizOpps archives past solicitations, so contracting officers can look over the history of a particular kind of procurement and see how its structure might have changed.

The site gives procurement executives control over the quality of solicitations, because executives can go online and see what people at the agency are posting, Sade says. He looks at documents to spot weaknesses and strengths so he can improve training and give people appropriate credit for crafting effective procurements and attracting new vendors. "In a nonobtrusive way, I can see what we're doing out there," he says.

FedBizOpps is widely used, but that doesn't necessarily mean it's easy to use. People with no familiarity with the procurement process and its unique jargon would probably be lost surfing around the site. Of course, FedBizOpps is a professional tool, intended for those who live and breathe the obscure purchasing lexicon, but Burman says the site's managers shouldn't take for granted their users' grasp of minutiae, especially as use of the site grows. "Too often, people [in government] fall into jargon and use terms that aren't all that understandable by the general public," Burman says.

Paying to keep FedBizOpps in business may be one of GSA's biggest challenges as the site evolves. "Funding is a big issue and hasn't been resolved," Drabkin says. "[The site] doesn't currently pay for itself." Officials have said it takes about $4.3 million a year to operate FedBizOpps. Agencies pay a fee for every solicitation they post. GSA agreed in the first year not to charge agencies more per posting than they paid for CBDNet, Drabkin says. Agencies end up paying about $5 per posting to use FedBizOpps.

However, Drabkin adds, many more agencies use FedBizOpps than ever used CBDNet. The number of postings in February alone exceeded CBDNet's annual rate, Drabkin says. Presumably, higher use might drive fees down. But even with its popularity, FedBizOpps has only collected $650,000 in fees this fiscal year, which is not enough to cover its operating costs, Drabkin says. GSA is considering ways to make the site self-funding. Vendors don't pay to register on the site or to receive e-mail notifications, but Drabkin says GSA might start charging them a small annual fee, which probably would not exceed $30.

GSA officials are looking to enhance FedBizOpps in several ways. One of the most significant would be creating a system to allow vendors to post bids online. Federal officials want agencies to have the capacity to receive online bids, whether through FedBizOpps or some other site. Members of the Procurement Executives Council, which includes procurement chiefs from across the government, are discussing how to do this. Sade says procurement officials who are members of the FedBizOpps users group will submit their ideas and suggestions to the council. Those users also want to implement electronic authentication tools for verifying vendors' and purchasers' identities. The Office of Management and Budget has participated in these ongoing discussions. But while a dialogue has started, no firm plans have been made on how to move into the next phase.

Drabkin says he's happy that FedBizOpps overcame the obstacles that have stalled similar efforts. "All of the agencies that came together to make this happen . . . could have kept it from happening," he says. Drabkin says the site is a testament to intergovernmental cooperation, something many agencies are trying to emulate these days with a new Homeland Security Department emerging.

Burman says FedBizOpps can serve as a model for the Bush administration's electronic government initiatives, a series of two dozen projects that aim to put government transactions online. FedBizOpps takes information from many sources and puts it in one accessible place, a model that has implications well beyond the scope of procurement.

August 15, 2002

FEDERAL REGISTER

The *Federal Register* is a daily newspaper that informs the public of congressional and federal enactments and regulatory activities. It is the official publication used by the federal government to announce changes to the FAR. The National Archives and Records Administration is responsible for publishing the *Federal Register*. The size of the *Federal Register* varies from 200 to 600 pages (or more), depending on the number and length of announcements.

Careful attention to the *Federal Register* will help you anticipate the government's priorities and program changes. The *Federal Register* is available online at:

WWW.GPOACCESS.GOV/fr/index.html

FEDERAL AGENCY ACQUISITION FORECASTS

Among the best sources a contractor can use to anticipate future contract actions or awards are federal agency acquisition forecasts. Each federal agency must compile and make available one-year projections of contracting opportunities that small and small disadvantaged businesses can perform. Most federal agencies announce their acquisition forecasts on the Internet. You can find these at each agency's website, or call the agency to request a copy.

BIDDERS LISTS

Contracting activities (or buying offices) maintain bidders lists to identify contractors that have expressed an interest in furnishing a particular supply or service. Bidders lists are also called "solicitation mailing lists," "bidders list catalogs," or "commodity lists."

Contracting activities typically keep separate bidders lists for the various types of supplies and services they purchase. For example, a contracting

Federal Register / Vol. 68, No. 166 / Wednesday, August 27, 2003 / Notices   **51565**

Personal Data Record, USAFA Form 146, OMB Number 0701–0064.

Needs and Uses: The information collection requirement is necessary to obtain data on candidate's background and aptitude in determining eligibility and selection to the Air Force Academy.

Affected Public: Individuals or households.

Annual Burden Hours: 3,617.

Number of Respondents: 7,233.

Responses per Respondent: 1.

Average Burden per Response: 30 Minutes.

Frequency: 1.

SUPPLEMENTARY INFORMATION:

Summary of Information Collection

The information collected on this form is required by 10 U.S.C. 9346. The respondents are students who are applying for admission to the United States Air Force Academy. Each student's background and aptitude is reviewed to determine eligibility. If the information on this form is not collected, the individual cannot be considered for admittance to the Air Force Academy.

Pamela Fitzgerald,

Air Force Federal Register Liaison Officer.

[FR Doc. 03–21846 Filed 8–26–03; 8:45 am]

BILLING CODE 5001–05–P

DEPARTMENT OF DEFENSE

Department of the Air Force

Proposed Collection; Comment Request

AGENCY: Department of the Air Force, DoD.

ACTION: Notice.

In compliance with Section 3506(c)(2)(A) of the Paperwork Reduction Act of 1995, Headquarters Air Force Recruiting Service announces the proposed extension of a currently approved public information collection and seeks public comment on the provisions thereof. Comments are invited on: (a) Whether the proposed collection of information is necessary for the proper performance of the functions of the agency, including whether the information shall have practical utility; (b) the accuracy of the agency's estimate of the burden of the proposed information collection; (c) ways to enhance the quality, unity, and clarity of the information to be collected; (d) ways to minimize the burden of the information collection on respondents, including the use of automated collection techniques or other forms of information technology.

DATES: Consideration will be given to all comments received by September 8, 2003.

ADDRESSES: Written comments and recommendations on the proposed information collection should be sent to Department of Defense, HQ AFRS/RSOC, 550 D Street West, Suite 1, Randolph AFB TX 78150–4527.

FOR FURTHER INFORMATION CONTACT: To request more information on this proposed information collection or to obtain a copy of the proposal and associated collection instruments, please write to the above addresses, or call HQ AFRS/RSOC, Officer Accessions Branch at (210) 652–4334.

Title, Associated Form, and OMB Number: Air Force Officer Training School Accession Forms, AETC Forms 1413 and 1422, OMB Number 0701–0080.

Needs and Uses: These forms are used by field recruiters and education counselors in the processing of Officer Training School (OTS) applications.

Affected Public: Civilian and Active Duty OTS Applicants.

Annual Burden Hours: 2,200.

Number of Respondents: 1,700.

Responses per Respondent: 1.

Average Burden per Response: 1 Hour (AETC Form 1413)/2 Hours (AETC Form 1422).

Frequency: On Occasion.

SUPPLEMENTARY INFORMATION:

Summary of Information Collection

Respondents are civilian and active-duty candidates applying for a commission in the United States Air Force. These forms provide pertinent information to facilitate selection of candidates for commission.

Pamela Fitzgerald,

Air Force Federal Register Liaison Officer.

[FR Doc. 03–21848 Filed 8–26–03; 8:45 am]

BILLING CODE 5001–05–P

DEPARTMENT OF DEFENSE

Department of the Air Force

Proposed Collection; Comment Request

AGENCY: Department of the Air Force, DoD.

ACTION: Notice.

In compliance with section 3506(c)(2)(A) of the Paperwork Reduction Act of 1995, Headquarters Air Force Recruiting Service announces the proposed extension of a currently approved public information collection and seeks public comment on the provisions thereof. Comments are invited on: (a) Whether the proposed collection of information is necessary for the proper performance of the functions of the agency, including whether the information shall have practical utility; (b) the accuracy of the agency's estimate of the burden of the proposed information collection; (c) ways to enhance the quality, unity, and clarity of the information to be collected; (d) ways to minimize the burden of the information collection on respondents, including the use of automated collection techniques or other forms of information technology.

DATES: Consideration will be given to all comments received by September 11, 2003.

ADDRESSES: Written comments and recommendations on the proposed information collection should be sent to Department of Defense, HQ AFRS/RSOC, 550 D Street West, Suite 1, Randolph AFB TX 78150–4527.

FOR FURTHER INFORMATION CONTACT: To request more information on this proposed information collection or to obtain a copy of the proposal and associated collection instruments, please write to the above addresses, or call HQ AFRS/RSOC, Officer Accessions Branch at (210) 652–4334.

Title, Associated Form, and OMB Number: Health Profession Accession Forms, AETC Forms 1402 and 1437, OMB Number 0701–0078.

Needs and Uses: These forms are used by field recruiters in the processing of health professions applicants applying for a commission in the United States Air Force.

Affected Public: Individuals or households.

Annual Burden Hours: 3,600.

Number of Respondents: 3,600.

Responses per Respondent: 1.

Average Burden per Response: 1 Hour.

Frequency: On Occasion.

SUPPLEMENTARY INFORMATION:

Summary of Information Collection

Respondents are civilian candidates applying for a commission in the United States Air Force as healthcare officers. These forms provide pertinent information to facilitate selection of candidates for commission.

Pamela Fitzgerald,

Air Force Federal Register Liaison Officer.

[FR Doc. 03–21849 Filed 8–26–03; 8:45 am]

BILLING CODE 5001–05–P

Sample Page of *Federal Register*

activity might have separate bidders lists for office supplies, motor vehicle parts, janitorial services, light fixtures, video equipment, technical support, and computers. The best way to get information about a contracting activity's bidders list procedures is to contact the small business specialist at that particular contracting activity.

Many contracting activities use Standard Form 129, Solicitation Mailing List Application, as its bidders list application. Standard Form 129 asks for the following information:

■ Type of organization (corporation, partnership, or individual)

■ Officers' names

■ Supplies and services offered (use descriptions that are as specific as possible; in addition, use government classification codes, standards, or specifications, if known)

■ Business size and average number of employees

■ Ownership type (e.g., small disadvantaged business, women-owned business)

■ Length of time in business

■ Financial status.

For example, if Rick Hanley, of Rick's Hardware, wanted to sell some of the tools his company manufactures to the Defense Logistics Agency, he would submit an SF 129 with the information shown in the sample.

Electronic registration via an agency's Internet home page is the best way to submit your bidders list application.

Placement on a bidders (or mailing) list does not guarantee that you will receive government orders. Government regulations require only that a sufficient number of offerors be solicited to ensure competition. If a particular bidders list includes many firms capable of supplying the products

SOLICITATION MAILING LIST APPLICATION	1. TYPE OF APPLICATION ■ INITIAL ❏ REVISION	2. DATE 3/30/06	FORM APPROVED OMB NO. 2900-0445

NOTE: Please complete all items on this form. Insert N/A in items not applicable. See reverse for instructions.

Public reporting burden for this collection of information is estimated to average .58 hours per response, including the time for reviewing instructions, searching existing data sources, gathering and maintaining the data needed, and completing and reviewing the collection of information. Send comments regarding this burden estimate or any other aspect of this collection of information, including suggestions for reducing this burden, to the FAR Secretariat (MVR), Federal Acquisition Policy Division, GSA, Washington, DC 20405.

3. SUBMIT TO

A. FEDERAL AGENCY'S NAME		
Defense Supply Center Columbus		
B. STREET ADDRESS		
3990 East Broad Street		

C. CITY	D. STATE	E. ZIPCODE
Columbus	OH	43216

4. APPLICANT

A. NAME		
Rick's Hardware		
B. STREET ADDRESS		C. COUNTY
128 K Street		

D. CITY	E. STATE	F. ZIPCODE
Wichita	KS	67201

5. TYPE OF ORGANIZATION (Check one)

❏ INDIVIDUAL
❏ NON-PROFIT ORGANIZATION
❏ PARTNERSHIP
■ CORPORATION, INCORPORATED UNDER THE LAWS OF THE STATE OF: KS

6. ADDRESS TO WHICH SOLICITATIONS ARE TO BE MAILED (IF DIFFERENT THAN ITEM 4)

A. STREET ADDRESS	B. COUNTY

C. CITY	D. STATE	E. ZIPCODE

6(A). EMAIL ADDRESS

7. NAMES OF OFFICERS, OWNERS, OR PARTNERS

A. PRESIDENT	B. VICE PRESIDENT	C. SECRETARY
Rick Hanley	Susan Snow	Judy Stevens

D. TREASURER	E. OWNERS OR PARTNERS
Joe Smith	N/A

8. AFFILIATES OF APPLICANT (Names, locations and nature of affiliation. See definition on reverse)

NAME	LOCATION	NATURE OF AFFILIATION

9. PERSONS AUTHORIZED TO SIGN OFFERS AND CONTRACTS IN YOUR NAME (Indicate if agent)

NAME	OFFICIAL CAPACITY	TELEPHONE NUMBER AREA CODE	NUMBER
Rick Hanley	President		999-888-5616
Susan Snow	Vice President		999-888-5617

10. IDENTIFY EQUIPMENT, SUPPLIES, AND/OR SERVICES ON WHICH YOU DESIRE TO MAKE AN OFFER, AND INCLUDE NORTH AMERICAN INDUSTRY CLASSIFICATION SYSTEM CODE (NAICS)
Stainless Steel Hammers and Stainless Steel Chisels

11A. SIZE OF BUSINESS (See definitions on reverse) ■ SMALL BUSINESS (IF CHECKED, COMPLETE ITEMS 11B AND 11C) ❏ OTHER THAN SMALL BUSINESS	11B. AVERAGE NUMBER OF EMPLOYEES (Including affiliates) FOR FOUR PRECEDING CALENDAR QUARTERS 25	11C. AVERAGE ANNUAL SALES OR RECEIPTS FOR PRECEDING THREE FISCAL YEARS $ 250,000

12. TYPE OF OWNERSHIP (See definitions on reverse) (Not applicable for other than small business) ❏ DISADVANTAGED BUSINESS　❏ WOMEN-OWNED BUSINESS ❏ HUBZONE SMALL BUSINESS　■ VETERAN-OWNED BUSINESS ❏ VERY SMALL BUSINESS　❏ SERVICE DISABLED VETERAN ❏ 8(A)	13. TYPE OF BUSINESS (See definitions on reverse) ■ MANUFACTURER OR PRODUCER ❏ SERVICE ESTABLISHMENT ❏ CONSTRUCTION COINCERN ❏ RESEARCH AND DEVELOPMENT ❏ SURPLUS DEALER

14. DUN AND BRADSTREET NUMBER (If applicable) 12-589-1684	15. HOW LONG IN PRESENT BUSINESS 5 years

16. FLOOR SPACE (In square feet)		17. NET WORTH	
A. MANUFACTURING	B. WAREHOUSE	A. DATE	B. AMOUNT
8,000	5,000	December 31, 2005	$ 50,000

18. SECURITY CLEARANCE (If applicable, check highest clearance authorized)

FOR	TOP SECRET	SECRET	CONFIDENTIAL	C. NAME OF AGENCIES WHICH GRANTED SECURITY CLEARANCES	D. DATES GRANTED
A. KEY PERSONNEL	N/A				
B. PLANT ONLY					

CERTIFICATION -- I certify that information supplied herein (including all pages attached) is correct and that neither the applicant nor any person (for concern) in any connection with the applicant as a principal or officer, so far as is known, is now debarred or otherwise declared ineligible by any agency of the Federal Government from making offers for furnishing materials, supplies, or services to the Government or any agency thereof.

19. NAME AND TITLE OF PERSON AUTHORIZED TO SIGN (Type or Print) Rick Hurley, President	20. SIGNATURE	21. DATE SIGNED 3/30/06

AUTHORIZED FOR LOCAL REPRODUCTION　　　　　　　　　　　　STANDARD FORM 129

Sample SF 129

or services sought, the contracting activity may select only a portion of those listed to solicit. However, a rotation system ensures that each offeror has a fair chance of being selected periodically. Even if you are listed, you should secure information about bids from other sources, such as FedBizOpps, to maximize your selling opportunities.

Effective October 1, 2003, federal contracting activities are no longer required to establish and maintain manual solicitation mailing lists. This change to the FAR is intended to broaden the use of e-business applications such as the Central Contractor Registration (CCR) system.

Bidders lists are slowly but surely becoming a thing of the past. In today's marketplace, they are used primarily by smaller contracting activities to purchase items that are under the micropurchase threshold of $2,500.

Using a Bidders List

The following example illustrates how Widget World, a small business, navigates through the Department of Transportation's bidders list system.

Julie Smith, the company's accountant, completes and submits an SF 129 application for widgets to a contracting activity in the Department of Transportation. On January 5, 2005, the application is received and approved by the contracting activity.

Luckily, Mike Mitchell, a contracting officer at this activity, happens to be issuing a solicitation for $2,000 worth of widgets. Currently, the contracting activity has 20 businesses on its widget bidders list. Mike Mitchell decides to solicit 10 businesses to help ensure full and open competition.

Although Mike Mitchell can randomly select businesses from the current bidders list or send a solicitation to all the businesses on the list, he decides to rotate the bidders list because it is excessively long. As is typical when a bidders list is rotated, he solicits from the previously successful bidder; firms that were added to the list since the last solic-

continued

continued

itation, which includes Widget World; and a certain other portion of the list. Julie Smith, the accountant, watches carefully for this solicitation because if Widget World is not on the initial bidders list and she has to request a copy of the solicitation, Mike Mitchell, the contracting officer, must provide one for her.

Many times, you will receive a solicitation for which you are not interested in submitting a bid. In that case, notify the contracting officer in writing that you are unable to submit a bid at this time but would like to be retained on the bidders list. Be sure to use your company's letterhead, so the contracting officer can clearly identify you as the sender. If you are removed from a bidders list, you will have to resubmit your SF 129.

PROCUREMENT MARKETING AND ACCESS NETWORK

The Procurement Marketing and Access Network (Pro-Net) is an electronic gateway of procurement information for and about small businesses. It is a search engine for contracting officers, a marketing tool for small firms, and a link to procurement opportunities and important information. Pro-Net is a virtual one-stop procurement shop.

Pro-Net is an Internet database that includes information on more than 220,000 small, disadvantaged, 8(a), HUBZone, and women-owned businesses. It is free to federal and state government agencies, as well as to prime and other contractors seeking small business contractors, subcontractors, or partnership opportunities. Pro-Net is also open to all small firms seeking federal, state, and private contracts. Businesses profiled on the Pro-Net system can be searched by NAICS codes, key words, location, quality certifications, business type, ownership race and gender, and other criteria.

Business profiles in the Pro-Net system include data from SBA's files and other available databases, plus additional business and marketing information, such as company specialties. Businesses listed on the system update their profiles, keeping all information current. Profiles are structured like executive business summaries, with specific data search fields that are user-friendly and designed to meet the needs of contracting officers and other potential users. These profiles also give vendors an opportunity to put a controlled marketing spin on their businesses. Companies with home pages can link their websites to their Pro-Net profiles, creating a very powerful marketing tool. To learn more about Pro-Net, visit SBA's website.

SUB-NET

Although there is no single point-of-entry for subcontracting opportunities in the federal marketplace, SBA's SUB-Net is a valuable source for obtaining information on subcontracting solicitations and notices. Prime contractors, federal agencies, state and local governments, and educational entities are encouraged to post solicitations and notices there.

SUB-Net allows users to search for opportunities by NAICS code, description (key word), or solicitation number. You can access SUB-Net through the PRO-Net home page by choosing the "Subcontracting Opportunities" button. Or, you can go directly to SUB-Net at:

http://web.sba.gov/subnet

TECH-NET

TECH-Net, the Technology Resources Network, is a search engine that features a database of high-tech small businesses. Business profiles are structured like executive business summaries, with specific data fields that are user-friendly and designed to meet the needs of researchers, contracting officers, investors, and other potential users. Small businesses can use their profiles to market their capabilities and accomplishments. TECH-Net also provides access to SBIR/STTR solicitations (see Chapter 5) and other technology procurement opportunities.

Businesses profiled on TECH-Net can be searched using a variety of data elements, including: NAICS code; key words; location; company name, ownership race and gender; technology code; and contract award year. For more information on TECH-Net, visit:

http://tech-net.sba.gov/

SBAEXCHANGE

SBAExchange is an electronic purchasing tool that allows federal agencies to award simplified acquisitions up to $100,000 (including micropurchases) and make purchases and payments electronically with a government-wide credit card. In other words, SBAExchange allows you to bid on government projects over the Internet.

When an award exceeds $25,000, the buying office must post a notice in FedBizOpps stating that the award will be made electronically using SBAExchange.

SBAExchange provides small businesses the following benefits:

- A fully hosted, supplier branded, e-commerce website

- Exposure to federal buying offices, prime contractors, and other buying officials

- An electronic catalog

- A centralized order management system for receiving and processing Internet-based orders from federal, state, local, and commercial buying authorities

- A management system for tracking new business and creating and submitting quotes

- Assistance in managing the new site.

Federal agencies receive a number of benefits as well, including credit toward small business goals, access to socioeconomic data and demographic reports, and online order approval and tracking.

The annual cost for a small business to participate in SBAExchange is $1,500. Additionally, a transaction fee of 2% is added to all orders. For more information on SBAExchange, visit the following website:

WWW.SBAEXCHANGE.GOV

FEDERAL PROCUREMENT DATA SYSTEM-NG

The Federal Procurement Data System (FPDS) was established in 1978 by Congress as a system for collecting, developing, and disseminating data on the $265 billion a year the government spends on supplies and services. Over the years, the FPDS became out-of-date, and its data became unreliable, so the next-generation FPDS (a.k.a. FPDS-NG) was developed to vastly improve the speed and accuracy of government procurement/sales data.

Among its many features, FPDS-NG:

■ Provides the public web access to all data in "real-time"

■ Provides users with extensive online reporting capabilities, including reports with charts and graphs

■ Collects data on over 13 million procurements valued at more than $2,500, including who bought what, from whom, the dollar amount of each transaction, when the contract was signed, and where the work is performed

■ Maintains an historical trail of all transactions, including interagency transactions conducted through government-wide acquisition contracts (GWACs), multi-agency contracts, and Federal Supply Schedule (FSS) contracts

■ Enables government acquisition officials worldwide to input and access purchase data via the web.

Unlike its predecessor, FPDS-NG is designed to serve as a federal-wide acquisition management information system. It provides unprecedented visibility into procurement and acquisition activities within federal agencies.

For more information on FPDS-NG, visit:

WWW.FPDS.GOV

YEAR-END PROCUREMENTS

The federal government operates on a fiscal-year basis, which begins on October 1 and ends on September 30. As mentioned in Chapter 2, Congress appropriates funds to federal agencies to run their operations or mission requirements. The appropriations can be for a single year, multiple years, or on an unrestricted basis. The majority of the appropriations are for a single year. If Congress appropriates funds to a federal agency on a single-year basis, the agency must spend those funds during that particular fiscal year or lose the funding. Use it or lose it! This situation gives federal agencies no incentive to save money. In fact, it encourages agencies to spend all available funds.

What quarter during the government's fiscal year historically has the highest level of procurement activity or number of acquisitions? If you guessed the fourth quarter, you're right. Why do you think this is? It's not because federal personnel have gone crazy from the heat; it's because the majority of government funds expire on September 30. If you receive a solicitation during May or June, the agency may have to award the contract before midnight on September 30 or lose its funding.

It is a fact of life that year-end procurements tend to be a little frantic. Mostly this is the result of poor planning by the agencies, internal bickering, and politics. These procurements are often poorly thought out, poorly designed, and fraught with errors that must be corrected after the procurement has been awarded. Knowing the government's situation at this time of the year gives you an advantage during the solicitation process.

There are exceptions to this requirement. For example, funds that are appropriated on an unrestricted basis (also referred to as no-year money) or funds that are appropriated for more than one year do not necessarily expire on September 30. Ask the contracting officer about the status of a contract's appropriated funds.

■   ■   ■

In spite of—or because of—the federal government's size, no one way exists to market your supplies and services. Each federal agency's procedures differ for purchasing supplies and services; therefore, the best way to market your supplies and services is to contact specific agencies to determine exactly how their procurement processes work.

To be successful in marketing to the federal government, you must be persistent. Visit each federal agency's website. Go to the programs and workshops that the agencies offer. Register your supplies and services with the agencies. Talk to each agency's small business specialist. Provide each contracting office (or contracting activity) with brochures or other information describing your company, supplies and services, area served, and other details. Do whatever it takes to get your supplies and services noticed!

■   ■   ■

Support Programs and Services for Contractors

© 1997 Randy Glasbergen
www.glasbergen.com

HAIR BALLS
50¢

GLASBERGEN

"Business is lousy. Maybe I should have done more market research first."

What's in this chapter?

- Small Business Administration
- Defense Logistics Agency
- General Services Administration
- A-76 Program
- Federal Information Center
- FirstGov
- National Contract Management Association

The government has established numerous programs and services to help small businesses participate in federal contracting. For example, each federal agency must provide small businesses with information on procurement opportunities, guidance on procurement procedures, and identification of both prime and subcontracting opportunities. Many nonfederal sources also offer services. This chapter discusses many of the support programs and services that are available to small business contractors.

SMALL BUSINESS ADMINISTRATION

The Small Business Administration (SBA) is in business solely to help the small business owner. It provides small businesses with a wide variety of programs and services covering various business areas, including financial, technical, and management assistance. Specifically, SBA offers five major programs:

- Business development assistance

- Procurement assistance

- Minority small business assistance

- Advocacy

- Financial assistance.

SBA also offers counseling services to business owners or potential business owners on all facets of small business matters.

Did You Know That SBA . . .

- Partners with more than 7,000 private sector lenders to provide capital to small businesses?

- Guaranteed more than 73,000 loans totaling $14 billion to small businesses during FY2003?

■ Maintains a portfolio guaranteeing more than $35 billion in loans to 200,000 small businesses that otherwise would not have such access to capital?

■ Extended management and technical assistance to nearly one million small businesses through its 1,100 Small Business Development Centers and 10,500 Service Corps of Retired Executives volunteers during FY2003?

■ Provides loan guarantees and technical assistance to small business exporters through U.S. Export Assistance Centers?

The best place to locate up-to-the-minute information about SBA programs and services is the Internet. SBA's website is:

WWW.SBA.GOV

This web page also offers detailed information about SBA and other business services.

SBA Answer Desk

The SBA answer desk is a toll-free information center that answers questions about starting or running a business and getting assistance. The toll-free number is (800) 827-5722 or (800) 8-ASK-SBA.

This answer desk can give you a list of SBA offices and their telephone numbers.

SBA Business Information Centers

Business Information Centers (BICs) are one-stop locations where current and future small business owners can receive assistance and advice. BICs combine the latest computer technology (hardware and software), an extensive small business reference library of books and publications, and current management videotapes to help entrepreneurs plan their strategies, expand existing businesses, or venture into new business areas. BICs also offer one-on-one counseling in conjunction with the Service Corps of Retired Executives.

Each BIC adds new materials and resources throughout the year to meet special needs in the small business community. BICs also inform the public about new initiatives and programs offered by SBA and reach business owners who might not otherwise take advantage of SBA's programs and services. Every BIC provides contractors access to SBA Online, the agency's national electronic bulletin board, and the Internet. Individuals who are in business or are interested in starting a business can use the BIC as often as they like at no charge.

Service Corps of Retired Executives

SBA developed the Service Corps of Retired Executives (SCORE) to provide one-on-one management counseling to aspiring entrepreneurs and business owners. SCORE's experienced business experts offer general business advice on everything from marketing and writing a business plan, to managing cash flow, to developing a small business advisory board. Assistance for aspiring entrepreneurs may involve investigating the market potential for a product or service and assessing the capital needs to start a business. Counselors also give insight into how to start, operate, buy or franchise, and sell a business. These services are free. Currently more than 10,500 volunteer business counselors are located at SBA field offices and BICs throughout the United States.

For a current list of SCORE locations and addresses, visit:

WWW.SCORE.ORG

or call (800) 634-0245.

SBA Small Business Development Centers

Numerous studies have shown that most small businesses fail as a result of poor management. SBA established the Small Business Development Center (SBDC) program to provide management assistance to current and prospective small business owners. This program coordinates efforts among universities across the country; local, state, and federal governments; and private sector businesses to provide assistance with management techniques and technology to the small business community. SBDC services include assisting small businesses with financial, marketing, production, organization, engineering, and technical problems and feasibility studies. In addition, these SBDCs offer special programs and services on international trade, business law, venture capital formation, and rural development.

Currently, there are 57 SBDCs, one in each state (except Texas, which has four), the District of Columbia, Puerto Rico, Guam, and the U.S. Virgin Islands. In each state a lead organization sponsors the SBDC and manages the program. The lead organization coordinates program services offered to small businesses through a network of subcenters and satellite locations in each state, providing more than 1,100 service locations. Subcenters are located at universities, colleges, community colleges, vocational schools, local government offices, and economic development centers.

The best way to locate information about these SBDCs is to contact your local SBA office.

SBA Women Business Centers

Women Business Centers (WBCs) provide women with long-term training and counseling in all aspects of owning and managing a business. SBA has a network of more than 60 WBCs located in 36 states, the District of Columbia, and Puerto Rico. You can access information about these WBCs by calling the SBA answer desk at (800) 8-ASK-SBA.

The answer desk will give you the telephone number of the Women's Business Ownership representative in your state or district. There are currently more than 70 Women's Business Ownership representatives, with at least one in each state.

SBA has also set up an Online Women's Business Center to provide comprehensive training, counseling, and information. Visit the Online WBC at the following address:

WWW.ONLINEWBC.GOV

SBA Office of Advocacy

SBA's Office of Advocacy encourages policies that support small business development and growth. In addition, the Office of Advocacy works to reduce the burdens that federal policies impose on small businesses and to maximize the benefits small businesses receive. To accomplish these objectives, Congress has specified five statutory duties for SBA's advocacy office:

■ Serve as a focal point for receiving complaints, criticisms, and suggestions concerning federal policies and activities that affect small businesses

■ Counsel small businesses on ways to resolve problems in dealing with the federal government

■ Represent small businesses before other federal agencies whose actions affect small business

■ Develop proposals that recommend government changes to better comply with the Small Business Act (see Chapter 4) and communicate such proposals to appropriate federal agencies

■ Work with federal agencies and private groups to examine ways in which small businesses can make better use of the government's programs and services.

The Office of Advocacy also provides statistics and research studies on small businesses. For more information about the SBA Office of Advocacy, contact:

Office of Advocacy
U.S. Small Business Administration
409 Third Street, SW
Washington, DC 20416
Phone (202) 205-6532

SBA Financial Assistance Programs

No matter how carefully you manage your company's cash flow, at some point, you will have to borrow money. The two primary reasons a company borrows money are to (1) cover temporary cash-flow shortages, and (2) provide working capital for business growth. One of the best places for a small business to look for financial assistance is SBA.

SBA provides financial assistance in the form of loan guarantees to qualified small businesses that are unable to obtain credit elsewhere. These loans are available for many business purposes, such as acquiring real estate, equipment, working capital, or inventory, or for expanding. To be eligible for an SBA loan, a business must meet the size standards established by industry type (published by SBA). Check with your local SBA lender to determine your eligibility.

SBA makes loans in conjunction with a bank or other lending institution, which provides the funds while SBA guarantees up to 90% of the loan. When funds are available to SBA, it can also consider a direct or immediate participation loan. The major benefit to borrowers who obtain loans through SBA programs is the terms of the loans, which are typically longer than those available from commercial lenders. SBA does not provide grants to start or expand a business.

SBA offers many different types of loans, including:

- International trade loans

- Minority prequalification loans

- Women's prequalification loans

- Physical disaster business loans

- Contract loans

- Surety bond guarantees

- Small business energy loans

- Microloans

- General contractor loans.

To be eligible for an SBA loan, you must first apply—and be rejected—for a loan from at least one qualified commercial lender. Reasons for rejection might include situations in which the repayment period was too long, the business had not been in operation long enough, or the loan request was too large. If the lender rejects your loan request for any reason other than your ability to repay the loan, ask if the lender would be willing to make the loan if SBA guaranteed it.

If the lender agrees to the SBA loan arrangement, the lender contacts SBA to determine if the agency will guarantee the loan. Assuming that the loan meets SBA's criteria, the lender decides whether or not to make the loan. If the lender agrees, it makes the necessary arrangements to secure the guarantee with SBA. If the lender refuses to make the loan, the borrower must look for another lender.

Borrowers should be prepared to pay closing costs on SBA-guaranteed loans. Closing costs vary, but most tend to be 3–5% of the total loan amount.

DEFENSE LOGISTICS AGENCY

The Defense Logistics Agency (DLA) is not a support program for contractors. It is, however, an organization that contractors interested in selling to the military should be aware of. DLA provides supply support, contract administration services, and technical and logistical services to all branches of the military and to several civilian agencies. DLA also manages a distribution system of approximately four million general supply items, including:

■ Food and clothing

■ Textiles

■ Fuel and petroleum products

■ Medical and dental equipment

■ Automotive parts

■ Electronic spare parts

■ Construction equipment.

DLA buys and manages these supplies at the following Lead Centers:

Defense Supply Center Columbus
3990 East Broad Street
Columbus, OH 43216-5000
(877) 352-2255

Defense Energy Support Center
8725 John J. Kingman Road,
Suite 4950
Fort Belvoir, VA 22060-6222
(800) 286-7633

Defense Supply Center Richmond
8000 Jefferson Davis Highway
Richmond, VA 23297-5764
(877) DLA-CALL

Defense Supply Center
   Philadelphia
700 Robbins Avenue
Philadelphia, PA 19111-5092
(877) DLA-CALL

Defense Distribution Center	Defense Reutilization and
2001 Mission Drive	Marketing Service
New Cumberland, PA 17070-5000	74 N. Washington Ave.
(877) DLA-CALL	Battle Creek, MI 49017-3092
	(888) 352-9333

Each of these centers manages very specific commodity groupings, so don't be misled by the center names. If you are interested in selling to the military, contact the small business specialist at the supply center that purchases your particular supplies (see Chapter 3). DLA has the following website:

WWW.DLA.MIL

(DOD websites typically end in .MIL, which is an abbreviation for "military.")

MILITARY OPPORTUNITIES

DOD has published a handbook called *Selling to the Military*, which furnishes general information about DOD contracting. If you plan to contract with DOD, this handbook will be very useful to you. For more information about this publication, visit:

WWW.ACQ.OSD.MIL/sadbu/publications/

GENERAL SERVICES ADMINISTRATION

The General Services Administration (GSA) is one of three management agencies in the federal government (the Office of Personnel Management and the Office of Management and Budget are the others). GSA provides federal agencies with the tools necessary to perform their day-to-day operations. In many respects, GSA could be considered the government's landlord or housekeeper. For example, GSA provides the following supplies and services to federal agencies across the country:

- Workspace and security

- Furniture

- Equipment and supplies (including tools, telephones, and computers)

- Travel and transportation services

- Federal motor vehicle fleet management

- Telecommuting and federal child care center management

- Historic building preservation

- Fine art program management

- Development, advocacy, and evaluation for governmentwide policies.

GSA disbursements amount to several billion dollars annually. The best place to access current information about GSA programs and services is on the Internet at:

WWW.GSA.GOV

GSA also distributes a handbook called *Doing Business With GSA,* which provides general information about agency contracting. This handbook is available at GSA Business Service Centers (BSCs). Use GSA's website to locate the address and telephone number of the BSC that services your area or call the Federal Information Center at **(800) FED-INFO.**

GSA Forecast of Contracting Opportunities

The Office of Enterprise Development makes GSA's forecast of contracting opportunities available in accordance with the Business Opportunity Development Reform Act of 1988. This forecast informs small, small disadvantaged, and small women-owned businesses of anticipated contracting opportunities with GSA and other federal agencies for the current fiscal year, as well as known opportunities for subsequent fiscal years.

GSA Business Service Centers

GSA Business Service Centers (BSCs) serve as a front door for small businesses seeking to market their products and services to GSA. These centers advise and counsel individuals interested in contracting with GSA and other federal agencies and departments. BSCs also distribute federal directories, publication lists, references, and a variety of technical publications concerning contracts and bidding forms. Currently 12 BSCs are located throughout the country. GSA's website provides the address and telephone number of the BSC that serves your area or region.

Each BSC is staffed with specialists who can give you information on how to:

■ Get onto GSA's bidders lists

■ Introduce items for government purchase

■ Learn about current bidding opportunities with GSA

■ Obtain copies of federal standards and specifications

■ Review bid abstracts to learn the bidding history of various contract awards (abstracts identify the names of successful bidders, other bidders, and the prices they bid)

■ Obtain publications and other documents about government procurements

■ Receive business counseling.

BSCs also play an important role in GSA's small business set-aside programs. The BSC may challenge a contracting officer's decision not to set aside a procurement for small business. It also reviews prime contracts to identify subcontracting opportunities for small and small disadvantaged businesses.

Offices of Small and Disadvantaged Business Utilization

Each major federal agency and department must have an Office of Small and Disadvantaged Business Utilization (OSDBU). The OSDBU provides small businesses with information on procurement opportunities, guidance on procurement procedures, and identification of both prime and subcontracting opportunities. For a current list of OSDBU locations and addresses, see:

WWW.OSDBU.GOV

A-76 PROGRAM

This program is a product of the Office of Management and Budget (OMB) Circular A-76, Performance of Commercial Activities, which establishes procedures for determining whether federal functions or activities should be performed under contract with commercial sources or in-house using government facilities and personnel. It is the policy of the government not to compete with its citizens and to rely on commercial sources to supply the products and services the government needs. The terms "downsizing," "privatization," and "outsourcing" are generally synonymous with the A-76 program. Unless otherwise provided by law, the A-76 Circular applies to all federal agencies.

Certain functions are inherently governmental in nature, being so intimately related to the public interest as to mandate performance only by federal employees. For example, monetary transactions and entitlements, such as tax collection and revenue disbursements, are inherently governmental functions. These functions are not in competition with the commercial sector and are therefore to be performed by federal employees.

On the other hand, the government should not start or carry on any activity to provide a product or service if that product or service can be procured more economically from a commercial source. Examples of activities suitable for outsourcing include:

■ Equipment installation, operation, and maintenance

■ Machine, carpentry, electrical, plumbing, painting, and other shops

■ Custodial and janitorial services

■ Office furniture and equipment

■ Laundry and dry cleaning

■ Guard and protective services

■ Scientific data studies.

The government is required perform a comparison of the cost of contracting (with a commercial vendor) and the cost of in-house performance to determine who will do the work. When conducting cost comparisons, the government must ensure that all costs are considered and that these costs are realistic and fair.

OMB Circular A-76 requires each federal agency to maintain a detailed inventory or record of all of its in-house activities that could be obtained from commercial sources. These inventories of commercial activities are submitted to the Office of Management and Budget on a yearly basis. After review and consultation by OMB, the agencies will submit a copy of the inventory to Congress and make the contents of the inventory available to the public.

Agencies are responsible for establishing one or more offices as central points of contact to carry out the provisions of the A-76 Circular. Each office has access to documents and data pertinent to actions taken under the Circular and will respond in a timely manner to all requests concerning inventories, schedules, reviews, results of cost comparisons, and cost comparison data. Contractors are encouraged to examine the inventories of commercial activities for outsourcing candidates. Agencies are also responsible for conducting cost comparisons when inventory activities do not meet established performance standards.

When an inventory activity is identified as a candidate for outsourcing, the contracting officer will place a synopsis of the activity in FedBizOpps to determine if sufficient commercial sources are available to perform the activity. Assuming that sufficient commercial sources are available, the contracting officer will issue the solicitation stating the method of procurement. All competitive methods of procurement are appropriate for cost comparison under the Circular (see Part IV).

The federal agency will then prepare a cost estimate according to the solicitation's statement of work (or performance work statement). The cost estimate represents the agency's total cost to continue performing the commercial activity. The agency will use Circular A-76, Attachment C—Calculating Public-Private Competition Costs, to prepare the cost estimate. This attachment provides detailed procedures for developing the cost estimate and specifically identifies such factors as tax rates, depreciation rates, fringe benefit rates, insurance costs, repair and maintenance costs, and similar costs. The competed cost estimate is sealed and stored with the other bids or proposals. Finally, the contract will be awarded to the offeror providing the best value to the government.

The A-76 program is not designed to simply outsource federal functions. Rather, it is designed to balance the interests of the parties to a make-or-buy cost comparison, provide a level playing field between public and private offerors, and encourage competition and choice in the management and performance of commercial activities. It empowers federal agencies to make sound and justifiable business decisions.

The A-76 Circular and its supplement are available online at:

WWW.WHITEHOUSE.GOV/omb/circulars/

Federal Procurement Conferences

Federal procurement conferences give small businesses the opportunity to meet with procurement specialists from both military and civilian agencies, as well as prime contractors. In addition, these conferences inform small businesses about federal procurement and contracting processes, assistance available to small businesses, and opportunities to sell to federal agencies and prime contractors. These conferences are held at various locations throughout the country. You can
locate information about these conferences and their exact times and
locations at:

WWW.ACQ.OSD.MIL/sadbu/conferences/

FEDERAL INFORMATION CENTER

The Federal Information Center (FIC) is a single point of contact for
questions about federal agencies, programs, and services. You can access
this information center at:

WWW.INFO.GOV
or
(800) FED-INFO

An FIC Information Specialist will answer your questions directly, refer
you to the correct office, or research your inquiry.

FIRSTGOV

FirstGov.gov is the federal government's attempt to create a one-stop
shopping mall for government information. By linking nearly all government resources, FirstGov allows users to search: a directory of agencies;
popular topics; reference sources, such as news releases, forms, and laws

and regulations; and online services for citizens, businesses, and federal, state, and local governments.

Federal Yellow Book

The Federal Yellow Book is an organizational directory of the departments and agencies of the federal government's executive branch. It lists positions, addresses, and telephone numbers for more than 40,000 federal officials. For more information about this publication, contact:

Leadership Directories, Inc.
1001 G Street, NW
Suite 200 East
Washington, DC 20001
Tel: (202) 347-7757

WWW.LEADERSHIPDIRECTORIES.COM/fyb.htm

NATIONAL CONTRACT MANAGEMENT ASSOCIATION

The National Contract Management Association (NCMA) is a professional association in the field of contract management with more than 21,000 members. NCMA offers the following programs and services:

■ Training programs

■ *Contract Management* magazine

■ *National Contract Management* journal

■ National and regional conferences

■ Credential programs.

For more information about NCMA, contact:

National Contract Management Association (NCMA)
8260 Greensboro Drive
Suite 200
McLean, VA 22102
Phone (800) 344-8096

WWW.NCMAHQ.ORG

■   ■   ■

In addition to the huge buyers like DOD and GSA, hundreds of lesser-known federal agencies buy from both large and small businesses. An excellent source of names and addresses for federal agencies is:

WWW.LIB.LSU.EDU/gov/fedgov.html

■   ■   ■

PART 4

How the Government Issues Procurement Opportunities

> Money is always there, but the pockets change.
>
> —*Gertrude Stein*

The government procures most of its products and services through "full and open competition." But how does the government determine who receives its awards? Is it the contractor who submits the lowest bid or the contractor with the best overall product or service? The answer is: It depends on the solicitation type. The government primarily uses three methods to solicit contractors' offers:

- Simplified acquisition or small purchase procedures (see Chapter 10)

- Sealed bidding procedures (see Chapter 11)

- Negotiated procurement procedures (see Chapter 12).

Each of these solicitation methods specifies the basis on which the award decision will be made. You will need to examine each solicitation carefully to determine exactly which factors the government will use to make its award decisions.

The Uniform Contract Format (UCF) is a blank solicitation package that prospective contractors can use to submit their bids. Chapter 13 walks you through the four parts and 13 sections of the UCF.

10 Simplified Acquisition or Small Purchase Procedures

© 1999 Randy Glasbergen.
www.glasbergen.com

GLASBERGEN

"Unless we receive the outstanding balance within ten days, we will have no choice but to destroy your credit rating, ruin your reputation, and make you wish you were never born. If you have already sent the ninety-seven cents, please disregard this notice."

What's in this chapter?

- Micropurchases
- Simplified acquisition methods

When the government makes major purchases (greater than $100,000), it must follow an extensive set of procedures to ensure that the funds are spent wisely. However, the government cannot afford to spend the same amount of time and money on small purchases or commercial items. (A commercial item is a supply or service that is sold competitively to the general public.) Therefore, the government uses "simplified acquisition procedures" to make these types of purchases.

By using simplified acquisition procedures, contracting officers avoid much of the red tape that slows down the purchase of supplies and services. These procedures not only lessen the government's burden, but they also reduce the time and resources a contractor spends in meeting government standards. These procedures may be carried out either orally or in writing. The Federal Acquisition Streamlining Act (FASA) of 1994 changed the term "small purchase procedures" to "simplified acquisition procedures" and established many of the current thresholds that apply to government acquisitions.

Simplified acquisition procedures apply to purchases that are $100,000 or less. This $100,000 limit is referred to as the simplified acquisition threshold (SAT). In addition, the Federal Acquisition Reform Act authorizes the use of simplified acquisition procedures on commercial items that cost $5 million or less. The act's primary goal is to simplify the procurement process to encourage private sector or commercial companies to sell to the government. If an agency estimates that an acquisition will exceed the SAT, that acquisition must be handled using formal acquisition procedures (see Sealed Bidding in Chapter 11 and Negotiated Procurements in Chapter 12).

Federal agencies must use simplified acquisition procedures to the maximum extent practicable for all purchases of supplies or services not exceeding the SAT. However, these procedures do not apply to ordering from Federal Supply Schedules (see Chapter 7) or to delivery orders placed against existing contracts (see Chapter 16). Simplified acquisition procedures account for more than 90% of the government's purchase transactions, although they account for less than 20% of the government's total procurement dollars.

Simplified acquisition procedures emphasize simplicity and reduced administrative costs.

These procedures are also used to improve contract opportunities for small businesses. Each acquisition of supplies or services that has an anticipated dollar value exceeding $2,500 but not over $100,000 is reserved exclusively for small businesses, provided that the contracting officer determines that there is a reasonable expectation of obtaining offers from two or more responsible small business concerns that are competitive in terms of market prices, quality, and delivery. If that doesn't convince you that government contracting offers exceptional opportunities for small businesses, nothing will.

MICROPURCHASES

Purchases that are $2,500 or less are referred to as "micropurchases." (The micropurchase limit is $2,000 in the case of construction.) These purchases typically cover routine supplies and services. Micropurchases allow the government to keep less extensive documentation, pay bills more quickly, and handle discrepancies more rapidly and less formally. Micropurchases account for 85% of the government's purchasing actions.

Purchasers must use the following guidelines when making micropurchases:

■ Purchases must be distributed equitably among qualified suppliers to the maximum extent practical.

■ Micropurchases may be awarded without soliciting competitive quotations if the contracting officer or appointed individual determines that the quoted price is reasonable.

The requirements of the Buy American Act do not apply to micropurchases (see Chapter 2). Federal agencies may authorize employees who are not acquisition officials (contracting officers) to make micropurchases to allow the contracting officer to concentrate on major purchases. In addition, micropurchases can be made from any type of seller, not just small businesses.

Acquisition Methods	
$2,500 or less	Micropurchase Procedures
$2,501 to $100,000	Simplified Acquisition Procedures
Over $100,000	Formal Solicitation Procedures

SIMPLIFIED ACQUISITION METHODS

Simplified acquisition procedures allow the government to use several authorized methods for entering into contracts without using formal solicitation procedures. Some common simplified acquisition methods include those outlined in the following sections.

Request for Quotation

A request for quotation (RFQ) is a solicitation document (Standard Form 18) that the government uses to solicit prices for purchases that are under the simplified acquisition threshold (less than $100,000). The government typically uses RFQs when it does not intend to award a contract on the basis of the solicitation, but wishes to obtain price, delivery, or other market information as the basis for preparing a purchase order. Your response to this type of solicitation is called a "quote."

For example, suppose James Statton, president of Answer Tech, Inc., receives an RFQ for a telephone answering machine and decides to submit a quote. James enters the price of the answering machine on Block 12 of SF 18, signs Block 15, and returns the form to Becky Harper, the contracting officer, by the date specified on Block 10. James' response to the RFQ is not considered to be an offer, and it cannot be used to form a binding contract. Becky also has the option of obtaining oral quotes from vendors.

REQUEST FOR QUOTATION *(This is not an order)*		THIS RFQ ☐ IS ☒ IS NOT A SMALL BUSINESS SET-ASIDE				PAGE OF PAGES 1 | 6	
1. REQUEST NO. RFQ-DC-03-00228	2. DATE ISSUED 05/29/2003	3. REQUISITION/PURCHASE REQUEST NO. PR-DC-03-01902		4. CERT. FOR NAT. DEF. UNDER BOSA REG. 2 AND/OR DMS REG. 1		RATING	

5a. ISSUED BY   US EPA   Mail Drop: 3805R
EMERGENCY RESPONSE SERVICE CENTER
1200 PENNSYLVANIA AVE., NW
WASHINGTON, DC 20460

6. DELIVER BY (Date)
07/30/2003

7. DELIVERY
☒ FOB DESTINATION   ☐ OTHER (See Schedule)

5b. FOR INFORMATION CALL: (No collect calls)

Name	TELEPHONE NUMBER
CHRISTINE EDWARDS	(202) 564-2182 Fax: (202) 565-2558

8. TO:

a. Name	b. Company
c. Street Address	
d. City	e. State	f. Zip Code

9. DESTINATION
a. Name of Consignee US EPA   Mail Drop:
U.S. EPA - ERT-EAST   MS101
b. Street Address
2890 WOODBRIDGE AVE., BLDG 18
c. City   EDISON
d. State NJ   e. Zip Code 08837 - 3679

10. PLEASE FURNISH QUOTATIONS TO THE ISSUING OFFICE IN BLOCK 5A ON OR BEFORE CLOSE OF BUSINESS (Date) 07/10/2003	IMPORTANT: This is a request for information, and quotations furnished are not offers. If you are unable to quote, please so indicate on this form and return it to the address in Block 5A. This request does not commit the Government to pay any costs incurred in the preparation of the submission of this quotation or to contract for supplies or services. Supplies are of domestic origin unless otherwise indicated by quoter. Any representations and/or certifications attached to this request for Quotations must be completed by the quoter.

12. SCHEDULE (Include applicable Federal, State and Local taxes)

ITEM NO. (a)	SUPPLIES/SERVICES (b)	QUANTITY (c)	UNIT (d)	UNIT PRICE (e)	AMOUNT (f)
1	Centech Chemical Agent Centech UC AP2Ce (or equivalent) Accesories to be included in the quote: Battery Charger Carrying Case Straps for carrying equipment (quote on any available) RS 232 cables and software for laptop computer Minimum Specifications: 1. Detects phosphoreus and sulphur compounds, nerve and blister agents 2. Detects vapors and liquids. 3. Flame photometric detector for HD, G, V agents. 4. Operational temperature range: -10 C to 55 C , not effected by relative humidity. Operational to 3000m altitude. 5. Storage temperature range: -39 C to	36	EACH		

12. DISCOUNT FOR PROMPT PAYMENT ▶	a.10 Calendar Days (%)	b.20 Calendar Days (%)	c.30 Calendar Days (%)	d. Calendar Days Number | Percent

NOTE: Additional provisions and representations   ☒ are ☐ are not attached.

13. NAME AND ADDRESS OF QUOTER	14. SIGNATURE OF PERSON AUTHORIZED TO SIGN QUOTATION	15. Date Of Quotation
a. NAME OF QUOTER		
b. STREET ADDRESS		
	16. SIGNER	
c. COUNTY	a. NAME (Type or Print)	b. TELEPHONE Area Code
d. CITY | e. STATE | f. ZIP CODE	c. TITLE (Type or Print)	Number

AUTHORIZED FOR LOCAL REPRODUCTION / Previous edition not usable   STANDARD FORM 18 (REV. 6-95) / Prescribed by GSA - FAR (48 CFR) 53.215-1(a)

Sample SF 18

Becky Harper then issues a purchase order to the contractor that submits the lowest quote. Assuming Answer Tech, Inc., submits the lowest quote, it will form a binding contract with the government, if James signs the purchase order. If James decides not to sign the purchase order, then Becky must find another contractor.

Purchase Order

A purchase order (PO) is a contract document that the government uses to buy supplies and services at a price quoted by a seller or vendor. Contracting officers typically use POs to make over-the-counter purchases. All POs are issued on a firm-fixed-price basis (see Chapter 14). The PO contains all information that the government and the seller must know to complete the sales transaction, including:

■ The quantity of supplies or scope of services ordered

■ When and where the supplies are to be delivered or the services performed

■ Inspection requirements (if applicable)

■ Contract and acquisition numbers

■ Any trade and prompt payment discounts.

Several contractual clauses may appear on the reverse of the PO or be attached to it. For the most part, these clauses apply during the performance of the work described on the PO.

The PO process typically works as follows:

■ The contracting officer lists the supplies or services he or she plans to purchase on Standard Form 44, Purchase-Order-Invoice-Voucher.

■ If the contracting officer pays cash, he or she signs the SF 44 and gives a copy of this PO to the seller as a record of the transaction.

- If the contracting officer doesn't pay at the time of sale, he or she signs the SF 44 and gives a copy to the seller to use as an invoice.

That's it! There's not much red tape with this process.

POs, however, are becoming endangered, thanks to the governmentwide commercial purchase card.

Governmentwide Commercial Purchase Card

A governmentwide commercial purchase card is a credit card. If your company already accepts credit cards, the transaction procedures are identical. This card allows an authorized purchaser to buy supplies and services that are under the micropurchase threshold ($2,500 for most goods and services). Authorized government employees are using these cards more and more frequently because they reduce the administrative expenses associated with government purchases.

These cards also reduce the amount of time it takes to purchase routine supplies or services. More than 130,000 government employees currently hold one of these credit cards. During FY2003, the federal government purchased over $14 billion worth of supplies and services using credit cards.

Anyone in possession of a government purchase card has procurement authority to use it, based on the fact that he or she has the purchase card. If you want additional verification that a buyer is eligible to use the card, ask to see his or her government identification card.

Blanket Purchase Agreement

A blanket purchase agreement (BPA) is a simplified method of filling anticipated repetitive needs for supplies or services by establishing charge accounts with qualified suppliers. BPAs reduce administrative costs by eliminating the need for issuing individual purchase orders for each purchase. When a supplier establishes a BPA, it agrees to fill orders at or below the lowest price paid by the supplier's most favored private sector customer. BPAs usually are established with local sources so that individual purchases can be made with minimal time and effort.

A contracting officer typically issues BPAs to several different suppliers for the same types of supplies or services. This gives a contracting officer greater flexibility and choice when making a purchase decision. The BPA may be limited to specific supplies or services, or it may cover all the supplies or services a supplier can furnish. BPAs also may limit the size of each order or the aggregate amount of each month's orders. Each BPA includes information about personnel who are authorized to place orders with the vendor, invoicing and payment procedures, delivery requirements, fixed price(s) of the covered items, or other pricing arrangements.

When a contracting officer makes a purchase using a BPA, he or she must comply with small business set-aside requirements. If two or more small businesses can perform the contract on time and at reasonable prices, the contracting officer must solicit only small business BPA suppliers. A contracting officer usually uses SF 1449 to place orders for commercial items and SF 347 to place orders for noncommercial supplies and services.

The following are typical circumstances under which a contracting officer may establish a BPA:

■ The agency purchases a wide variety of items in a broad class of supplies or services but does not know the exact items, quantities, and delivery requirements in advance.

■ Using the BPA would eliminate numerous purchase orders.

■ There are no existing contract requirements for the same supply or service that the contracting activity is required to use.

BPAs may be established with:

■ More than one contractor (or supplier) for the same types of supplies or services to provide maximum practicable competition

- A single firm from which numerous individual purchases at or below the simplified acquisition threshold will likely be made

- Federal supply schedule contractors, if using the BPA would not be inconsistent with the terms of the applicable schedule contract (see Chapter 7).

A supplier can obtain a BPA from a contracting activity in many ways. One is for a contracting officer to contact the suppliers with whom he or she typically does business and ask them if they would like to establish BPAs. Suppliers may also ask a contracting officer to issue BPAs for their supplies or services. BPAs are usually issued for a one-year period. Once a contracting officer issues a BPA to a company, the firm must provide the authorized supplies or services upon request by the contracting officer. BPAs can typically be canceled by either party with advance written notice (e.g., in 30 days).

The government maintains a list of BPA suppliers. When a contracting officer decides to place an order for supplies or services, the list is used to obtain competitive quotations. Once the contracting officer obtains three or more quotations, the order is placed with the BPA supplier that quoted the lowest price. The contracting officer typically places this order over the telephone. The supplier then fills the order or performs the service, charges it to the contracting activity's account, and submits a summary invoice at least monthly.

Imprest Fund Method

Most federal agencies use an imprest fund to purchase routine supplies and services. This fund is basically a "petty cash" account. An authorized government purchaser may use an imprest fund to make small purchases when the transaction amount is not more than $500. These small purchases usually include postage, C.O.D. charges, local delivery charges, and travel advances.

Fast Payment Procedure

The fast payment procedure allows a contractor to receive payment before the government verifies that supplies have been received and accepted. This procedure improves a contractor's cash flow by speeding up the payment process. The government can use these procedures only for purchases that are less than $25,000. Fast payment procedures require a contractor to submit an invoice with the following certifications:

- The supplies were delivered to a post office, common carrier, or point of first receipt by the government.

- The contractor is responsible for replacing, repairing, or correcting the supplies not received at the destination, damaged in transit, or not conforming to purchase agreements.

The contractor also must prepay the transportation costs and postage. Title to the supplies passes to the government on delivery to the post office or common carrier. If the supplies are shipped by means other than the Postal Service or common carrier, the title passes upon receipt by the government. Not all federal agencies use the fast payment procedure.

■ ■ ■

This chapter detailed the various thresholds for simplified acquisition or small purchase procedures. You must know these thresholds, so you will be aware of the policies and procedures that apply when you sell your supplies or services to the government. For acquisitions that exceed the simplified acquisition threshold, the government uses two basic methods of procurement: sealed bidding and negotiated procurement procedures.

■ ■ ■

Sealed Bidding

"This is my final offer, Fred. I'll give you a 15% discount on all orders, free shipping for six months, two of my pickles, half of my fries **and** my little packet of crackers."

What's in this chapter?

- The solicitation process
- The sealed bidding (IFB) process
- Solicitation methods
- Preparing your bid
- Late bids
- Bid opening
- Bid evaluations
- Bid award
- Two-step sealed bidding

Sealed bidding is a rigid procurement process designed to protect the integrity of the competitive bidding system. It typically is used to purchase noncommercial supplies or services that are estimated to exceed $100,000. While there is no dollar limit on the use of sealed bidding procedures, the federal government is authorized to use sealed bidding only under the following conditions:

- The government's specifications can be described clearly and accurately.

- Two or more bidders are expected to compete individually for the contract.

- There is adequate time to perform the sealed bidding process.

- The award will be made on the basis of price and other price-related factors.

The price-related factors might include: the costs or savings that could result from making multiple awards; federal, state, and local taxes; application of the Buy American Act; or costs or delays resulting from inspection, supply location, and transportation differences. Without these conditions, the contracting officer must use negotiated procurement procedures (see Chapter 12). The primary purpose of sealed bidding is to give all qualified contractors the opportunity to compete for government contracts while avoiding favoritism, collusion, or fraud, and to benefit from competition.

THE SOLICITATION PROCESS

The sealed bidding process begins when a contracting officer publicizes a synopsis or notification for a solicitation package, called an invitation for bid (IFB), in FedBizOpps (see Chapter 8) 15 days before the solicitation is issued. A synopsis briefly describes the desired supplies and services. It also provides information on obtaining a copy of the solicitation from the responsible contracting activity. Most solicitations can be downloaded directly from the Internet.

Sealed Bidding (IFB) Process

The contracting officer
prepares an IFB

↓

The contracting officer
posts a synopsis
of the IFB
on FedBizOpps

↓

The IFB is posted
to FedBizOpps

↓

Bids are received
and opened at
a public bid opening

↓

The contracting officer
evaluates the bids
without discussion

↓

The lowest responsive
and responsible bidder
is awarded the contract

↓

The contractor performs
the contract

THE SEALED BIDDING (IFB) PROCESS

After this 15-day period, the contracting officer publicizes the actual IFB in FedBizOpps. The contracting officer may also mail the IFB to companies on its solicitation mailing (or bidders) list. Each IFB describes the needs of the procuring activity in sufficient detail to permit bidders to compete on an equal basis. Because an IFB contains everything a bidder must know to fulfill the contract, it tends to be a sizable document. To be considered for an award, the bidder must agree to comply in all material respects with the IFB at the bid price.

The IFB is divided into sections and subsections, and includes a transmittal sheet and a table of contents. The transmittal sheet generally shows the solicitation number, the supplies or services to be acquired, the contract period, and other pertinent information. This transmittal sheet should not be submitted with your bid.

An IFB should always include the following information:

- Description of supplies or services

- Specifications or statement of work

- Packaging and marking requirements

- Inspection and acceptance criteria

- Delivery or performance schedules

- Deadline for submission of bids

- Special contract requirements (if necessary).

IFBs also include technical data in the form of drawings and specifications, or describe where to access the necessary information.

The contracting officer must allow at least 30 days between the IFB's issuance and the bid opening, unless the contracting officer uses a "Streamlined Synopsis/Solicitation for Commercial Items." Sealed bidding results in a firm-fixed-price (FFP) contract or a fixed-price contract with an economic price adjustment (FP/EPA). (See Chapter 14.)

SOLICITATION METHODS

A contracting officer will use one of four formats in preparing an IFB: (1) Solicitation/Contract/Order for Commercial Items (SF 1449), (2) Streamlined Synopsis/Solicitation for Commercial Items, (3) Uniform Contract Format (UCF), or (4) Simplified Contract Format (SCF).

Solicitation/Contract/Order for Commercial Items

The contracting officer must use Standard Form 1449 if:

■ The commercial items being acquired are expected to exceed the simplified acquisition threshold, which is $5 million for commercial items.

■ A paper solicitation or contract will be issued.

■ Procedures for Streamlined Synopsis/Solicitation for Commercial Items are not being used.

Using SF 1449 is not mandatory, but is encouraged for commercial acquisitions under the simplified acquisition threshold.

Streamlined Synopsis/Solicitation for Commercial Items

The contracting officer typically uses the Streamlined Synopsis/Solicitation for Commercial Items procedure to reduce the time required to solicit and award commercial item contracts. This procedure combines the synopsis and the solicitation issuance into a single document, thereby eliminating the 15 days between the synopsis publication and the IFB issuance. This solicitation method has the following limitations:

■ The combined synopsis and solicitation may not exceed 12,000 textual characters (approximately 3 1/2 single-spaced pages).

SOLICITATION/CONTRACT/ORDER FOR COMMERCIAL ITEMS *OFFEROR TO COMPLETE BLOCKS 12, 17, 23, 24, & 30*		1. REQUISITION NO. 06-06PP00323	PAGE 1 OF 17
2. CONTRACT NO.	3. AWARD/EFFECTIVE DATE	4. ORDER NO.	5. SOLICITATION NO. DE-RP06-06PP00323	6. SOLICITATION ISSUE DATE 05/18/2006

7. FOR SOLICITATION INFORMATION CALL ▶ a. NAME Pat Thom — b. TELEPHONE NO. *(No collect calls)* 202-426-8568 — 8. OFFER DUE DATE/LOCAL TIME 06/18/2006 5 pm

9. ISSUED BY CODE MA-541
U.S. Department of Energy
HQ Procurement Services/MA-541
1000 Independence Ave., SW
Washington, DC 20585

10. THIS ACQUISITION IS ■ UNRESTRICTED ☐ SET ASIDE: % FOR ☐ SMALL BUSINESS ☐ SMALL DISADV. BUSINESS ☐ 8(A)
NAICS: 517410 SIZE STD: 12.5 mil

11. DELIVERY FOR FOB DESTINATION UNLESS BLOCK IS MARKED ☐ SEE SCHEDULE
12. DISCOUNT TERMS
13a. THIS CONTRACT IS A RATED ORDER UNDER DPAS (15 CFR 700)
13b. RATING N/A
14. METHOD OF SOLICITATION ☐ RFQ ■ IFB ☐ RFP

15. DELIVER TO CODE
U.S. Department of Energy
16. ADMINISTERED BY See Clause B.3 CODE

17a. CONTRACTOR/OFFEROR CODE FACILITY CODE
E-Watch, Inc.
401 West Peachtree St.
Atlanta, GA 30365
404-331-5159

18a. PAYMENT WILL BE MADE BY CODE
U.S. Department of Energy

☐ 17b. CHECK IF REMITTANCE IS DIFFERENT AND PUT SUCH ADDRESS IN OFFER
18b. SUBMIT INVOICES TO ADDRESS SHOWN IN BLOCK 18a UNLESS BLOCK BELOW IS CHECKED ☐ SEE ADDENDUM

19. ITEM NO.	20. SCHEDULE OF SUPPLIES/SERVICES	21. QUANTITY	22. UNIT	23. UNIT PRICE	24. AMOUNT
	See Clause B.5 and Statement of Work. Cable/Broadcast television and radio news/commentary monitoring service for energy-related news. *(Attach Additional Sheets as Necessary)*	See B.5	See B.5		

25. ACCOUNTING AND APPROPRIATION DATA — 26. TOTAL AWARD AMOUNT *(For Govt. Use Only)*

■ 27a. SOLICITATION INCORPORATES BY REFERENCE FAR 52.212-1, 52.212-4. FAR 52.212-3 AND 52.212-5 ARE ATTACHED. ADDENDA ■ ARE ☐ ARE NOT ATTACHED.
☐ 27b. CONTRACT/PURCHASE ORDER INCORPORATES BY REFERENCE FAR 52.212-4. FAR 52.212-5 IS ATTACHED. ADDENDA ☐ ARE ☐ ARE NOT ATTACHED.

■ 28. CONTRACTOR IS REQUIRED TO SIGN THIS DOCUMENT AND RETURN ___ COPIES TO ISSUING OFFICE. CONTRACTOR AGREES TO FURNISH AND DELIVER ALL ITEMS SET FORTH OR OTHERWISE IDENTIFIED ABOVE AND ON ANY ADDITIONAL SHEETS SUBJECT TO THE TERMS AND CONDITIONS SPECIFIED HEREIN.
☐ 29. AWARD OF CONTRACT: REFERENCE ___ OFFER DATED ___. YOUR OFFER ON SOLICITATION (BLOCK 5), INCLUDING ANY ADDITIONS OR CHANGES WHICH ARE SET FORTH HEREIN, IS ACCEPTED AS TO ITEMS:

30a. SIGNATURE OF OFFEROR/CONTRACTOR — 31a. UNITED STATES OF AMERICA *(SIGNATURE OF CONTRACTING OFFICER)*
30b. NAME AND TITLE OF SIGNER *(TYPE OR PRINT)* — 30c. DATE SIGNED — 31b. NAME OF CONTRACTING OFFICER *(TYPE OR PRINT)* — 31c. DATE SIGNED

32a. QUANTITY IN COLUMN 21 HAS BEEN ACCEPTED, AND CONFORMS TO THE ☐ RECEIVED ☐ INSPECTED ☐ CONTRACT, EXCEPT AS NOTED
33. SHIP NUMBER ☐ PARTIAL ☐ FINAL — 34. VOUCHER NUMBER — 35. AMOUNT VERIFIED CORRECT FOR
36. PAYMENT ☐ COMPLETE ☐ PARTIAL ☐ FINAL — 37. CHECK NUMBER
32b. SIGNATURE OF AUTHORIZED GOVT REPRESENTATIVE — 32c. DATE
38. S/R ACCOUNT NO. — 39. S/R VOUCHER NO. — 40. PAID BY
42a. RECEIVED BY *(Print)*
41a. I CERTIFY THIS ACCOUNT IS CORRECT AND PROPER FOR PAYMENT
41b. SIGNATURE AND TITLE OF CERTIFYING OFFICER — 41c. DATE — 42b. RECEIVED AT *(Location)*
42c. DATE REC'D *(YY/MM/DD)* — 42d. TOTAL CONTAINERS

AUTHORIZED FOR LOCAL REPRODUCTION Computer Generated — SEE REVERSE FOR OMB CONTROL NUMBER AND PAPERWORK BURDEN STATEMENT — **STANDARD FORM 1449 (10-95)** Prescribed by GSA - FAR (48 CFR) 53.212

Sample SF 1449

■ The combined synopsis/solicitation is appropriate only for a relatively simple solicitation.

Uniform Contract Format

The federal government generally uses the Uniform Contract Format (UCF) to purchase supplies and services. All IFBs for noncommercial supplies and services must use the UCF, unless:

■ The simplified contract format is used.

■ The solicitation is for construction, shipbuilding, ship repairs and maintenance, subsistence, architect/engineering services, and supplies and services that require special contract forms.

See Chapter 13 for more detailed information about the UCF.

Simplified Contract Format

A contracting officer may use the simplified contract format (SCF) instead of the UCF for firm-fixed-price or fixed-price with economic price adjustment acquisitions of supplies and services. The SCF is being used more and more because it allows the contracting officer greater flexibility in preparing and organizing the IFB. This solicitation format should include the following information to the maximum practical extent:

■ **SF 1447, Solicitation/Contract.** SF 1447 is the first (or cover) page of the solicitation. This form includes the solicitation number, the solicitation issue date, the issuing contracting activity, and a place for the signature of the contractor and the contracting officer.

■ **Contract schedule.** The contract schedule includes the: (1) contract line item number; (2) supplies or services description; (3) unit price and amount; (4) packaging requirements; (5) delivery place, performance, and dates of performance period; and (6) other information.

SOLICITATION/CONTRACT BIDDER/OFFEROR TO COMPLETE BLOCKS 11, 13, 15, 21, 22 & 27			1. THIS CONTRACT IS A RATED ORDER UNDER DPAS (15 CFR 350) N/A		RATING N/A	PAGE 1 OF 1
2. CONTRACT NO.	3. AWARD/EFFECTIVE DATE	4. SOLICITATION NUMBER DE-FB01-06AD66850	5. SOLICITATION TYPE [X] IFB [ ] RFP		6. SOLICITATION ISSUE DATE 11/10/06	

7. ISSUED BY   CODE HR-541

U.S. Department of Energy
1000 Independence Ave., SW
Washington, DC 20585

8. THIS ACQUISITION IS:
[ ] UNRESTRICTED   [ ] LABOR SURPLUS AREA CONCERNS
                   [ ] COMBINED SMALL BUSINESS &
[X] SET ASIDE: 100% FOR [ ] LABOR SURPLUS AREA CONCERNS
[X] SMALL BUSINESS   [ ] OTHER

NAICS: 561720   SIZE STANDARD: $ 14 Million

9. (AGENCY USE)

10. ITEMS TO BE PURCHASED (BRIEF DESCRIPTION)
[ ] SUPPLIES [X] SERVICES   Janitorial Services

11. IF OFFER IS ACCEPTED BY THE GOVT BY _____, THE CONTRACTOR AGREES TO HOLD ITS OFFERED PRICES FIRM FOR THE ITEMS SOLICITED HEREIN AND TO ACCEPT ANY RESULTING CONTRACT SUBJECT TO THE TERMS AND CONDITIONS STATED HEREIN.

12. ADMINISTERED BY   CODE HR-541
U.S. Department of Energy
1000 Independence Ave., SW
Washington, DC 20585

13. CONTRACTOR OFFEROR CODE: N/A FACILITY _____
Joe's Janitorial Services
1500 East Bannister Rd.
Kansas City, MO 64131

TELEPHONE NO. (816) 926-7203
[ ] CHECK HERE IF REMITTANCE IS DIFFERENT & PUT ADDRESS IN OFFER

14. PAYMENT WILL BE MADE BY   CODE CR-541-2
U.S. Department of Energy
P.O. Box 500
Germantown, MD 20874

SUBMIT INVOICES TO ADDRESS SHOWN IN BLOCK 7

15. PROMPT PAYMENT DISCOUNT
N/A

16. AUTHORITY FOR USING OTHER THAN FULL & OPEN COMPETITION
10 USC 2304   41 USC 253
[ ] (c) ( )   [ ] (c) ( )

17. ITEM NO.	18. SCHEDULE OF SUPPLIES/SERVICES	19. QUANTITY	20. UNIT	21. UNIT PRICE	22. AMOUNT
0001	Provide the U.S. Department of Energy with janitorial services in accordance with the Statement of Work found in Clause B.10 for the DOE Forrestal Complex and Child Development Center.				

23. ACCOUNTING AND APPROPRIATION DATA
SEE SECTION G

24. TOTAL AWARD AMOUNT (FOR GOVT USE ONLY)

25. CONTRACTOR IS REQUIRED TO SIGN THIS DOCUMENT AND RETURN ALL COPIES TO ISSUING OFFICE. CONTRACTOR AGREES TO FURNISH AND DELIVER ALL ITEMS SET FORTH OR OTHERWISE IDENTIFIED ABOVE AND ON ANY CONTINUATION SHEETS SUBJECT TO THE TERMS AND CONDITIONS SPECIFIED HEREIN.

26. AWARD OF CONTRACT: YOUR OFFER ON SOLICITATION NUMBER SHOWN IN BLOCK 4 INCLUDING ANY ADDITIONS OR CHANGES WHICH ARE SET FORTH HEREIN, IS ACCEPTED AS TO ITEMS:

27. SIGNATURE OF OFFEROR/CONTRACTOR

28. UNITED STATES OF AMERICA (SIGNATURE OF CONTRACTING OFFICER

NAME AND TITLE OF SIGNER (TYPE OR PRINT)	DATE SIGNED	NAME OF CONTRACTING OFFICER	DATE SIGNED

NSN 7540-01-218-4366
Prescribed by GSA

1447-101

STANDARD FORM 1447 (5-88)
FAR (48 CFR 53.215-1(g))

Sample SF 1447

- **Clauses.** Clauses include those required by the FAR and those considered necessary by the contracting officer.

- **List of documents and attachments.**

- **Representations and instructions.** These typically are divided into: (1) representations and certifications; (2) instructions, conditions, and notices; and (3) award evaluation factors.

PREPARING YOUR BID

Responding to a solicitation requires considerable time and effort. Generally, the cost of preparing a winning proposal is 3–5% of the contract's total dollar value. Prospective bidders should examine each solicitation carefully to decide if preparing a bid is worth their time and effort.

If your company decides to prepare a bid, you should start to work on it immediately upon receipt of the solicitation document (IFB). This is particularly important if the contract is large or if you must obtain and read several documents before bidding. Carefully examine the IFB's specifications, including all instructions, clauses, and other documents. Questions about the IFB should be directed to the contracting officer or the person named in the solicitation. Make no assumptions without authorized clarification.

The solicitation package should indicate where to obtain essential specifications, standards, and other documents cited. If it doesn't, the contracting officer will provide this information. Bidders must meet the requirements of all the documents cited in the package.

Once you have read the IFB and the required documentation carefully, you should prepare a work plan and a delivery schedule. The work plan should detail the time and material costs of fulfilling the contract (information you'll need in determining your bid price). The delivery schedule should detail distances to the locations to which you'll ship the products. Some solicitations require bidders to submit a work plan and a delivery schedule as part of the offer. The solicitation may also require bidders to submit information about the company's financial stability and relevant experience. Your proposal must address performance and delivery at least equal to the IFB's minimum standards.

Bidders should not substitute items that they deem to be just as good as the specified items. A bid must meet the exact specifications called for in the bid request or the bid may be declared nonresponsive. Because price is the primary evaluation factor in sealed bidding, it is to your advantage to determine the price that the government paid for a similar supply or service in the past. Among the sources for this information are past bids and Freedom of Information Act requests (see Chapter 2).

After a contracting activity issues an IFB, but before bid opening, it may make changes to the IFB. Typical changes involve quantities, specifications, delivery schedules, or opening dates. Such changes are accomplished through an IFB amendment (SF 30, Amendment of Solicitation/ Modification of Contract). Any amendments made by a contracting officer to an IFB must be sent to each contractor that was sent a solicitation or invitation. Upon submitting bids, bidders must acknowledge all issued amendments. Failure to acknowledge an amendment may cause a bid to be declared nonresponsive.

Once you have completed your bid, review it for clarity, consistency, and accuracy. Compare your work plan, budget, and schedule to ensure that they agree. Double check cost figures and computations to be sure that all information has been included.

If everything checks out, the next step is to submit your bid. Be sure to review the submission instructions. In addition, review the address to which the bid should be sent and allow enough time to meet the deadline. Keep in mind that an IFB is actually a contractual document. If a prospective bidder submits an erroneous bid and is awarded a contract on the basis of that bid, the result may be little or no profit, or even serious financial loss.

LATE BIDS

If you receive a solicitation, the first thing to do is to note the date and time your bid is due. This is extremely important because the government will not accept bids that are even five seconds late.

This rule has a few exceptions. Late bids may be considered if the bid was:

■ Mishandled by (and within) the government

■ Sent by the U.S. Postal Service Express Mail Next Day Service, no later than 5:00 P.M. at the place of mailing, two working days before the bid opening date

■ Sent by registered or certified mail, postmarked no later than the fifth calendar day before the deadline

■ Sent electronically and received by the government no later than 5:00 P.M. one working day before the bid opening date

■ The only offer received.

The government may also, at any time, consider late modifications to an otherwise successful bid that make its terms more favorable to the government.

If hand delivering the bid, be sure that the room number and any other special requirements for hand delivery are met. Security concerns can delay hand delivery of a bid, so be sure to allow extra time or use a bonded courier. When a bid is received late and it cannot be considered, the government notifies the bidder and holds the bid unopened.

BID OPENING

All bids in response to an IFB are secured until the bid opening, which takes place in a public location at the time specified on the IFB. Anyone may attend a bid opening. At the time designated for opening, a bid opening officer publicly opens all unclassified bids.

A bidder may withdraw its bid at any time before the bid opening date. Once the bids have been opened, the contracting officer will allow withdrawals or corrections to bids only if the offeror substantiates a mistake, the manner in which it occurred, and the intended bid. For example, an obvious clerical error may be corrected and the bid considered with the other offers if the offeror verifies the error and the intended bid.

BID EVALUATIONS

A bid opening officer, who is generally not the contracting officer, opens, announces, and records all the bids. They are recorded on a form called an "abstract of bids." Interested parties may examine the bids at the time of recording but will be denied access to financial and other proprietary information of the bidders. Following the recording, the bid opening officer reveals the results to the contracting officer.

The contracting officer evaluates the bids, considering such items as price, options, economic price adjustments, transportation costs, and other areas controlled by regulations. Discounts, such as prompt payment discounts (see Chapter 17), are not considered during the evaluation of bids. Any discount that the bidder offers, however, becomes part of the contract award.

To be eligible for the award, the offeror must be both "responsive" and "responsible."

- To be *responsive*, the otherwise successful bidder must not have taken exception to the IFB's specifications, work statement, or other terms of the proposed contract. A bid usually will be rejected as nonresponsive if its prices are subject to change without notice.

- To be *responsible*, the otherwise successful bidder must be able to produce the supplies or services, meet the delivery schedule, follow the terms and conditions, have adequate financial capabilities, and have integrity.

The contracting officer uses the following "pre-award survey" to determine if a bidder is both responsive and responsible:

■ Does the bidder have adequate financial resources to perform the contract or the ability to obtain them?

■ Can the bidder comply with the proposed delivery or performance schedule, considering all existing business commitments?

■ Does the bidder have a satisfactory performance record?

■ Does the bidder have a satisfactory record of integrity and business ethics?

■ Does the bidder have the necessary organization, experience, accounting and operational controls, and technical skills?

■ Does the bidder have the necessary production, construction, and technical equipment and facilities?

■ Is the bidder qualified and eligible to receive an award under the applicable laws and regulations?

The pre-award survey may be informal or formal. The informal pre-award survey includes a review of the bidder's capabilities, performance records, and previous contracts and/or telephone inquiries of previous customers. The informal survey typically is used for small and straightforward contracts.

The formal pre-award survey, on the other hand, involves the assistance of another federal agency, the Defense Contract Management Command (DCMC). DCMC is the contract administration branch of the Defense Logistics Agency. The contracting officer may ask DCMC to review all or some of following items: technical capabilities, production capacity, quality assurance procedures, financial capability, purchasing system, transportation, packaging, security, environmental/energy considerations, and any other areas of concern. Formal procedures typically are used for large contracts that involve a number of products or services.

If the apparent low or otherwise successful bidder is determined to be nonresponsive or nonresponsible by the contracting officer and it is a small business, the findings must be referred to SBA for further investigation. SBA then performs its own investigation to determine if the small business can perform the contract.

If SBA determines that the small business is competent, it issues a Certificate of Competency, which binds the contracting officer for that particular procurement (see Chapter 4). Contractors who fail to perform acceptably, or who commit crimes or other acts indicating their irresponsibility, may be temporarily suspended or debarred from receiving any new government contracts for a period of three or more years.

BID AWARD

The lowest bidder that meets the contracting officer's evaluation criteria is awarded the contract. Each bidder must keep its bid open (or available) during the evaluation period. The contracting officer conducts these procedures based strictly on the sealed bids. There are no discussions with the bidders.

When the contracting officer receives two or more equal low bids, the contract is awarded in the following order:

1. To a small business that is also in a Historically Underutilized Business Zone (HUBZone)

2. To another small business

3. To a business in a labor surplus area

4. To another business.

The contracting officer may reject all bids received if he or she believes that this action is in the government's best interest. For example, if the bids were submitted in bad faith or were calculated in collusion by the bidders, the contracting officer may reject them.

The successful bidder receives a properly executed award document, or Notice of Award (NOA). An NOA has no specified format; however, it should include the contract number, its effective date, the authorized funding provided, the initial tasks that the bidder will perform, and the contracting officer's approval (or signature). An NOA's primary purpose is to serve as the bidder's go-ahead. The award is effective when the bidder receives it. Once the contracting officer signs the contract, the bidder becomes responsible for performing the contract's specifications.

The contracting officer notifies the unsuccessful bidders in writing or orally (usually within three days of contract award). If an unsuccessful bidder requests additional information, the contracting officer must provide the:

■ Successful bidder's name and address

■ Contract price

■ Location of a copy of the abstract of bids that may be inspected.

Contracting officers must consider all contract award protests or objections, whether received before or after the award is issued. If the contracting officer receives a written protest, he or she will not award the contract until the matter is resolved, unless the items being procured are urgent or the delivery or performance will be unduly delayed by failure to make the award promptly. However, no bidder has the right to prevent award to another bidder, to make an agency award it a contract, or to recover damages for losing the award.

TWO-STEP SEALED BIDDING

Two-step sealed bidding combines sealed bidding procedures with negotiated procurement procedures. This approach is designed to obtain the benefits of sealed bidding when adequate specifications are unavailable. This method is especially useful for complex acquisitions (or acquisitions requiring technical proposals). It can also be used for multiyear contracts (see Chapter 16), government-owned facilities or government-furnished property contracts, and small business or labor surplus area set-asides (see Chapter 5).

The government uses two-step sealed bidding under the following conditions:

■ The contracting officer can define the criteria for evaluating technical proposals.

■ The contracting officer expects more than one technically qualified source to bid.

■ Sufficient time is available to apply the two-step method.

■ The contracting officer will use a firm-fixed-price contract or a fixed-price contract with economic price adjustment.

■ The contracting officer cannot provide definite or complete specifications or purchase descriptions; therefore, a technical evaluation must ensure a mutual understanding between each source and the government.

The two-step sealed bidding solicitation method is more flexible than the IFB because it allows discussions to occur during step one but maintains the integrity of the bidding process with a public bid opening in step two. Step one allows vendors to propose alternative technical solutions. In addition, step one allows the government to discuss with vendors the technical acceptability of their proposals. Step two is conducted as a public bid opening that reveals competitors and pricing. Awards are based on the lowest cost.

Government personnel need to be well educated in this process to ensure that information does not leak inadvertently among vendors. The two-step sealed bidding solicitation method requires a long-term effort, usually several months.

Step One

During step one, each bidder submits a technical proposal describing its offered supplies or services, along with an explanation of its proposed approach for providing these. The solicitation document for this technical proposal is usually called a Request for Technical Proposals (RFTP). No pricing is involved during step one. The primary purpose of step one is to clarify the solicitation's technical requirements.

The solicitation document (or the RFTP) must, at a minimum, include:

■ A description of the supplies or services to be provided.

■ A statement of intent to use the two-step method.

■ The technical proposal's requirements.

■ The evaluation criteria.

■ A statement that the technical proposal will not include prices or pricing information.

■ The date and time by which the proposals must be received.

■ A statement that, in the second step, only bids based on technical proposals determined to be acceptable will be considered for awards and each bid in the second step will be based on the bidders' own technical proposals.

■ A statement that bidders should submit proposals that are acceptable without additional explanation or information.

■ A statement that a notice of unacceptability will be forwarded to the bidder upon completion of the proposal evaluation.

■ A statement either that only one technical proposal may be submitted by each bidder or that multiple technical proposals may be submitted. When specifications permit different technical approaches, it is generally in the government's interest to authorize multiple proposals.

Any proposal that modifies or fails to conform to the essential requirements or specifications of the RFTP is considered to be nonresponsive and is categorized as unacceptable.

Step Two

Step two uses conventional sealed bidding procedures; however, the government issues IFBs only to those bidders that submitted adequate technical proposals in step one. Bidders submit a price (or bid), and the contracting officer evaluates those bids under standard sealed bidding procedures. Step two is not synopsized in FedBizOpps or publicly posted as a new acquisition opportunity. However, FedBizOpps lists bidders that submitted acceptable proposals in step one for the benefit of prospective subcontractors. Despite the use of negotiated procedures in step one, this method is still considered to be sealed bidding.

■   ■   ■

Sealed bidding is perceived to be the fairest procurement method because it involves a public bid opening during which all prices and proposals are revealed and the contract is awarded based on the lowest overall cost. This method is thought to prevent fraud more effectively than other procurement methods because the public bid opening gives vendors only one chance to offer the federal government a price with which the bidder will win or lose. In general, the IFB allows for a shorter solicitation time frame, a fast evaluation process, and a quick award at the lowest price.

On the other hand, the use of sealed bidding procedures requires the government to clearly articulate its product specifications. The government is less likely to procure state-of-the-art products because bidders can bid older models that meet the specifications at a lower price than newer technology. The government must accept the low bid unless it is judged to be nonresponsive or nonresponsible. Technical superiority and extra features cannot be evaluated.

■   ■   ■

12 Negotiated Procurements

© 1999 Randy Glasbergen.

GLASBERGEN

"Lemont is our finest negotiator. Perhaps you've read his book, *The Art of Pouting.*"

What's in this chapter?

- Exchanges with industry before proposal receipt
- Advisory multistep process
- The solicitation process
- Preparing your proposal
- Oral presentations
- Late proposals
- Proposal evaluation
- Source selection processes and techniques
- Changes and discussions
- Final proposal revision and award
- Debriefings
- Protests

The federal government uses negotiated procurement procedures to make competitive acquisitions when it prefers to hold discussions with offerors before making a final source selection. Negotiated procurement procedures, unlike sealed bidding procedures, permit bargaining and afford offerors the opportunity to revise their offers before award of a contract. It is the federal government's most flexible procurement method, but it is also the most complicated.

Negotiated procurement procedures take many forms. They may call for competitive proposals, involve restricted competition, or even be sole source (when a federal agency enters into an acquisition after soliciting and negotiating with only one source). Eighty percent of the contracts that exceed the simplified acquisition threshold of $100,000 use negotiated procurement procedures. A request for proposal (RFP) is the solicitation document issued under negotiated procurement procedures and contains information necessary for prospective contractors to prepare proposals. A "bid set" includes all the documents that make up the RFP, including technical and cost matters.

The RFP, like the IFB, is a request for an offer and most follow the same format as the IFB. A contractor's response to an RFP represents an offer, which the government may accept without change or negotiation, resulting in a binding contract. However, the solicitation must state if proposals will be evaluated and awarded: (1) after discussions with offerors, or (2) without discussions with offerors.

If the contracting officer intends to enter into discussions, he or she must conduct written or oral discussions with all responsible offerors that submit proposals within the competitive range. The contracting officer may negotiate price, terms and conditions, technical requirements, performance or delivery schedules, and other parts of the contract that law or regulation do not mandate. In addition, the contracting officer may talk to offerors about their proposals and decide that the government's best interests might be better served by a contract that is significantly different from the original solicitation. Negotiation is frequently used for research and development of new systems, for which each contractor takes a different approach to meeting the government's requirements.

When a contracting officer uses negotiated procedures, the following conditions are supposed to be met:

■ All competitors or offerors are treated equally.

■ The contract complies with federal regulations.

■ The contract gives the winning contractor incentive to perform the contract on time and at the lowest possible cost to the government.

■ The contract does not contain add-on or nice-to-have features; the solicitation should contain only the minimum, essential requirements of the contract.

■ The contract price is fair and reasonable.

EXCHANGES WITH INDUSTRY BEFORE PROPOSAL RECEIPT

The government encourages information exchanges among interested parties, from the earliest identification of a requirement through proposal receipt. These exchanges can improve understanding of government requirements and industry capabilities, thereby allowing potential offerors to determine if or how to satisfy the requirements. Interested parties typically include potential offerors, end users, government acquisition personnel (such as the contracting officer and program manager), and others involved in the conduct or outcome of an acquisition. These exchanges also help identify and resolve concerns regarding the acquisition strategy, including the proposed contract type, the feasibility of requirements, and other industry concerns or questions. These exchanges must be consistent with procurement integrity requirements.

Some techniques that the government might use to promote these early exchanges include:

■ Industry or small business conferences.

■ Public hearings.

■ Market research.

■ One-on-one meetings with potential offerors.

■ Presolicitation notices.

■ Draft RFPs.

■ Requests for information (RFIs), which may be used when the government currently does not intend to award a contract but wants to obtain price, delivery, or other market information or capabilities for planning purposes. (Responses to these notices are not offers and the government cannot accept a response to an RFI as a binding contract. There is no required format for RFIs.)

■ Presolicitation or preproposal conferences.

■ Site visits.

Active participation in these early exchanges will give you a great head start on your competition. Once the solicitation is issued or released, the contracting officer will be the focal point of exchanges among potential offerors.

ADVISORY MULTISTEP PROCESS

The government encourages federal agencies to publish presolicitation notices, which provide contractors with information about potential acquisitions. Contractors that are interested in a presolicitation notice must submit information that allows the government to advise them about their potential to compete for a specific contract. Presolicitation notices identify the information that a potential contractor must submit and the criteria that will be used for the initial evaluation. This information may be limited to a statement of qualifications and other information, which might include proposed technical concept, past performance, and limited pricing information. At a minimum, this notice contains sufficient information to permit potential contractors to determine whether to participate in the acquisition.

Federal agencies evaluate each response based on the criteria stated in the notice. In addition, federal agencies notify the respondents in writing if they are invited to participate in the resultant acquisition or if, based on the information submitted, they are unlikely to be viable competitors. Any contractors that are not considered to be viable competitors may still participate in the acquisition.

THE SOLICITATION PROCESS

The process of negotiation starts in a way that is similar to sealed bidding. The contracting officer publishes a synopsis or notification of an RFP in FedBizOpps 15 days before issuing the solicitation. After this period, the contracting officer publishes the actual RFP in FedBizOpps. The contracting officer may also post the RFP on a bid board or mail it to companies on the agency's solicitation mailing list. In addition, the contracting officer may hold a preproposal conference if one is necessary. (A preproposal conference is a briefing held by the contracting officer to explain complicated specifications and requirements to prospective offerors.)

Negotiated (RFP) Process

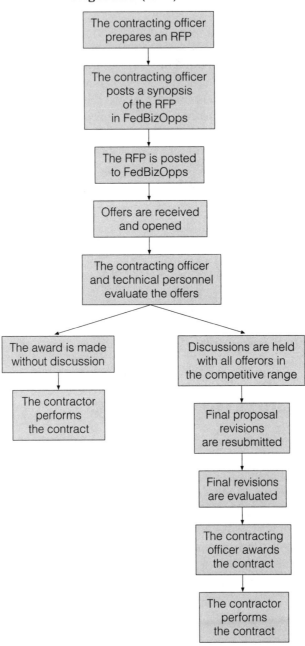

Solicitation Methods

The contracting officer uses one of the following formats to prepare RFPs:

■ Solicitation/Contract/Order for Commercial Items (SF 1449)

■ Uniform Contract Format (SF 33) (see Chapter 13)

■ Simplified Contract Format (SF 1447).

At first glance, these solicitation methods look identical to those used for IFBs. FedBizOpps synopsizes both IFBs and RFPs to solicit full and open competition. Differences between IFBs and RFPs include the solicitation provisions, proposal preparation instructions, and evaluation factors. The quickest way to differentiate between an IFB and an RFP is to look at Block 4 of SF 33, Block 5 of SF 1447, or Block 14 of SF 1449 (see Chapter 11 and Chapter 13 for copies of these forms).

RFP Requirements

At a minimum, RFPs for competitive acquisitions must provide:

■ The government's requirements.

■ The contract's anticipated terms and conditions. (For example, the solicitation may authorize offerors to propose alternative terms and conditions.)

■ Information required for the offeror's proposal.

■ Factors and significant subfactors that will be used to evaluate the proposal and their relative importance.

PREPARING YOUR PROPOSAL

Awards are made based on evaluation factors, which may include:

■ Cost/pricing data

■ Technical requirements

■ Management capabilities (if applicable)

■ Relevant experience and past performance.

Evaluation factors tell potential offerors what considerations will be used to evaluate and grade proposals compared to the requirements set forth in the statement of work (SOW) or specification (see Chapter 13). The contracting officer tailors the evaluation factors and subfactors to each acquisition's characteristics and requirements. In addition, the contracting officer identifies the relative order of importance or weight of these factors. Selected factors and subfactors enable the contracting officer to determine, based on the proposal submitted, how well the offeror understands—and the degree to which the offeror could successfully meet—the RFP's requirements. Evaluation factors are not used to compare one offeror with another.

Cost/Price Proposal

Offerors develop detailed cost and pricing data to convince the government purchaser of the reasonableness of their proposed costs. Detailed cost and pricing data include estimates of the expected costs of performance and the offeror's expected profit or fee (i.e., cost + profit = total price).

The cost/price evaluation criteria differ for fixed-price, incentive, and cost-reimbursement contracts. (Part 5 of this book discusses the various contract types the government uses.) For a fixed-price contract, the offer-or's proposed price is considered in the evaluation. Incentive contracts, on the other hand, are structured and evaluated as a package of cost factors, including target cost, share ratio, ceiling price, or maximum/minimum fee. Finally, cost-reimbursement contracts require federal agencies to use estimates of expected costs (plus the proposed fee or profit) to measure the cost realism of the proposed contract costs. The RFP states the contract type to be awarded and its applicable terms.

Cost/price proposals are not required when the award is based on adequate price competition or when the contractor is exempt from certified cost and pricing data submission (see the Truth in Negotiations Act in Chapter 2). Cost/price evaluation factors include:

■ Proposed cost/price completeness

■ Proposed cost/price reasonableness

■ Proposed cost/price realism

■ Cost/price risk assessment.

Technical Proposal

The primary purpose of the technical proposal is to assure the government that you possess the know-how and resources to perform the contract requirements. The technical proposal may cover the RFP's management aspects, or the contracting activity may require separate technical and management proposals. The RFP details specific technical criteria that your technical proposal must meet.

Technical and management proposals are generally prepared according to the Instructions to Offerors (Section L) of the Uniform Contract Format (see Chapter 13), which are often called proposal preparation instructions. In large, technically complex procurements, a representative from an agency's technical and operational areas may help develop the factors for award. In many cases, technical proposals are more significant than price proposals. Technical evaluation factors might include:

- Soundness of proposed technical approach

- Innovation of proposed technical approach

- Requirement compliance

- Requirement understanding

- Key personnel or other resources

- Available facilities

- Technical risk assessment.

Federal specifications and standards are a prescribed set of rules, conditions, and requirements established to achieve uniformity in materials and products for interchangeability of parts. They specify performance requirements and the quality and construction of materials and equipment needed to produce an acceptable product. The General Services Administration issues and controls federal specifications, standards, and commercial item descriptions, which are mandatory for use by all federal agencies.

Management Proposal

The management proposal's primary purpose is to explain how the contractor intends to manage the proposed program if awarded the contract. The management proposal's key element is the description of your type of management. Specifically, your management proposal should explain the organizational structure, management capability, management controls, and assignment of key personnel with experience directly related to the contract. If you do not intend to form a specific management group, describe your overall operation method.

A management proposal is evaluated based on:

- Soundness of the proposed management plan

- Corporate resources for overseeing and performing the work

- Logical, timely pursuit of work schedules

- Quality plan

- Management risk.

Developing the factors and determining their relative importance should be the joint responsibility of the requiring organization's contracting officer and the program manager or technical representative. Ideally, the contracting officer should develop evaluation factors and subfactors as early as possible in the acquisition's planning phase.

ORAL PRESENTATIONS

The government may ask offerors to substitute or enhance written information with oral presentations. Oral presentations may occur at any time during the acquisition process and are subject to the same restrictions as written information regarding timing and content. Oral presentations provide an opportunity for dialogue between government personnel and offerors. Prerecorded videotaped presentations that lack real-time interactive dialogue are not considered oral presentations, although they may be included in an offeror's submission, when appropriate. All members of the evaluation team—including the contracting officer, the program manager, and technical representatives—should attend all oral presentations. Substitution of oral presentations for portions of a proposal streamlines the source-selection process.

The solicitation may also require that offerors submit part of their proposals orally. Information pertaining to such areas as an offeror's capability, past performance, work plans or approaches, staffing resources, or transition plans may be suitable for oral presentations. Offerors are not, however, required to discuss technical or management approaches during their oral presentations. Instead, offerors may provide the government with a written description of their planned approach for carrying out the work upon the completion of their presentation. Each offeror must also submit in writing a signed offer sheet and any certifications and representations (including exemptions from the government's terms and conditions).

When a solicitation calls for oral presentations, it provides offerors with sufficient information to prepare them. For example, the solicitation may describe:

- Types of information to be presented orally and the associated evaluation factors

- Qualifications of the personnel who will give the oral presentation

- Requirements for, and any limitations on, written material or other media to supplement the oral presentations

- The oral presentation's location, date, and time

- Time restrictions for each presentation

- The scope and content of exchanges that may occur between the government's participants and the offeror's representatives during the presentations, including whether or not discussions will be permitted during oral presentations.

The contracting officer maintains records of the oral presentations and documents the evaluation factors for the source-selection decision. The source-selection authority determines the method and level of detail of this record (e.g., videotaping, audiotape recording, written records). Following the selection, you may request a copy of this record by calling the contracting officer.

LATE PROPOSALS

Negotiated procurement procedures have no formal public bid opening, as sealed bidding does, but you must submit your proposal by the date and time stated on the RFP (the closing date). Late proposals will only be considered if:

■ The government mishandled the proposal.

■ You sent the proposal by the U.S. Postal Service Express Mail Next-Day Service no later than 5:00 P.M. at the place of mailing, two working days before the proposal opening date.

■ You sent the proposal by registered or certified mail, postmarked no later than the fifth calendar day before the deadline.

■ You sent the proposal electronically and the government received it no later than 5:00 P.M. one working day before the proposal opening date.

■ Only one proposal is received.

The government will also consider, at any time, late modifications to an otherwise successful proposal that make the proposal's terms more favorable to the government.

If you hand deliver the proposal, make sure you have the right room number and meet any other special requirements for hand delivery.

PROPOSAL EVALUATION

The time the government takes to perform an evaluation depends on the number of proposals received and the complexity of the items or services being evaluated. The process of selecting the winning contractor is called "source selection." The purpose of source selection is to select the contractor whose proposal has the highest degree of credibility and whose performance is expected to best meet the government's needs at a reasonable price. The selection process must be fair and reflect a comprehensive evaluation of the competitors' proposals. The source selection authority (SSA) is the official appointed to direct the source selection process. Throughout the evaluation process, the contracting officer is the government's exclusive agent with the authority to enter into and administer contracts.

The selection process typically includes the evaluation of technical and cost/price proposals, negotiations between the contracting officer and the offerors, and preparation and selection of a best and final offer. When certain evaluation factors affect the selection decision more than others, it may be necessary for the contracting officer to weight the factors in such a way that their relative importance influences the evaluation category's final scoring appropriately.

The relative importance of evaluation factors and significant subfactors corresponds with the stated solicitation requirements to ensure that the source selection authority awards the contract to the offeror whose proposal is most advantageous to the government. Offerors should understand the basis on which their proposals will be evaluated and how best to prepare their proposals.

Contracting officers evaluate past performance in all RFPs that are estimated to exceed $100,000. Your past performance will indicate your ability to perform the contract requirements for which you submitted your proposal. The RFP will allow you to provide references for items or services that you provided for similar contracts. Contractors that lack relevant past performance information receive a neutral evaluation for past performance.

The technical proposal should contain no cost reference. It should, however, include resource information, such as labor hours and categories, materials, and subcontracts (if applicable), so that the offeror's understanding of the scope of work can be evaluated. The contracting officer typically uses technical personnel to evaluate technical proposals. Technical evaluators do not see price proposals because the contracting officer does not want price to influence the technical evaluation. RFPs are not opened publicly, so the competitive position of the various offerors is not disclosed.

Proposals that merely offer to conduct the project or program "in accordance with the requirements of the government's work statement" are ineligible for award (see Chapter 13). Offerors must submit an explanation of the proposed technical approach and the tasks to be performed in achieving the project objectives.

SOURCE SELECTION PROCESSES AND TECHNIQUES

Some of the more common acquisition processes and techniques include the following.

Best Value Continuum

The contracting officer tries to obtain the best value in negotiated acquisitions by using any one or a combination of source selection approaches. For acquisitions in which the requirements are clearly definable and the risk of unsuccessful contract performance is minimal, cost/price may dominate the source selection. When successful contract performance is less certain and more development work is required, technical and past performance considerations might play a more important role in the source selection.

For example, if a contracting officer issued a solicitation for standard office supplies, such as copier toner, cost/price would dominate the source selection. On the other hand, if the solicitation was for a specifically designed product, such as a computer chip, technical performance considerations would play a more dominant role.

Tradeoff Process

A tradeoff process occurs when the government may possibly benefit by awarding the contract to other than the lowest priced offeror or other than the highest technically rated offeror. When a contracting officer uses the tradeoff process, the following requirements apply:

■ The solicitation must clearly state all evaluation factors and significant subfactors (and their relative importance) that affect the contract award.

■ The solicitation must state whether all evaluation factors other than cost/price, when combined, are significantly more important than, approximately equal to, or less important than cost/price.

The perceived benefits of a higher priced proposal must merit the additional cost, and the rationale for tradeoffs must be documented.

Lowest Priced, Technically Acceptable Source Selection Process

The lowest priced, technically acceptable source selection process is appropriate when the best value to the government is expected to result from the selection of a technically acceptable proposal with the lowest evaluated price. For this method, the following requirements apply:

■ The solicitation must set forth the evaluation factors and significant subfactors that establish the requirements of acceptability.

■ Tradeoffs are not permitted.

■ Proposals are evaluated for acceptability but not ranked using the non-cost/price factors.

CHANGES AND DISCUSSIONS

Unlike sealed bidding procedures, negotiated procedures allow offerors to propose changes to the RFP's terms and conditions. The offeror could propose changes to the statement of work, propose alternative performance schedules (or delivery schedules), or even suggest an alternative product or service. For example, if the contracting officer issues a solicitation for red widgets, the offeror, for whatever reason, could submit a proposal for blue widgets. The contracting officer must consider the proposal as long as it conforms to the significant or material aspects of the RFP. However, in proposing changes to the RFP, you take the chance that the government will award the contract without discussion to a competitor.

When discussions or negotiations are necessary, the regulations require the contracting officer to conduct written or oral discussions with all responsible offerors whose proposals are within the competitive range. Discussions may be as specific as pointing out particular proposal problems or as broad as complete negotiations. However, these discussions may not disclose any information about competing proposals.

The competitive range consists of offerors that the contracting officer believes to have a reasonable chance of winning the contract, based on the initial proposal evaluation. The contracting officer would consider:

■ Strengths and weaknesses of each technical proposal

■ Offeror's understanding of the contract requirements and the reasonableness of its cost and pricing data

■ Management proposal (if applicable) and any other special requirements of the RFP.

Offerors outside the competitive range are eliminated from further consideration. If a contracting officer has any doubt about whether a proposal is in the competitive range, the proposal is included.

FINAL PROPOSAL REVISION AND AWARD

At the conclusion of the discussions, the offerors that are still within the competitive range receive a reasonable opportunity to revise their proposals. The government then notifies all offerors to submit their final proposal revision (previously called "best and final offer") by a certain time and date. A final proposal revision is, in effect, an opportunity to enhance your proposal. Be sure to submit your final proposal revision on time.

The contracting officer will not reopen discussions with contractors after receiving the final proposal revisions unless the government could benefit. For example, additional discussions would be necessary if it is clear to the contracting officer that the information provided in the final proposal revisions is insufficient to justify contractor selection and award. Once these additional discussions are complete, the contracting officer will issue another request for final proposal revisions to all remaining offerors.

The final source selection (or the contract award) is based on the content of the final proposal revisions. Just as in sealed bidding, however, an offeror must be "responsible" to receive the contract (see Bid Evaluations, Chapter 11). The contract award is usually accomplished in one of three ways:

- By sending the successful offeror a copy of the award contract. (For example, if SF 33, Solicitation, Offer and Award [see Chapter 13], is used as the cover sheet for the RFP, the contracting officer would complete and sign the award section of this form.)

- By notifying the successful offeror by telephone with written confirmation.

- By notifying the successful offeror by letter.

Contracting officers usually notify unsuccessful offerors within three business days of contract award.

Sealed Bidding vs. Negotiated Procurement Procedures		
Characteristics	**Sealed Bidding**	**Negotiated Procurement Procedures**
Initial solicitation document	IFB	RFP
Response (offer)	Bid	Proposal
Specification or requirements	Must be precise	Less precise (discussions are allowed)
Minimum prospective bidders	Two	May be sole source
Amendments to solicitation after closing	Not allowed	Allowed
Selection criteria	The lowest responsive and responsible bidder is awarded the contract	Award is made in accordance with the stated evaluation criteria
Types of contracts	Fixed-price only	Fixed-price or cost-reimbursement may be used

DEBRIEFINGS

Once the contract is awarded, the contracting officer may tell unsuccessful offerors the number of offers solicited, the number of offers received, the name and address of each firm receiving an award, the quantities and prices of each award, and in general terms, the reasons their proposals were not accepted. Unsuccessful offerors may also request a debriefing by the contracting officer. A debriefing is a meeting between government personnel involved in the proposal evaluation, usually the contracting officer, and an unsuccessful offeror, during which the government explains why the offeror's proposal was not chosen for award. (Debriefings are conducted with only one offeror at a time.) The debriefing should occur within five days after receipt of the written request.

An offeror that was excluded from the competitive range at any point in the evaluation process may also request a preaward debriefing.

The debriefing should foster an open, nonadversarial environment that encourages the exchange of information about the offeror's proposal. However, the debriefing should not compromise the integrity of the source selection process or disclose proprietary information about other offerors.

At a minimum, the debriefing information should include:

■ Government's evaluation of the significant strengths and weaknesses or deficiencies in the offeror's proposal

■ Overall evaluated cost/price and technical rating, if applicable, of the successful offeror

■ Overall ranking of all offerors

■ Summary of the rationale for award

■ For acquisitions of commercial items, a description of the services or the make and model of the item to be delivered by the successful offeror

■ Reasonable responses to concerns about source selection procedures and applicable regulations.

The contracting officer will not provide point-by-point comparisons of the proposals. In addition, the contracting officer is prohibited from disclosing the following information:

■ Trade secrets

- Privileged or confidential manufacturing processes and techniques

- Privileged or confidential commercial and financial information

- The names of individuals providing reference information about an offeror's past performance.

Don't expect to be satisfied with the debriefing results. Debriefings generally are unsuccessful because government evaluators are naturally inhibited by the fear of triggering a protest. You can help alleviate this fear by communicating your intentions not to protest the award before the debriefing.

PROTESTS

Protests are written objections by interested parties to a solicitation, proposed award, or award of a contract. Interested parties include actual or prospective offerors whose direct economic interest would be affected by the award of or failure to award a particular contract. Unfortunately, protests are common in federal procurements.

The contracting officer must consider all protests, whether submitted before or after contract award. Successful protests may change a planned award, cause cancellation of an award already made, or reimburse the protester for the cost of the protest or the bid preparation effort. Protests are usually initiated by filing a written protest with the General Accounting Office (GAO). A protest may also be filed directly with the contracting activity, the General Services Board of Contract Appeals, or in some cases, the U.S. Claims Court. Protests should be filed no later than 10 days after the date on which the basis for the protest was either known or should have been known.

Once filed, you must provide a copy of your protest to the contracting officer no later than the next day. GAO's Office of General Counsel then requests a report on the matter from the contracting officer. When this report is received, a copy is provided to the protester, who is given the opportunity to comment.

Many times, GAO holds an informal conference to give the contractor an opportunity to present its views. GAO then considers the facts and issues raised by the protest and adjudicates a decision in the name of the Comptroller General (decisions are usually made within 100 days of the initial receipt of the protest). Both the protester and the contracting officer receive a copy of the decision. The contracting officer usually takes action in accordance with the decision.

If a protester disagrees with the GAO decision, it may appeal the decision to the federal district court. If the protester disagrees with that decision, it may appeal the matter all the way to the Supreme Court. FAR 33.1 provides detailed information on protests.

■ ■ ■

Negotiated procurement procedures enable the government to evaluate desirable features and technical superiority. RFPs allow the government and industry to correct errors in understanding and specifications by permitting discussions and negotiations.

However, the RFP usually requires a long-term effort. Price leaks may occur. Leveling of proposals may occur during negotiations. Vendors often learn who their competitors are. Contracting officers may have difficulty controlling communications between technical staff and vendors. Multiple final proposal revisions are common, which tends to erode the integrity of the procurement process.

■ ■ ■

13 The Uniform Contract Format

© 1997 Randy Glasbergen.

"I haven't read your proposal yet, Bob, but I already have some great ideas on how to improve it."

What's in this chapter?

- Part I: The schedule
- Part II: Contract clauses
- Part III: List of documents, exhibits, and other attachments
- Part IV: Representations and instructions
- Amendments to the solicitation
- Typical proposal weaknesses
- Procurement instrument identification numbers
- Unsolicited proposals
- Contingent fees

The Uniform Contract Format (UCF) is a blank solicitation package that the contracting officer sends out to prospective contractors. It is the most common solicitation format used by the federal government to purchase supplies and services. During FY2002, the federal government used the UCF for more than 100,000 solicitations. This format can be used for both IFBs and RFPs. A completed solicitation package can be anywhere from 20 to 10,000 pages in length, depending on the complexity of the procurement.

Prospective contractors tend to be intimidated by the sheer volume or size of the UCF. Don't be! Once you become familiar with the UCF's organization, you will be able to anticipate and understand its content. The four parts and 13 sections of the UCF are shown below.

Uniform Contract Format

Part I—The Schedule

Section A	Solicitation/contract form
Section B	Supplies or services and prices/costs
Section C	Description/specifications/statement of work
Section D	Packaging and marking
Section E	Inspection and acceptance
Section F	Deliveries or performance
Section G	Contract administration data
Section H	Special contract requirements

Part II—Contract Clauses

Section I	Contract clauses

Part III—List of Documents, Exhibits, and Other Attachments

Section J	List of attachments

Part IV—Representations and Instructions

Section K	Representations, certifications, and other statements of offerors or respondents
Section L	Instructions, conditions, and notices to offerors or respondents
Section M	Evaluation factors for award

The UCF may not be used for the following acquisitions:

■ Construction and architect-engineering contracts

■ Shipbuilding (including design, construction, and conversion), ship overhaul, and ship repair

■ Subsistence contracts

■ Supplies or service contracts requiring special contract formats

■ Letter requests for proposals

■ Contracts exempted by the agency head or designee

■ Firm-fixed-price or fixed-price with economic price adjustment acquisitions that use the simplified contract format.

Contracting officers are encouraged to use the UCF to the maximum extent practicable. One of the UCF's primary benefits is that it ensures that the same general information appears in the same order in most federal solicitations. This familiar format enables the reader to focus on the proposal's content rather than its form. Federal agencies must ensure that the various sections of the solicitation are in agreement.

The contracting officer will delete any section of the UCF that does not apply to the solicitation. Part IV, Representations and Instructions, usually is not included in the resulting contract, but the contracting officer retains it in the contract file. Each solicitation package includes all the necessary forms, along with the scheduled time and place for bid opening.

PART I: THE SCHEDULE

The purpose of the schedule is to explain the products or services being acquired, along with contractual requirements and specifications. The schedule provides detailed descriptions of the items being solicited; technical information about production, marking, packaging, packing, delivery, and inspection; and other information necessary to meet the contract requirements.

Section A - Solicitation/Contract Form

SF 33, Solicitation, Offer, and Award, is typically the first page and serves as the cover sheet of the solicitation package. It contains information about the time and place at which offerors should submit proposals. It also itemizes a table of required contents that each offeror must provide.

The offer section of this form, which the offeror completes, constitutes a legally binding offer. The award section is completed by the contracting officer after making the source selection or award decision. Once the contractor receives this signed solicitation package, it becomes an executed contract.

If the contracting officer does not use SF 33, the cover sheet of the UCF must include the following information:

- Name, address, and location of issuing activity (including room and building where proposals or information must be submitted)

- Solicitation type

- Solicitation number (each federal agency uses its own contract numbering system)

- Issuance date

- Closing date and time

- Number of pages

- Requisition or other purchase authority

- Brief description of item or service

SOLICITATION, OFFER AND AWARD		1. THIS CONTRACT IS A RATED ORDER UNDER DPAS (15 CFR 700)		RATING		PAGE	OF	PAGES
2. CONTRACT NUMBER	3. SOLICITATION NUMBER	4. TYPE OF SOLICITATION	5. DATE ISSUED		6. REQUISITION/PURCHASE NUMBER			
DE-AC06-98FD00036	DE-RP06-98FD00036	[X] SEALED BID (IFB) [ ] NEGOTIATED (RFP)	03/17/06		01-98FD00036.000			
7. ISSUED BY CODE HR-541			8. ADDRESS OFFER TO (If other than Item 7)					

U.S. Department of Energy
1000 Independence Ave., SW
Washington, DC 20585

NOTE: In sealed bid solicitations "offer" and "offeror" mean "bid" and "bidder".

SOLICITATION

9. Sealed offers in original and _____ 2 _____ copies for furnishing the supplies or services in the Schedule will be received at the place specified in Item 8, or if

handcarried, in the depository located in Room 505, Building A   until 04:30 local time   06/15/06
                                                                                                        (Hour)   (Date)

CAUTION - LATE Submissions, Modifications, and Withdrawals: See Section L, Provision No. 52.214-7 or 52.215-1. All offers are subject to all terms and conditions contained in this solicitation.

10. FOR INFORMATION CALL:	A. NAME Sam Mills, Contract Officer	B. TELEPHONE (NO COLLECT CALLS)			C. E-MAIL ADDRESS
		AREA CODE	NUMBER	EXT.	
		202	426-0150		

11. TABLE OF CONTENTS

(X)	SEC.	DESCRIPTION	PAGE(S)	(X)	SEC.	DESCRIPTION	PAGE(S)
		PART I - THE SCHEDULE				PART II - CONTRACT CLAUSES	
X	A	SOLICITATION/CONTRACT FORM	1	X	I	CONTRACT CLAUSES	52-62
X	B	SUPPLIES OR SERVICES AND PRICES/COSTS	2-20			PART III - LIST OF DOCUMENTS, EXHIBITS AND OTHER ATTACH.	
X	C	DESCRIPTION/SPECS./WORK STATEMENT	21-28	X	J	LIST OF ATTACHMENTS	63
X	D	PACKAGING AND MARKING	29			PART IV - REPRESENTATIONS AND INSTRUCTIONS	
X	E	INSPECTION AND ACCEPTANCE	30-31	X	K	REPRESENTATIONS, CERTIFICATIONS AND OTHER STATEMENTS OF OFFERORS	64-80
X	F	DELIVERIES OR PERFORMANCE	32				
X	G	CONTRACT ADMINISTRATION DATA	33-36	X	L	INSTRS., CONDS., AND NOTICES TO OFFERORS	81-95
X	H	SPECIAL CONTRACT REQUIREMENTS	37-51	X	M	EVALUATION FACTORS FOR AWARD	96-98

OFFER (Must be fully completed by offeror)

NOTE: Item 12 does not apply if the solicitation includes the provisions at 52.214-16, Minimum Bid Acceptance Period.

12. In compliance with the above, the undersigned agrees, if this offer is accepted within _____ calendar days (60 calendar days unless a different

period is inserted by the offeror) from the date for receipt of offers specified above, to furnish any or all items upon which prices are offered at the price set opposite each item, delivered at the designated point(s), within the time specified in the schedule.

13. DISCOUNT FOR PROMPT PAYMENT (See Section I, Clause No. 52.232-8)	10 CALENDAR DAYS (%)	20 CALENDAR DAYS (%)	30 CALENDAR DAYS (%)	CALENDAR DAYS (%)

14. ACKNOWLEDGMENT OF AMEND-MENTS (The offeror acknowledges receipt of amendments to the SOLICITATION for offerors and related documents numbered and dated):	AMENDMENT NO.	DATE	AMENDMENT NO.	DATE

15A. NAME AND ADDRESS OF OFFER-OR	CODE 8711	FACILITY	16. NAME AND TITLE OF PERSON AUTHORIZED TO SIGN OFFER (Type or print)
	TechNet 450 Garden Gate Ave. Denver, CO 80225		Scott Turner, President

15B. TELEPHONE NUMBER			15C. CHECK IF REMITTANCE ADDRESS IS DIFFERENT FROM ABOVE - ENTER SUCH ADDRESS IN SCHEDULE.	17. SIGNATURE	18. OFFER DATE
AREA CODE	NUMBER	EXT.	[ ]		05/30/2007
303	867-5301	123			

AWARD (To be completed by Government)

19. ACCEPTED AS TO ITEMS NUMBERED	20. AMOUNT	21. ACCOUNTING AND APPROPRIATION

22. AUTHORITY FOR USING OTHER THAN FULL AND OPEN COMPETITION: [ ] 10 U.S.C. 2304(c) ( ) [ ] 41 U.S.C. 253(c) ( )	23. SUBMIT INVOICES TO ADDRESS SHOWN IN (4 copies unless otherwise specified)	ITEM

24. ADMINISTERED BY (If other than Item 7) CODE	25. PAYMENT WILL BE MADE BY CODE

26. NAME OF CONTRACTING OFFICER (Type or print)	27. UNITED STATES OF AMERICA (Signature of Contracting Officer)	28. AWARD DATE

IMPORTANT - Award will be made on this Form, or on Standard Form 26, or by other authorized official written notice.

AUTHORIZED FOR LOCAL REPRODUCTION
Previous edition is unusable

STANDARD FORM 33 (REV. 9-97)
Prescribed by GSA - FAR (48 CFR) 53.214(c)

Sample SF 33

■ Requirement for the offeror to provide its name and complete address (including street, city, county, state, zip code, and electronic address)

■ Offer expiration date.

SF 33 also has a section for any price discounts you're willing to offer. The Prompt Payment Act (see Chapter 17) requires the government to make payments within 30 days of receipt of a properly prepared invoice. However, if a contractor wants a faster payment turnaround, it may offer the government a prompt-payment discount. For example, the contractor may offer the government a 1% discount on the payment (or contract) amount if the government makes payment within 15 days. Prompt-payment discounts are not considered in determining the low offeror.

This required information must be signed by an authorized company representative. Do not use a transmittal letter to forward an offer, unless the contracting officer specifically requires you to do so. Any such letter attached to an offer will be considered part of the offer. Stock phrases, such as "prices subject to change without notice," or even letterhead slogans, could invalidate an offer.

Section B - Supplies or Services and Prices/Costs

Section B is basically the government's ordering form. Anything the government intends to buy and have delivered should show up here. In this section, the offeror records its bid price. Also, offerors must include a brief description of the supplies and services they offer, including item number; national stock number/part number, if applicable; title or name identifying the supplies or services; and quantities. This section may also include information about the contract type, renewal options, delivery requirements, ordering procedures, or other considerations.

The Federal Acquisition Regulation (FAR) lists no specific structure requirements for this section, but the Department of Defense (DOD), the General Services Administration (GSA), and the Department of Energy (DOE) all have specific formats for their procurements or purchases. For example, DOD would use the following format to purchase 30 office desks:

DOD Price/Cost Format					
ITEM NO.	SUPPLIES/ SERVICE	QUANTITY	UNITS	UNIT PRICE	AMOUNT
0001	Office Desk	30	EA	$ 1,000.00	$ 30,000.00

As you can see, DOD uses a four-digit contract line item number (CLIN). If DOD also purchased chairs with this solicitation, CLIN 0002 would be the chairs' item number. When the purchased supply or service has separate parts, different prices, or different delivery schedules, each line item is further subdivided. The following shows a breakdown for a computer system being purchased by DOD.

DOD Computer System Purchase					
ITEM NO.	SUPPLIES/ SERVICE	QUANTITY	UNITS	UNIT PRICE	AMOUNT
0001	Computer System				
0001AA	Monitor	5	EA	$ 300.00	$ 1,500.00
0001AB	Keyboard	5	EA	$ 50.00	$ 250.00
0001AC	CPU	5	EA	$ 800.00	$ 4,000.00
0002	Setup	As Reqd			$ 500.00
0003	Maintenance Agreement	As Reqd			$ 1,000.00

Subline items, which provide a further breakdown of the CLIN, receive a two-digit alphanumeric identifier, such as 0001AA. In many cases, subline items help in monitoring or administering contract performance.

Solicitations usually require price lists, catalogs, or GSA schedule contracts to justify prices for commercial off-the-shelf items that are based on the contractor's commercial prices. Service contracts, on the other hand, are based on estimated costs. The solicitation usually requires a detailed breakdown of costs for labor, overhead, general and administrative services, subcontracts, and materials (with fee or profit expressed as a cost percentage).

Section C - Description/Specifications/Statement of Work

Section C provides detailed and critical information about the supplies and services being purchased and addresses what the seller must do to perform the contract. The FAR provides no specific structure requirements for this section. Section C also describes minimum or mandatory requirements. If a contractor fails to satisfy any of the stated requirements, the government may reject the proposal as nonresponsive. Please read this section carefully!

The description of the products or services may reference specifications, standards, technical data packages, or other descriptive resources. If the contract is for products, Section C includes purchase descriptions or specifications that the products must meet. If the contract is for services, Section C contains a statement of work that describes the tasks to be performed. If the procurement requires a large number of specifications, they may be grouped together and listed as an exhibit in Section J.

Section D - Packaging and Marking

This section protects against liability for deterioration or damage of products during shipping and storage. Contractors must preserve, pack, and mark all items in accordance with standard commercial practices or other special requirements if the products are subject to a more hostile environment. Packaging and marking requirements may exceed the cost of the unit itself, so be sure to include these costs in your proposal or bid price. If there are no packaging and marking requirements, as in service contracts, this section will be omitted from the proposal.

Section E - Inspection and Acceptance

Section E contains the contractor inspection and acceptance instructions, as well as quality assurance and reliability requirements. These instructions tell the contractor where the inspection will take place and specify sampling criteria, first-item test requirements, or other inspection requirements. For most procurements or purchases, the standard inspection requirement directs the contractor to maintain an inspection system that is acceptable to the government, maintain records of inspections conducted, and allow the government to make its own inspections. This section may also identify specific tests that the contractor must conduct during the manufacturing process or, if the contract is for services, during specific phases of the work.

Before any product is accepted, the government verifies that the materials meet all contractual requirements. The government also has the right to require a contractor to replace or correct defective products. Rejections, late deliveries, and other performance failures are recorded in the contract file by the contracting officer. Contracting officers review this file before making new awards to the contractor.

Section F - Deliveries or Performance

This section specifies the time, place, and method of delivery or performance. For products, the delivery (or performance) schedule usually states the calendar date or a specified period after the contract has been awarded. It also lists the place of delivery, usually stated as: F.O.B. origin or F.O.B. destination. Service deadlines are usually specified by a contractual period (or period of performance).

A free-on-board (F.O.B.) origin contract requires the government to pay shipping costs and to assume the risk of loss or damage to the goods en route. The contractor is responsible only for delivering the goods to a common carrier or to the U.S. Postal Service. Delivery is complete once this occurs.

With F.O.B. destination, the contractor is responsible for the arrival of goods to the location specified in the contract. The contractor pays all shipping costs and retains the risk of loss or damage to the goods until they arrive at their destination.

Section G - Contract Administration Data

Section G supplements the administrative information contained in Section A. This information typically includes:

■ The contracting officer's name and address, the contracting officer's technical representative, the transportation office, and the contract administrative officer

■ Accounting and appropriation data

■ Procedures for preparing and submitting invoices

■ Seller's payment address

■ Contract administration office instructions.

This section may become important as a company tries to collect payment.

Section H - Special Contract Requirements

Section H contains the customized clauses that do not fit elsewhere in the UCF. Policies concerning placement of these clauses vary among federal agencies and even among the buying offices within a federal agency. Such clauses might include:

■ Option terms

■ Economic price adjustment provisions

■ Government-furnished property or facilities

■ Foreign sources

■ Total system performance responsibility

■ Multiyear provisions

■ Limitations on the federal government's obligations

■ Service Contract Act wage determinations

■ Payment of incentive fees

■ Technical data requirements.

The contracting officer (or authorized government official) has several hundred clauses and provisions to choose from when drafting Section H. Every clause included in this section must be there for a reason—either a regulation requires it or the administration of the contract necessitates it. The contracting officer carefully selects clauses in this section because they add to the contract cost and can raise contractors' objections.

PART II: CONTRACT CLAUSES

Part II of the UCF contains a variety of contract clauses.

Section I - Contract Clauses

This section contains clauses that laws or regulations require. The circumstances of the proposed contract predetermine the clauses in this section, although the contracting officer may include any additional clauses that he or she expects to apply to the resulting contract. As a general rule, only those clauses included in FAR Part 52 (and a federal agency's FAR supplement, Part 52) are included in this section. These laws or regulations are commonly referred to as "boilerplate clauses." The contracting officer has little or no leeway in preparing this section. Each clause derives its authority from the FAR or from a public law, statute, or executive order.

Most clauses included in this section are referenced by the clause number, title, date, and regulation source. Instead of printing an entire clause within a contract, an agreement may merely refer to the clause, e.g., FAR 52.203-3, Gratuities. Contractors are still liable for the legal consequences of the clause's terms, even if the clause is not expressly quoted or spelled out. Clauses must be written out or incorporated in full text if the:

■ FAR specifically requires full text

■ Seller must complete the clause

■ Clause is based on a FAR or agency regulation but will not be printed verbatim in the contract

■ Contracting officer's boss directs it.

Most clauses included in Section I must "flow down" to subcontractors. In other words, the same clauses that apply to the prime contractor also apply to the subcontractor. If you are unfamiliar with a referenced clause, be sure to obtain a copy of it, so you will know exactly what the government requires of you. The easiest way to obtain a copy of a referenced clause is to download it directly from the FAR website at:

WWW.ARNET.GOV/far/

Provisions do not typically appear in this section. How does a provision differ from a clause? A "clause" is a term or condition that is used in both contracts and solicitations that can apply either after contract award or both before and after contract award, such as a clause requiring a contractor to maintain a drug-free workplace. A "provision" is a term or condition that is used only in solicitations and applies only before contract award, such as procedures for handling late proposals. Provisions provide information and direction to the seller and are typically found in Sections K, L, or M.

PART III: LIST OF DOCUMENTS, EXHIBITS, AND OTHER ATTACHMENTS

Part III contains a variety of attachments.

Section J - List of Attachments

Requirements that don't fit into any other section of the UCF appear in Section J. This section is essentially an inventory of documents. The FAR provides little guidance on the format or content of these attachments. The FAR does, however, direct the contracting officer to provide a list of the title, date, and number of pages for each attached document. Some examples of these attachments include:

■ System requirements and specifications

■ Architectural drawings

■ Exhibits

■ Work statements

■ Technical or engineering data

■ Government-furnished property

When you receive an IFB or RFP, be sure that it includes all the attachments listed in this section.

PART IV: REPRESENTATIONS AND INSTRUCTIONS

This section includes instructions for preparing your bid and presents questions you must answer (or a questionnaire you must fill out) for your bid to be considered. Items ranging from definitions of contracting terms to statements about contract conditions are contained in this section. Part IV is not included in the final contract award, but the contracting officer retains the winning contractor's representations and certifications. Be sure to fill in and sign all sections as required; if you don't, you may be considered nonresponsive and your bid may be rejected.

Section K - Representations, Certifications, and Other Statements of Offerors or Respondents

In Section K, the offeror provides information about itself and certifies that it complies with all applicable laws and regulations. The contracting officer typically uses FAR Subpart 52.3 as a guide for selecting the provisions that apply to the contract. Some examples of these representations and certifications include:

■ Is the offeror's workplace drug-free?

■ Is the offeror a small business?

■ Is the offeror minority-owned?

■ Has the offeror performed the requirements for Certification of Procurement Integrity?

These representations and certifications usually require several pages of "fill-in-the-blank" answers. Many questions will be difficult to answer if your government contracting background is limited. The small business specialist at the contracting activity issuing the solicitation can help you answer these questions, which must be submitted and signed with your bid. Be sure to complete all the representations, certifications, and other statements included in this section.

Contracting officers will generally accept a contractor's self-certification, unless there is a reason to challenge it (or unless a competitor challenges it). If an offeror makes a false representation or certification, the contracting officer can terminate the contract for default and turn the matter over to the Department of Justice for prosecution.

Section L - Instructions, Conditions, and Notices to Offerors or Respondents

Section L tells the offeror how the contracting officer wants the proposal to be prepared. Each evaluation factor and significant subfactor, as outlined in the source-selection plan and stated in Section M, should have a corresponding instruction in Section L. The contracting officer will use the matrices contained in FAR Subpart 52.3 as a guide for selecting solicitation provisions. These instructions are designed to facilitate the evaluation process. For example, Section L may specify a limitation on the number of pages or volumes in the proposal, require that a certain font size and margins be used, and lay out the order of presentation.

Section L also contains information on the various conditions and circumstances that may affect the proposal, such as:

■ Whether the proposal is set aside for small businesses

■ Contract type expected to result from the solicitation

■ Procedures for handling late proposals.

In general, Section L should include information that allows you to submit your best possible proposal, while providing the source-selection team with sufficient data to make an award decision. The information requested from offerors must also correlate with the Section C requirements and Section M evaluation factors.

Section M - Evaluation Factors for Award

This section identifies the federal government's criteria for evaluating the proposals and selecting the winning contractor. Section M must include and adequately describe all factors and significant subfactors the government will consider in making the selection (e.g., the government will award up to 10 points for originality). The solicitation also informs offerors of minimum requirements that apply to particular evaluation factors and significant subfactors, such as the requirement that the contractor's proposal be technically sound.

In sealed bidding procurements, the evaluation criteria are limited to price and price-related factors. Negotiated procurements allow the contracting officer to evaluate price, terms and conditions, technical requirements, performance schedules (or delivery schedules), management proposals, or other parts of the contract that law or regulation do not mandate. However, cost and price always must affect the evaluation.

Section M often shows each factor's relative weight in the evaluation process. For example, the technical requirements may be twice as important as the management proposal. If no relative order is stated, the evaluation factors are of equal importance. Prospective offerors should carefully examine Section M before developing a proposal. The government will consider only those factors specified in this section.

To help ensure that your proposal addresses all the elements of Section C, Section L, and Section M, you might consider preparing a compliance matrix that identifies exactly where each item is addressed within the proposal.

AMENDMENTS TO THE SOLICITATION

Many times, a contracting officer issues solicitation amendments before the offerors' proposals are due. The contracting officer may issue an amendment to clarify ambiguities or add or delete requirements to the specifications or statement of work. Amendments should be taken very seriously because their content could dictate significant changes to the original solicitation, as well as the time allowed for performance. Now that most procurements are available online, a contractor should be sure to check the website of the procurement daily to see if any amendments are forthcoming.

To amend a solicitation, the contracting officer must furnish an SF 30, Amendment of Solicitation/Modification of Contract, to all prospective offerors who received a copy of the original solicitation. (The sample shows an amendment to extend the date that proposals are due from April 5, 2006, to April 19, 2006.) Each prospective' offeror must acknowledge receipt of the amendment by:

■ Completing Blocks 8 and 15 on SF 30 and returning the form with the bid.

■ Identifying receipt of the amendment on each copy of the offer. You will need to enter the amendment number and date of the amendment in the spaces provided on Block 14 of SF 30.

■ Submitting a separate letter or fax (if permitted by the solicitation) that includes the solicitation number and the amendment's number and date, as well as your name or your company's name, address, and telephone number.

If the offeror does not acknowledge or sign the amendment, the contracting officer may disqualify the bid as nonresponsive.

Don't confuse amendments to a solicitation with modifications to a solicitation or changes to the contract. Amendments to a solicitation generally add new requirements, change requirements, clarify discrepancies in the solicitation, or delete something before the proposal's due date. Modifications to a solicitation, on the other hand, are made after discussions between the offerors and the contracting officer. If a contracting officer requests a final proposal revision, your revised proposal must make final changes or corrections. Finally, changes to a contract result from events that happen after the contract is awarded, while work is being performed.

TYPICAL PROPOSAL WEAKNESSES

Some common proposal weaknesses include:

■ Noncompliance with the solicitation's specifications and requirements

■ Unrealistic cost estimates (either too high or too low)

AMENDMENT OF SOLICITATION/MODIFICATION OF CONTRACT		1. CONTRACT ID CODE	PAGE OF PAGES
			1 / 1

2. AMENDMENT/MODIFICATION NO. 0001	3. EFFECTIVE DATE 03/19/2006	4. REQUISITION/PURCHASE REQ. NO. 01-06NN63100.000	5. PROJECT NO. *(If applicable)*

6. ISSUED BY	CODE	MA-542	7. ADMINISTERED BY *(If other than Item 6)*	CODE

6. ISSUED BY

U.S. Department of Energy
Headquarters Office of Procurement Services
1000 Independence Ave., SW
Washington, DC 20585

8. NAME AND ADDRESS OF CONTRACTOR *(No., street, county, State, and Zip Code)*	(x)	9A. AMENDMENT OF SOLICITATION NO. DE-RP01-06NN63100
Happy's Office Furniture 850 Taylor St. Fort Worth, TX 76102	X	9B. DATED *(SEE ITEM 11)* March 3, 2006
		10A. MODIFICATION OF CONTRACT/ORDER NO.
		10B. DATED *(SEE ITEM 13)*

CODE	FACILITY CODE

11. THIS ITEM ONLY APPLIES TO AMENDMENTS OF SOLICITATIONS

[X] The above numbered solicitation is amended as set forth in Item 14. The hour and date specified for receipt of Offers [X] is extended, [ ] is not extended.

Offers must acknowledge receipt of this amendment prior to the hour and date specified in the solicitation or as amended, by one of the following methods:
(a) By completing Items 8 and 15, and returning __2__ copies of the amendment; (b) By acknowledging receipt of this amendment on each copy of the offer submitted; or (c) By separate letter or telegram which includes a reference to the solicitation and amendment numbers. FAILURE OF YOUR ACKNOWLEDGEMENT TO BE RECEIVED AT THE PLACE DESIGNATED FOR THE RECEIPT OF OFFERS PRIOR TO THE HOUR AND DATE SPECIFIED MAY RESULT IN REJECTION OF YOUR OFFER. If by virtue of this amendment you desire to change an offer already submitted, such change may be made by telegram or letter, provided each telegram or letter makes reference to the solicitation and this amendment, and is received prior to the opening hour and date specified.

12. ACCOUNTING AND APPROPRIATION DATA *(If required)*

13. THIS ITEM APPLIES ONLY TO MODIFICATIONS OF CONTRACTS/ORDERS, IT MODIFIES THE CONTRACT/ORDER NO. AS DESCRIBED IN ITEM 14.

(x)	
	A. THIS CHANGE ORDER IS ISSUED PURSUANT TO: *(Specify authority)* THE CHANGES SET FORTH IN ITEM 14 ARE MADE IN THE CONTRACT ORDER NO. IN ITEM 10A.
	B. THE ABOVE NUMBERED CONTRACT/ORDER IS MODIFIED TO REFLECT THE ADMINISTRATIVE CHANGES *(such as changes in paying office, appropriation date, etc.)* SET FORTH IN ITEM 14, PURSUANT TO THE AUTHORITY OF FAR 43.103(b).
	C. THIS SUPPLEMENTAL AGREEMENT IS ENTERED INTO PURSUANT TO AUTHORITY OF:
	D. OTHER *(Specify type of modification and authority)*

E. IMPORTANT: Contractor [ ] is not, [ ] is required to sign this document and return ____ copies to the issuing office.

14. DESCRIPTION OF AMENDMENT/MODIFICATION *(Organized by UCF section headings, including solicitation/contract subject matter where feasible.)*
The purpose of this amendment is to extend the date that proposals are due from April 5, 2006 to April 19, 2006. Accordingly, Part II, Section L, Provision L.8 – Time, Date and Place Bids/Proposals are Due is revised to reflect the following: 1:00 p.m. on April 19, 2006

15A. NAME AND TITLE OF SIGNER *(Type or print)* Happy Gilmore, CEO		16A. NAME AND TITLE OF CONTRACTING OFFICER *(Type or print)* David J. Smith Contracting Officer
15B. CONTRACTOR/OFFEROR	15C. DATE SIGNED March 19, 2006	16B. UNITED STATES OF AMERICA BY _____	16C. DATE SIGNED March 19, 2006
(Signature of person authorized to sign)		*(Signature of Contracting Officer)*	

NSN 7540-01-152-8070 PREVIOUS EDITION UNUSABLE	30-105	STANDARD FORM 30 (Rev. 10-83) Prescribed by GSA FAR (48 CFR) 53.243

Sample SF 30

- Insufficient understanding of the contract's requirements

- Poor proposal organization

- Wordiness or unclear writing style

- Unsubstantiated rationale for the proposed approach

- Insufficient resources to accomplish the contract's requirements

- Incomplete response to the solicitation.

To avoid these problems, set up a checklist of solicitation requirements as you read the IFB or RFP. Use the checklist in your proposal's final review.

PROCUREMENT INSTRUMENT IDENTIFICATION NUMBERS

Each solicitation/contract issued by the government receives a procurement instrument identification number (PIIN). The government uses a standard system for numbering solicitations/contracts, which typically consists of 13 digits (or positions). The first six digits of each PIIN identify the contracting activity (or buying office) issuing the solicitation/contract. For example, here are a few of the PIINs used by DOD buying offices:

Major Army Buying Offices:

U.S. Army Industrial Operations Command   PIIN DAAA09

U.S. Army Research Laboratory (Adelphi, MD)   PIIN DAAD17

Major Navy Buying Offices:

Office of Naval Research (Arlington, VA)   PIIN N00014

Naval Air Warfare Center (China Lake, CA)   PIIN N68936

Major Air Force Buying Offices:

10th Air Base Wing (10ABW/LGCP—Academy, CO)   PIIN F05601

Air Intelligence Agency (San Antonio, TX)   PIIN F41621

Defense Logistics Agency Supply Centers:

Defense Industrial Supply Center—Philadelphia, PA   PIIN DLA500

Defense Electronic Supply Center—Dayton, OH   PIIN DLA900

The next two digits in the PIIN identify the fiscal year of the solicitation or contract. The ninth character identifies the solicitation type being used, such as an invitation for bid (B) or a request for proposal (R). The remaining digits identify the particular solicitation or contract. For example, the following is a PIIN for a request for proposal issued in FY2004 by the Office of Naval Research.

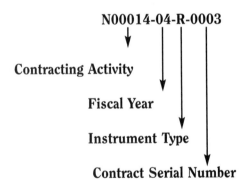

N00014-04-R-0003

Contracting Activity

Fiscal Year

Instrument Type

Contract Serial Number

UNSOLICITED PROPOSALS

An unsolicited proposal is a written offer submitted to a federal agency on the offeror's initiative to obtain a government contract. These proposals are not in response to formal or informal solicitation requests. (Sometimes they are actually "solicited" by technical personnel rather than contracting personnel.) The government typically encourages the submission of new and innovative ideas in response to Broad Agency Announcements, Small Business Innovation Research topics, Small Business Technology Transfer Research topics, or any other government-initiated solicitations or programs. If your new and innovative idea does not fall under any of these programs, you may still submit it as an unsolicited proposal. Each federal agency uses different procedures for handling unsolicited proposals. To get information on an agency's submission procedures, contact the small business specialist at the agency of interest to you (see Chapter 3).

A major advantage of submitting an unsolicited proposal is that your offer is typically one-of-a-kind. That is, you probably won't have competition. Federal agencies are not, however, responsible for costs incurred in proposal preparation. It is always a good idea to consult with appropriate agency officials before starting on an unsolicited proposal.

A valid unsolicited proposal must:

■ Be innovative and unique

■ Be independently originated and developed by the offeror

■ Be prepared without government supervision, endorsement, direction, or direct government involvement, although detailed discussions with the government about the need or requirement for the equipment or service often serve to encourage the contractor to prepare and submit an unsolicited proposal.

■ Include sufficient detail to determine that government support could be worthwhile and the proposed work could benefit the agency's research and development or other mission responsibilities

■ Not be an advance proposal for a known federal agency requirement that can be acquired by competitive methods.

Advertising material, commercial item offers, contributions, or routine correspondence on technical issues are not considered to be unsolicited proposals.

Unsolicited proposals should contain the following basic information to permit objective and timely consideration:

- The offeror's name, address, and organization type (such as profit, non-profit, educational, small business)

- Names and telephone numbers of technical and business personnel to be contacted for evaluation or negotiation purposes

- Identification of proprietary (or confidential) data to be used only for evaluation purposes

- Submission date

- Signature of a person authorized to represent and contractually obligate the offeror

- A title and abstract of the proposed effort (the abstract should be approximately 200 to 300 words, stating the basic purpose, summary of work, and expected end result)

- A report or narrative that discusses the activity's objectives, the approach and extent of effort to be employed, the nature and extent of the anticipated results, and the manner in which the work will support the agency's mission

- Names and biographical information of the offeror's key personnel

- Type of support needed from the agency (such as facilities, equipment, materials, or personnel resources)

- Proposed price or total estimated cost

- Time period for which the proposal is valid (a six-month minimum is suggested)

- Preferred contract type

■ Brief description of the organization, previous experience, relevant past performance, and facilities of the offeror.

Federal agencies have procedures for controlling the receipt, evaluation, and timely disposition of unsolicited proposals. These procedures include control of the reproduction and disposition of proposal material, particularly data identified by the offeror as subject to duplication or disclosure restrictions. In addition, federal agencies have contact points to coordinate the receipt and handling of unsolicited proposals. If the agency determines that it doesn't need the services, it returns the unsolicited proposal to the offeror, citing the reasons for its return.

Government personnel should not use any data, concept, idea, or other part of an unsolicited proposal as the basis for a solicitation or in negotiations with any other firm, unless the offeror is notified of and agrees to the intended use, or the proposed information is available from another unrestricted source. In addition, government personnel may not disclose restrictively marked information included in an unsolicited proposal. The disclosure of such information could result in criminal penalties.

CONTINGENT FEES

Contingent fee arrangements are a very complicated area in government contracting. Simply stated, a contingent fee means any commission, percentage, brokerage, or other fee that is contingent on the success that a person or concern has in securing a government contract award. For example, if a company hires a consultant to help prepare a proposal for a government contract and the agreement states that payment is contingent upon the company winning the contract, that would be considered a contingent fee arrangement.

Contractor arrangements to pay contingent fees for soliciting or obtaining government contracts have long been considered contrary to public policy because such arrangements may lead to attempted or actual exercise of improper influence. Therefore, in every negotiated contract, the government requires the contractor to provide a certification or warranty that it has not paid contingent fees to secure the contract. If a contractor fails to provide this documentation, the government may annul the contract without liability or deduct from the contract price the full amount of the contingent fee.

There is, however, an exception to this certification requirement. If contingent fee arrangements are made between contractors and "bona fide employees" or "bona fide agencies," they are permitted. A "bona fide employee" is a person employed by a contractor who is subject to the contractor's supervision and control with respect to time, place, and manner of performance, and who neither exerts nor proposes to exert improper influence to solicit or obtain government contracts, nor holds himself or herself out as being able to obtain a government contract through improper influence.

Federal regulations also allow this same type of bona fide employee relationship on a part-time basis to small businesses because small firms typically do not have the resources to employ salespeople full-time. For example, if a small business hires a consultant to help prepare price proposals, the consultant would be considered a bona fide employee, if he or she is supervised by the company's president and performs the company's services two days a week throughout the year. A bona fide employee may represent more than one firm but should not bid for more than one firm in the same line of work.

A "bona fide agency" is an established commercial or selling agency, hired by a contractor to secure business. If such an arrangement exists, the contractor must detail it in the format prescribed in OMB Circular A-34. The contracting officer evaluates the arrangement to ensure compliance with government regulations.

Contingent fee arrangements are complex. Be sure to obtain legal advice if you have questions or concerns about any of your contractual arrangements.

■   ■   ■

In the world of government contracting, proposals represent the "point of sale" for companies looking to do business with the federal government. Effective and efficient proposal development, preparation, management, and design are essential to your company's success. To be successful, you must plan carefully, make informed decisions, and know your client's requirements.

■   ■   ■

PART 5

What Are the Contract Types and Administrative Requirements?

The trouble with the race race is that even if you win, you are still a rat!

—Lily Tomlin

There is a perception in government contracting that the lowest bidder always wins the contract. For example, sealed bidding procedures enable the bidder with the lowest priced proposal to win the contract. Low bids do not apply, however, to federal supply schedule orders, best-value procurements, or sole-source acquisitions. How comfortable would you be riding on the space shuttle if you knew it was built by the bidder with the lowest priced proposal?

The government contracts for supplies and services at fair and reasonable prices, but no set of standard rules defines a "fair and reasonable price." Eventually, no matter how the problem is approached, the decision comes down to a matter of good personal judgment.

Every solicitation method, whether simplified acquisition, sealed bidding, or negotiated, states the basis of the award decision. The contracting officer chooses a procurement method that best fits the contract's requirements. To purchase an item that can be clearly and accurately described, such as office furniture, the contracting officer would probably use sealed bidding procedures. If the contracting officer is unsure of a bidder's ability to provide acceptable supplies or services, negotiated procedures might be used. However, cost and pricing data must always be part of the evaluation criteria.

The selection of a contract type requires negotiation and the exercise of good judgment. A contracting officer generally considers several factors, including:

- Contract's expected length (or period of performance)

- Price competition

- Contract's technical complexity

- Urgency of the need

- Dollar value of the contract

- Contract's performance risks

- Market conditions

- Contractor's motivation to perform the contract.

In addition, the offeror may also propose an alternative contract type.

The federal government uses two basic types of contracts: fixed-price contracts (see Chapter 14) and cost-reimbursement contracts (see Chapter 15). The primary differences between the two basic contract types are the amount of responsibility placed on the contractor and the amount of profit incentive offered to the contractor for achieving or exceeding specified standards or goals. With fixed-price contracts, the contractor assumes the risk of contract performance (or cost risk), and its performance determines its profit. With cost-reimbursement contracts, the government assumes the risk of contract performance, and it reimburses the contractor for the expenses incurred during the contract's performance. The solicitation document always indicates the contract type.

The other contract types available (discussed in Chapter 16) are modifications of either fixed-price or cost-reimbursement contracts:

■ Indefinite-delivery contracts

■ Time and materials contracts

■ Labor-hour contracts

■ Letter contracts

■ Basic ordering agreements.

14 Fixed-Price Contracts

Berry's World

"Remember, money can't buy happiness, but in Washington it CAN BUY access, jobs and influence."

11-5-96

What's in this chapter?

- Firm-fixed-price contract
- Fixed-price contract with economic price adjustment
- Fixed-price incentive contract
- Fixed-price contract with prospective price redetermination
- Fixed-ceiling-price contract with retroactive price redetermination

Under a fixed-price contract, the government agrees to pay a specific price (which includes the contractor's profit) for completed work and delivered products. Fixed-price contracts are used primarily to acquire commercial items, but are being increasingly used for acquiring services. When a contract is fixed-price, acceptable performance by the contractor is the basic criterion for payment (a contractor's "bill" under a fixed-price contract is called an invoice). The federal government prefers fixed-price contracts because the contract price is not subject to adjustment on the basis of the contractor's cost experience in performing it. If a contractor wins a fixed-price government contract, it must perform the contract at the award price, even if its actual costs of performance exceed the award price.

Fixed-price contracts place the "cost risk" on the contractor. However, there is no statutory limit on the profits that can be earned under fixed-price contracts. Maximum profit can be earned by managing fixed-price contracts aggressively and identifying, understanding, and controlling risk. Fixed-price contracts are typically used when:

■ Price competition is adequate.

■ Reasonable price comparisons with past purchases of the same or similar supplies or services made on a competitive basis or supported by valid cost or pricing data are available.

■ Available cost or pricing information permits realistic estimates of the probable performance costs.

■ Performance uncertainties can be identified and reasonable estimates of their cost impact can be made.

The government uses fixed-price contracts in simplified acquisition and sealed bidding procedures. In addition, fixed-priced contracts are used in 80% of negotiated procurement procedures. Both fixed-price and cost-reimbursement contracts may contain incentives that increase or decrease a contractor's profit or fee depending on the contractor's performance in holding down costs, improving technical performance, or making prompt (or early) deliveries. These are known as fixed-price incentive contracts and cost-plus-incentive-fee contracts (see Chapter 15).

FIRM-FIXED-PRICE CONTRACT

In a firm-fixed-price (FFP) contract, the government agrees to pay a specific amount (or price) when a contractor's performance has been completed and accepted. The contract price does not change, regardless of the contractor's actual cost experience. A contractor accepts full cost responsibility when agreeing to this type of contract. FFP contracts are typically used when:

■ The statement of work or specification can be clearly and accurately described. (FFP contracts are generally used for purchasing commercial items and standard services.)

■ A fair, accurate, and reasonable contract price can be established before contract award.

The government prefers this contract type because the contractor bears all the risk and the government's administrative burden is minimal. FFP contracts require no cost or pricing data if the contracting officer determines that the agreed-upon prices are based on adequate price competition. (See the Truth in Negotiations Act in Chapter 2 for more information about cost and pricing data.)

The government establishes the firm contract price and performance requirements during the pre-award negotiation phase. For example, suppose three contractors were awarded contracts to supply office furniture, as follows:

	RJC Furniture	Joe's Office Supplies	All Office, Inc.
	100 Executive Chairs	5 Conference Tables	20 Office Desks
Contract value	$75,000	$150,000	$200,000
Actual costs	$50,000	$185,000	$200,000
Profit (or loss)	**$25,000**	**($ 35,000)**	**$ —**

In this example, RJC Furniture made a profit of $25,000, which the government pays once the chairs are delivered and accepted. Joe's Office Supplies incurred unexpected costs during contract performance and lost

$35,000. Joe's Office Supplies must fulfill the contract requirements despite its loss. All Office, Inc., broke even on its contract.

With limited exceptions, solicitations for FFP contracts include FAR provision 52.203-2, Certificate of Independent Price Determination. This provision requires offerors to certify that they have not prepared their price proposals in collusion with another person or firm. A contractor's failure to submit a certificate (or submission of a false certificate) may be grounds for rejection of the proposal and possible criminal or civil action.

FFP Advantages

■ You can obtain a higher profit under an FFP contract if you control your costs.

■ Because the government awards most FFP contracts under adequate price competition, your reporting requirements are minimal.

■ FFP contracts require less administration for both the government and the contractor.

FFP Disadvantages

■ FFP contracts offer little flexibility. (Price cannot be adjusted.)

■ If you do not control your costs, you could lose money.

FIXED-PRICE CONTRACT WITH ECONOMIC PRICE ADJUSTMENT

Suppose the U.S. Treasury Department awarded a contract to Coppermine, Inc., to supply the government with copper for minting pennies for two years. Because the price of copper tends to fluctuate over time, the contracting officer makes the copper price subject to an economic price adjustment. The contract pricing links to a price index for metals, so it can be adjusted to reflect market changes. The contract requires Coppermine, Inc., to deliver 5,000 pounds of copper each year.

	Year 1	Year 2
5,000 pounds of copper	$250,000	$275,000*
Labor costs	$50,000	$50,000
Shipping costs	$75,000	$75,000
Profit	$25,000	$25,000
Total contract value	**$400,000**	**$425,000**

* Per examination of the price index for metals, the price of 5,000 pounds of copper went up $25,000 in Year 2 of the contract. This contract has a 10% ceiling, so the fluctuation could not exceed $40,000 (400,000 x 10% = $40,000).

In this contract, the price of copper was isolated to provide for a foreseeable economic price adjustment, but the other requirements remained the same. The labor, shipping, and profit are handled as an FFP contract. Allowance for increased profit never justifies an economic price adjustment.

A fixed-price contract with economic price adjustment (FP/EPA) is designed to protect against contingencies that threaten multiyear contracts. It is basically an FFP contract with a clause that allows the contract price to be revised (either upward or downward) in case of economic uncertainties. An FP/EPA contract may be used when there is serious doubt about market stability or labor conditions that will exist during the contract performance, and when contingencies that would otherwise be included in the contract price cannot be identified and covered separately in the contract.

The contracting officer chooses an FP/EPA contract that meets the government's requirements for the supply or service being purchased, including elements subject to cost fluctuations. The government generally allows for three types of economic price adjustments:

■ *Adjustments based on established prices.* These price adjustments are based on increases or decreases of an agreed-upon published or otherwise established price.

■ *Adjustments based on actual costs of labor or material.* These price adjustments are based on increases or decreases in specified costs of labor or material that the contractor actually experiences during contract performance.

■ *Adjustments based on cost indexes of labor or material.* These price adjustments are based on increases or decreases in labor or material cost standards or indexes that the contract specifically identifies. The standards or indexes are largely dependent on two general series of publications put out by the Department of Labor, Bureau of Labor Statistics. These are the Industrial Commodities portion of the Wholesale Price Index for material and the Wage and Income Series by North American Industry Classification System for labor.

Economic price adjustments usually are restricted to industrywide contingencies. If the price adjustment is based on labor and material costs, it should be limited to contingencies beyond the contractor's control. Usually a ceiling on the upward adjustments is set at 10% of the unit price, but there is never a floor on downward adjustments. Determining a price that may be adjusted is typically done in three steps:

1. The government accepts a contract free of contingencies.

2. The contracting officer identifies the items subject to adjustment before contract performance. Next, the contracting officer sets a ceiling for the contingency and determines the ground rules for adjustments.

3. The contracting officer revises the prices up or down during the contract's performance as defined by market conditions. The contracting officer must support any adjustments.

An FP/EPA is used only when the contracting officer determines that both the contractor and the government need protection against significant fluctuations in labor or material costs or to provide for contract price adjustment in the event of changes in the contractor's established prices. As with an FFP contract, FP/EPA contracts must include FAR provision 52.203-2.

> ### FP/EPA Advantages
>
> ■ The contract price can be revised to reflect the effects of economic aberrations or changes in the marketplace.
>
> ■ FP/EPA contracts offer many of the same benefits as FFP contracts.
>
> ### FP/EPA Disadvantages
>
> ■ Price adjustments are limited to contingencies beyond the contractor's control.
>
> ■ There is usually a ceiling on upward adjustments but no floor for downward adjustments.

FIXED-PRICE INCENTIVE CONTRACT

Whereas a fixed-price contract allows for no profit adjustment, a fixed-price incentive (FPI) contract does. The government offers incentive contracting in the belief that a contractor will be motivated to enhance its performance if there is a chance of increased profits (kind of like a tip). By achieving better performance results and controlling contract costs, the contractor can earn a higher profit. A fixed-price incentive contract is typically used for development contracts, such as a highway construction contract.

FPI contracts are appropriate when:

■ The government and the contractor can negotiate at the outset: (1) a firm target cost, target profit, and profit adjustment formula that offers a fair and reasonable incentive, and (2) a ceiling to ensure that the contractor assumes an appropriate share of the risk.

■ The contractor assumes a major share of the cost responsibility under the adjustment formula, which is reflected in the target profit.

The contracting officer calculates the final contract price (or the profit or loss on the contract) by applying a formula based on the relationship of total actual cost of performance to total target cost. To understand this formula, you need to be familiar with the following terms:

- *Target cost* is the estimated cost to complete the contract. Both parties agree to the target cost after analysis and negotiation. A contractor usually has an equal chance of overrunning or underrunning the total estimated cost.

- *Target profit* is the profit a contractor would earn if its costs equaled the target costs. The profit must be fair and reasonable.

- *Target price* is the sum of the target cost and the target profit.

- *Ceiling price* is the maximum amount the government will pay for the contract. When the contract costs reach this point, the contractor's profit is zero and it assumes responsibility for any additional costs.

- *Sharing formula* apportions the cost overruns or underruns between the government and the contractor. There may be two separate formulas—one for the overrun and one for the underrun—or the same formula may be used for both expressions. The share ratio is generally between 50/50 and 75/25. For example, suppose a contractor had an overrun of $50,000 and the sharing formula was 75/25.

The Government's Portion:	
Overrun	($ 50,000)
Sharing formula	x 75%
	($ 37,500)
The Contractor's Portion:	
Overrun	($ 50,000)
Sharing formula	x 25%
	($ 12,500)

Here's an illustration of how the FPI contract works: Suppose the Department of Transportation (DOT) awarded Street Works, Inc., a contract to add a ramp to an existing highway. Street Works, Inc., negotiated the following contract cost projections:

Target cost	=	$ 6,000,000
Target profit	=	$ 500,000
Target price	=	$ 6,500,000
Ceiling price	=	$ 6,750,000
Sharing formula	=	60/40

The contracting officer used a sharing formula of 60/40 to strongly encourage Street Works, Inc., to perform the contract for less than the contract cost projections. Therefore, if Street Works, Inc., actually incurred $5,750,000 in contract costs, it would make the following profit on the contract:

Actual cost	$ 5,750,000
Less: target cost	$ 6,000,000
Contract underrun	$ 250,000
Contractor sharing %	40%
Total underrun profit	$ 100,000
ADD: target profit	$ 500,000
Total profit	**$ 600,000**
ADD: actual cost	$ 5,750,000
Total contract value	**$ 6,350,000**

If, on the other hand, Street Works, Inc., had actually incurred $6,800,000 in contract costs, its profit on the contract would be the following:

Actual cost	$ 6,800,000
Less: target cost	$ 6,000,000
Contract overrun	$ (800,000)
Contractor sharing %	40%
Total overrun profit	$ (320,000)
ADD: target profit	$ 500,000
Total profit	**$ 180,000**
ADD: actual cost	$ 6,800,000
Total contract value	**$ 6,980,000**

In this second example, Street Works, Inc., exceeded the projected target cost, so its total profit was reduced. However, Street Works, Inc., also exceeded the contract ceiling price of $6,750,000. The sharing formula changes from 60/40 to 0/100 once Street Works, Inc., reaches the ceiling price. The ceiling price is also referred to as the point of total (cost) assumption. Therefore, Street Works, Inc., must absorb the portion of the actual contract cost that exceeded the ceiling price:

Total contract value	$ 6,980,000
Ceiling price	$ 6,750,000
Additional loss to contractor	**($ 230,000)**

There are two types of FPI contracts: (1) firm target, and (2) successive target. This chapter discusses only the FPI firm target contract because the FPI successive target contract is used only when available cost or pricing information is not sufficient to permit the negotiation of a realistic firm target cost and profit before award. Because of the uncertainties involved with successive target contracts, they are rarely used. (See FAR 16.403-2 for information on successive target contracts.)

FPI Advantages

■ FPI contracts combine the sharing incentive feature and the FFP feature into one contract type.

■ The government shares in any cost overrun (up to the ceiling price).

FPI Disadvantages

■ The contractor is responsible for all costs beyond the ceiling price.

■ The government shares in the cost savings.

FIXED-PRICE CONTRACT WITH PROSPECTIVE PRICE REDETERMINATION

Suppose the Department of Justice (DOJ) awarded Make It Shine, Inc., a five-year contract to provide janitorial services. This contract originally was awarded at $100,000 a year, starting on January 1, 2005, and it has a redetermination date of January 1, 2008.

Contract Year	Contract Amount
2005	$ 100,000
2006	$ 100,000
2007	$ 100,000
2008	$ 125,000 *
2009	$ 125,000
Total contract value	**$ 550,000**

*On January 1, 2008, the contracting officer approved a price redetermination for this contract. The contract price was redetermined to be $125,000 a year. In this case, the annual contract amount was increased; however, in many cases, the contract amount will be lowered on the redetermination date.

A fixed-price contract with prospective price redetermination provides for a firm-fixed price for the initial period of contract performance and a prospective redetermination of the contract price (either up or down) at a stated date during contract performance. The government may use this contract type to acquire products or services for which the contractor can negotiate a fair and reasonable firm-fixed price for an initial period, but not for subsequent periods of contract performance.

This contract type is used when:

■ Negotiations have established that neither an FFP contract nor an FPI contract is appropriate.

■ The contracting officer can provide reasonable assurance that price redetermination actions will take place promptly at the specified times.

The initial period should be the longest period for which it is possible to negotiate a fair and reasonable firm-fixed price. Each subsequent pricing period should be at least 12 months. The contract may establish a ceiling price based on uncertainties involved in the contract's performance and their possible cost impact. This ceiling price should ensure that a reasonable amount of risk is given to the contractor.

> **Prospective Price Redetermination Advantages**
>
> ■ This contract type allows for a price redetermination during con-
> tract performance.
>
> **Prospective Price Redetermination Disadvantages**
>
> ■ This contract type is typically used for multiple-year contracts only.
>
> ■ Each price redetermination period should be at least 12 months
> apart.

FIXED-CEILING-PRICE CONTRACT WITH RETROACTIVE PRICE REDETERMINATION

Suppose the Environmental Protection Agency (EPA) awarded Virus
Tech, Inc., a six-month contract to develop software to protect against
certain computer viruses. The contracting officer determined the contract's estimated cost of $80,000 with a ceiling of $100,000 to be fair and
reasonable.

Contract Period	Contract Amount
Jan. 1, 2005, through	
June 30, 2005	$ 80,000
Redetermination date	
July 20, 2005	($ 5,000)
Total contract value	**$ 75,000**

On July 20, 2005, the contracting officer redetermined the value of this
contract. The total contract price was redetermined to be $75,000. In this
case, the total contract price was decreased; however, in many cases, the
total contract price will be increased on the redetermination date.

A fixed-ceiling-price contract with retroactive price redetermination
allows a fixed ceiling price and a price redetermination after the contract
is completed (retroactive), provided that it is under the contract's ceiling
price. This contract type is used when an FFP contract cannot be negotiated and the other types of fixed-price contracts would be impractical to

use as a business arrangement. The negotiated ceiling price used with this contract ensures that the contractor assumes a reasonable amount of risk. The contracting officer considers the contractor's management effectiveness and ingenuity when the contract price is redetermined retroactively.

This contract type is used only when:

■ The contract is for research and development (R&D) and the estimated cost is $100,000 or less. The contract period of performance should be no longer than 12 months.

■ The contracting officer can provide reasonable assurance that the price redetermination will take place promptly at the specified time.

■ The head of the contracting activity (or a higher level official, if required by agency procedures) approves the use of this contract type in writing.

Retroactive Price Redetermination Advantages

■ This contract type allows for a price redetermination once the contract is completed.

Retroactive Price Redetermination Disadvantages

■ The estimated contract costs must be $100,000 or less.

■ The contract period is typically less than 12 months.

■ ■ ■

The government uses fixed-price contracts for most of its purchases or procurements. The government prefers these because they tend to be the simplest contract type to administer and evaluate. In addition, the government prefers fixed-price contracts because they place the maximum amount of cost risk on the contractor. Why should the government bear the risk if it can make you bear it?

Once the government signs a fixed-price contract, it must pay the full amount, even if it subsequently determines the price to be too high. The only exception is if the contractor provided noncurrent, incomplete, or inaccurate cost and pricing data at the time of price agreement. In that case, the government may recover the amount by which the contractor was unjustifiably enriched.

■   ■   ■

Cost-Reimbursement Contracts

**"Paying close attention to every detail.
That's the key to my success, Bob!"**

What's in this chapter?

- Determining your contract cost
- Calculating contract cost
- Understanding rates
- Fee/profit
- Types of cost-reimbursement contracts

In some cases, the government contracts for supplies and services that involve uncertainties in contract performance and contract costs that cannot be estimated with sufficient accuracy to use a fixed-price type contract. For example, it would be almost impossible to estimate the costs for goal-directed R&D work, such as finding a cure for AIDS. In these cases, the government prefers to enter into a cost-reimbursement contract. Many service-type projects also would be eligible for cost-reimbursement contracts, such as repair and maintenance services.

With cost-reimbursement contracts, the government reimburses the contractor for the reasonable, allocable, and allowable costs it incurs under the terms and conditions of the contract. The government essentially carries all the risk with a cost-reimbursement contract. Because cost-reimbursement contracts provide contractors with little incentive to control costs, contracting officers are hesitant to use them. When a cost-reimbursement contract is used, the contracting officer must closely monitor the contractor's performance to ensure that it performs the contract effectively and efficiently.

If a contracting officer insists on using a fixed-price contract for a job that would be better suited for a cost-reimbursement contract, the contractor would have to inflate the proposed contract price to protect itself from the uncertainties involved with performing the contract. The contracting officer must use negotiated procurement procedures when a cost-reimbursement contract is used.

Each cost-reimbursement contract establishes a total cost estimate for the purpose of obligating funds and establishing a ceiling that the contractor may not exceed (except at its own risk). The contractor agrees to put forth its best effort to get the job done within a mutually agreed-upon cost estimate. In addition, the contractor must notify the contracting officer when its expenditure rate reaches a specified percentage of the agreed-upon cost estimate. If the estimated cost to complete becomes greater than the originally agreed-upon cost estimate, the contractor is required to submit a revised cost estimate to the contracting officer.

The contracting officer then decides whether to modify the contract and increase the estimated cost, or to end the contract, accepting whatever work has been completed. If the contractor completes the job for less than the estimated cost, the contracting officer can use the excess funds for other projects. A contractor's bill under a cost-reimbursement contract is called a public voucher.

DETERMINING YOUR CONTRACT COST

Before the government issues a cost-reimbursement contract, it must determine whether the contractor's accounting system can accumulate costs by contract (commonly referred to as a job order cost accounting system). The government will also want to determine whether the contractor's accounting system can segregate direct costs and indirect costs.

Direct costs are costs that can be specifically identified with a particular contract. Some examples of direct costs are labor performed and materials purchased specifically for the contract.

Indirect costs are expenses incurred by a contractor that cannot be attributed to any one particular contract. An example of an indirect cost is the lighting in a manufacturing area that houses the work of several contracts. The lighting benefits all the contracts, and therefore cannot be specifically identified to a particular contract. Indirect costs are allocated to a contract during the period in which they are incurred and accumulated.

Indirect costs are further classified as either overhead (O/H) expenses or general and administrative (G&A) expenses.

O/H expenses are general in nature, such as indirect labor, rent, supplies, insurance, and depreciation. O/H expenses are distinct from those costs necessary for the overall business operation. A contractor recovers these expenses by including a portion of them in the charges made to each customer. By charging each customer for part of these O/H expenses, the contractor recoups enough money to meet its total O/H expenses. This is sometimes called "burden" or "loading."

G&A expenses are any management, financial, or other expenses that are incurred by or allocated to a business unit for the general management and administration of the business unit as a whole. For example, the salary of a company's president is generally considered a G&A expense. A contractor recovers these expenses by including a portion of them in the charges made to each customer.

The total operating cost of a company for a period of time, such as a year, is the sum of all the direct and indirect costs the company pays that year. The company must get these costs back just to break even on the total cost of doing business. This is done by including these costs in billings.

The total cost of a cost-reimbursement contract is the sum of the direct and indirect costs allocable to the contract. In ascertaining what constitutes a cost, the contractor may use any generally accepted method of determining or estimating costs that is equitable and is consistently applied. In addition, the costs must be reasonable, allocable, and allowable.

Reasonable Costs

A cost is accepted as reasonable if, by its nature and amount, it does not exceed that which would be incurred by a prudent person in the conduct of a competitive business. Determining cost reasonableness is mostly a matter of common sense. When a contractor's business is in a highly competitive industry, its costs are probably reasonable because the business must keep its costs competitive. If the government contracts for specially designed products or services in a business market that is not highly competitive, it will need to ensure that the proposed costs are reasonable. If a specific cost is challenged, the contractor bears the burden of proving its reasonableness.

Allocable Costs

Contractors accumulate indirect expenses into logical cost groupings to permit distribution of expenses in relation to benefits received by the cost objectives. Accordingly, an indirect cost is allocable to a government contract if it:

■ Is incurred specifically for the contract

■ Benefits the contract and can be distributed in reasonable proportion to the benefits received

■ Is necessary to the overall operation of the business, although a direct relationship to any particular cost objective cannot be shown.

Each contractor must allocate its indirect costs to contracts (or cost objectives) in an equitable, logical, and consistent way. The FAR does not suggest or require the use of any particular cost distribution base. Instead, it allows for the use of alternative distribution bases that will bring about a substantial matching of the indirect costs with the appropriate cost objectives. The example presented under Calculating Contract Cost (later in this chapter) uses direct labor to allocate O/H expenses.

Determining what is equitable should be objective, but often it is not. For example, if a contractor hires a security guard for a specific contract, but the guard's services are allocated to all contracts, the expense of the guard probably wouldn't be considered an equitable allocation. On the other hand, if a security guard provides services for the entire company, this could be considered a benefit to all contracts, in which case allocating such costs to all contracts would be appropriate if done in an equitable manner. As a general rule, costs are allocable if they are the types of costs that it makes sense for the government to pay for a particular contract effort.

Allowable Costs

An allowable cost meets the tests of reasonableness and allocability, is in agreement with generally accepted accounting principles, and otherwise conforms to specific limitations or exclusions set forth in the FAR (Part 31) or agreed-to terms between contractual parties. If the government determines a cost to be unallowable, the law prohibits its payment. This is a very hard concept for many contractors to understand, because many of these unallowable costs are legitimate business expenses in the eyes of the Internal Revenue Service.

For example, bad debt expenses are not allocable to government contracts, because the government always pays its debts. The reason for the apparent inconsistency of these unallowable costs is that the government pays the contractor for only those costs from which the government benefits. The decision for determining the allowability of a particular cost ultimately rests with the contracting officer.

Some of the more common unallowable costs are:

■ *Public relations and advertising costs.* Public relations includes all functions and activities dedicated to maintaining, protecting, and enhancing the image of a concern or its products or maintaining or promoting favorable community relations. Advertising, the most common means for promoting public relations, includes conventions, exhibits, free goods, samples, magazines, newspapers, trade papers, direct mail, dealer cards, window displays, outdoor advertising, radio, and television. Public relations and advertising costs include the costs of media time and space and purchased services performed by outside organizations, as well as the applicable portion of salaries, travel, and fringe benefits of employees engaged in these functions and activities.

The only allowable advertising costs are those that the contract specifically requires or that arise from government contract requirements and are exclusively for: (1) recruiting personnel required for performing contractual obligations; (2) acquiring scarce items for contract performance; and (3) disposing of scrap or surplus materials acquired for contract performance.

Allowable public relations costs include costs specifically required by contract and costs of: (1) responding to inquiries on company policies and activities; (2) communicating with the public, press, stockholders, creditors, and customers; (3) conducting general liaison with news media and government public relations officers; (4) participating in community service activities, such as blood bank drives, charity drives, savings bond drives, and disaster assistance; and (5) conducting plant tours and holding open houses. All other advertising and public relations costs are unallowable.

■ **Bad debts.** Bad debts, including actual or estimated losses arising from uncollectible accounts receivable due from customers and other claims, and any directly associated costs, such as collection and legal costs, are unallowable.

■ **Contributions or donations.** Contributions or donations, including cash, property, and services, are unallowable.

■ **Entertainment costs.** Costs of amusement, diversions, social activities, and any directly associated costs, such as tickets to shows or sports events, meals, lodging, rentals, transportation, and gratuities, are unallowable. Costs of membership in social, dining, or country clubs or other organizations having the same purposes are also unallowable, regardless of whether the cost is reported as taxable income to the employees. Moreover, the government prohibits its employees from accepting contractor-provided gratuities or entertainment. The rationale behind this provision is that entertaining with government-provided funds is against public policy.

■ **Fines, penalties, and mischarging costs.** Costs of fines and penalties resulting from the contractor's violations of or failure to comply with federal, state, local, or foreign laws and regulations are unallowable, except when incurred as a result of compliance with specific terms and conditions of the contract or written instructions from the contracting officer. Costs incurred in connection with the mischarging of costs on government contracts are unallowable when the costs result from alteration or destruction of records or other false or improper charging or recording of costs. Such include those incurred to measure or otherwise determine the magnitude of the improper charging and costs incurred to remedy or correct the mischarging, such as costs to reconstruct records.

■ *Interest and other financial costs.* Interest on borrowings (however represented), bond discounts, costs of financing and refinancing capital, legal and professional fees paid in connection with preparing a prospectus, costs of preparing and issuing stock rights, and directly associated costs are unallowable. However, interest assessed by state or local taxing authorities is allowable.

■ *Organization costs.* The following organizational costs are unallowable: (1) costs for planning or executing the organization or reorganization of the business's corporate structure (including mergers and acquisitions); (2) costs associated with raising capital; and (3) expenditures that include incorporation fees and the costs of attorneys, accountants, brokers, promoters, organizers, management consultants, and investment counselors (whether or not they are company employees).

■ *Alcoholic Beverages.* Alcoholic beverage charges are unallowable.

The contract also will contain a variety of terms and conditions that will affect cost allowability. It will cite the contract requirements and deliverables, which will define the scope of work to be performed. The scope of work usually is contained in the statement of work of a solicitation (Section C in the Uniform Contract Format). Other contract clauses will address cost-associated matters. For example, you will find clauses dealing with such topics as reimbursement for travel, relocation, and other advance agreements peculiar to that specific contract.

This list does not cover all the unallowable costs, just those most common to commercial contractors. See Part 31 of the FAR for a complete listing of unallowable costs. Keep in mind that the contracting officer must analyze the application of any FAR cost principle on a case-by-case basis.

As a contractor, you must maintain your cost records in enough detail and depth for the government to audit. Auditors will seek to identify unallowable costs, including directly associated costs incurred in the contract performance. This requirement enables the government to identify and eliminate unallowable costs from your billing, claim, or proposal.

CALCULATING CONTRACT COST

The following is a simple example of how to calculate the total contract cost for each cost-reimbursement contract owned by a company. Suppose Microtech, Inc., a network and computer systems consulting firm, incurred the following direct and indirect costs as of December 31, 2005:

Direct Costs

Direct labor	$ 700,000
Direct materials	$ 650,000

Indirect Costs

Overhead:		**General and Administrative:**	
O/H labor $	110,000	G&A labor $	126,000
O/H vacation expense	25,000	Marketing labor	5,000
O/H sick leave	15,000	G&A vacation expense	28,000
Holidays	12,000	G&A sick leave	18,000
FICA expense	8,000	Holidays	14,000
Unemployment taxes	700	FICA expense	9,000
Workers comp.	500	Unemployment taxes	1,000
Disability insurance	1,200	Workers comp.	800
Group health insurance	10,000	Disability insurance	1,500
Conferences & seminars	500	Group health insurance	11,500
Consultants	850	Bank service charges	8,000
Depreciation	20,000	Conferences & seminars	3,000
Dues & subscriptions	700	Consultants	8,000
Copy charges	5,450	Postage & shipping	750
Equipment rentals	2,000	Depreciation	3,500
Recruiting	400	Dues & subscriptions	2,000
Repairs & maintenance	700	Copy charges	2,800
Postage & shipping	200	Equipment rental	850
Rent	80,000	Legal costs	6,500
Office supplies	5,500	Recruiting	1,500

Travel costs	520	Office supplies	3,600
Misc. expenses	2,780	Rent	15,000
		Repairs & maintenance	3,500
		Taxes	1,000
		Travel	2,400
		Misc. expenses	2,800
Total O/H claimed	**302,000**	**Total G&A expenses**	**280,000**

These accumulated costs are referred to as "pools." Accordingly, Microtech, Inc., has an overhead pool and a G&A pool. (If applicable, bid and proposal [B&P], independent research and development [IR&D], and other business development costs are included in the G&A pool.)

The first step in determining your total cost for a cost-reimbursement contract is to calculate your O/H and G&A rates. An O/H rate is typically determined by dividing your indirect O/H costs (or expenses) by your total direct labor. However, any allocation base (or denominator) can be used if you can establish and defend a causal/beneficial relationship, such as labor hours, machine hours, square footage, or units of production. Microtech, Inc., had the following rates:

O/H Rate Calculation:

$$\frac{\text{Indirect O/H costs}}{\text{Total direct labor*}} = \frac{\$\,302{,}000}{\$\,700{,}000} = \mathbf{43\%}$$

*Microtech, Inc., uses direct labor dollars for its allocation base in this example.

Microtech, Inc., calculates its G&A rate by dividing its G&A costs (or expenses) by all other costs (total cost input):

G&A Rate Calculation:

$$\frac{\text{Indirect G\&A costs}}{\text{Total cost input*}} = \frac{\$\,280{,}000}{\$\,1{,}652{,}000} = \mathbf{17\%}$$

*In this example, Microtech's total cost input consisted of:

Direct labor	$ 700,000
Direct materials	$ 650,000
O/H costs	$ 302,000
Total cost input	**$ 1,652,000**

Now that Microtech, Inc., has determined its rates, the next step is to apply these rates to its various contracts.

		O/H Rate 43%	Direct		G&A Rate 17%	Total
Contract #	Direct Labor		Materials	Subtotal		Contract Cost
Cost-Reimbursement Contracts:						
6000	150,000	64,710	125,000	339,710	57,580	397,290
6001	200,000	86,300	175,000	461,300	78,185	539,485
Time and Materials Contracts:						
6200	100,000	43,140	50,000	193,140	32,735	225,875
Fixed-Price Contracts:						
6300	150,000	64,710	150,000	364,710	61,815	426,525
Commercial Fixed-Price Contracts:						
6301	100,000	43,140	150,000	293,140	49,685	342,825
Totals	**700,000**	**302,000**	**650,000**	**1,652,000***	**280,000**	**1,932,000**

Microtech, Inc.
Analysis of Incurred Costs
For the Year Ending 12/31/05

*This subtotal balance ties to Microtech's G&A base (total cost input).

This schedule details the allocation of the O/H rate and the G&A rate to Microtech's various contracts (both government and commercial).

UNDERSTANDING RATES

Rates are typically calculated yearly, because O/H and G&A costs tend to fluctuate from month to month. For example, rent may be paid quarterly. Most businesses establish temporary or proposed rates at the beginning of each business year. These are commonly referred to as "billing" or "provisional" rates. The government compares proposed rates with the actual rates incurred in previous years to determine their reasonableness.

By establishing these provisional rates at the beginning of each business year, a contractor can seek government reimbursement using these rates at interim dates. These rates are then adjusted as necessary by the contractor as indirect cost rates are finalized. Final indirect cost rates are established and agreed upon by the government and the contractor after the contractor's business year closes. The primary purpose of final indirect cost rates is to effect uniformity of approach to multiple contracts with more than one federal agency.

Settlement of final indirect cost rates is a lengthy process. The contractor submits a proposed set of final indirect cost rates for the year. However, negotiation of the current year's rates will begin only after the previous year's rates are settled. Once these final indirect cost rates are approved, they are not subject to change. The contractor needs to prepare a schedule to recognize any differences between the final indirect cost rates and the billing rates.

Suppose PharmCo, a pharmaceutical company, determined its provisional (or billing) rates as follows:

Provisional (or Billing) Rates:
O/H rate   **44%**
G&A rate   **18%**

The government approved these rates for the business year beginning January 1, 2005. On March 31, 2006, PharmCo and the government determined the final indirect cost rates to be:

Final Indirect Cost Rates:
O/H rate   **43%**
G&A rate   **17%**

As a result, PharmCo had to reimburse the government for these rate differences. This difference was calculated as follows for contract # 6001:

		Provisional Rates		Final Indirect Rates	Difference
Direct labor		200,000		200,000	—
O/H	44%	88,000	43%	86,300	1,700
Direct materials		175,000		175,000	=
Subtotal		463,000		461,300	1,700
G&A	18%	83,340	17%	78,185	5,155
Total billed		546,340		539,485	6,855

PharmCo owes the government $6,855 for this contract. If PharmCo's final indirect cost rates had exceeded its provisional rates, it would be entitled to reimbursement for the difference (up to any ceiling rates stated in the contract, if applicable).

Cost Calculation Recap

The FAR contains no specific requirements for the allocation of indirect costs. It merely dictates that indirect costs be allocated to provide for logical cost groupings that permit the costs to be distributed to the cost objectives receiving the corresponding benefits. The FAR does indicate, however, that manufacturing overhead costs, selling costs, and G&A costs are usually accounted for separately.

Most small to medium-sized contractors use two cost pools: one for O/H and one for G&A. In addition, the use of a fringe benefits pool is becoming increasingly popular, probably because it creates the appearance of lower O/H rates. Fringe benefit costs typically include compensated absences, health insurance, bonuses, retirement plans, and payroll taxes. If a contractor performs work at more than one location (including government sites), then the use of additional O/H pools may be advisable. These additional O/H pools enable the contractor to better associate its O/H costs with the specific activities receiving the corresponding benefits.

Contractors are always concerned about their rates because the rates express a percentage relationship between the contractors' indirect costs and their base costs, and many contracting officers use these rates to determine a contractor's competitiveness. The problem with

continued

continued

examining the contractor's rates for competitiveness is that the rates themselves do not show the whole picture. For example, a manufacturing company that uses old, fully depreciated machinery equipment may have a low O/H rate but be very inefficient. A manufacturing company that uses modern equipment may have a high O/H rate, yet it will be very efficient at manufacturing products at a low overall cost. The contracting officer must look at the total cost of a proposal, as well as the individual cost elements, to make an accurate evaluation. An O/H rate is simply a device for allocating indirect costs; the rate by itself is meaningless.

FEE/PROFIT

The government defines "profit" as that element of the total remuneration that contractors may receive for contract performance over and above allowable costs. In laymen's terms, profit is whatever monies are left after all costs are paid. When talking about a particular contract, profit is the amount a contractor receives above its out-of-pocket costs. It is the reward for undertaking the contract in the first place. All contractors, except the narrow category of not-for-profit institutions, are interested primarily in profit.

Although the government wants to see businesses make a profit, that margin of profit is carefully examined to verify the contract's fairness. The government looks at various factors to justify the profit percentages, including risk, the economy, the time involved in the project, previous R&D expenditures, and the contractor's professional expertise.

The government puts statutory limitations on the amount of profit that can be earned on cost-reimbursement contracts. Profit on a cost-reimbursement contract is termed "fee." The profit is a percentage of the total estimated (not actual) cost. For example, the profit on a cost-plus-fixed-fee R&D contract cannot exceed 15% of the agreed-to cost estimate (excluding the fee estimate). Most cost-plus-fixed-fee contracts have a profit ceiling of 10%. As a general rule, cost-reimbursement contracts always limit the profit to some dollar amount. There is no limit on the profit you may include in your price on fixed-price contracts, but it must be reasonable. In fact, many government procurements are so competitive, contractors will use absurdly small fees in an attempt to lower the overall proposal cost to win the contract.

Federal law also prohibits the use of cost-plus-a-percentage-of-cost contracting. This contracting method encourages contractors to spend, not manage, costs, because profit is tied to increased expenditures and not to cost control or reduction. The more a contractor spends, the greater the profit it receives. The government requires all prime contracts (other than firm-fixed-price contracts) to prohibit cost-plus-a-percentage-of-cost subcontracts.

TYPES OF COST-REIMBURSEMENT CONTRACTS

The following are some common cost-reimbursement contract types.

Cost Contract

A cost contract is a cost-reimbursement contract in which the government reimburses the contractor for all allowable costs incurred during the contract's performance. The contractor receives no profit. This contract type is typically used for R&D, particularly with nonprofit educational institutions or other nonprofit organizations and for facilities contracts.

Cost-Sharing Contract

A cost-sharing contract is a cost-reimbursement contract in which the government agrees to reimburse the contractor for a predetermined portion of the allowable and allocable costs of contract performance. With this contract type, the contractor agrees to absorb a portion of the contract costs, in expectation of substantial compensating benefits. These benefits might include enhancing the contractor's operational capabilities and expertise or enhancing its position for follow-on work. For example, a contractor would be in an ideal position for obtaining additional work on a development contract, if the jobs are awarded in stages (or phases) of development. The contractor receives no profit/fee for its efforts.

Sample Cost-Sharing Contract

Rockwell Collins, Inc., Cedar Rapids, Iowa, was awarded a $6.5 million cost-sharing contract ($4 million, government portion; $2.5 million, contractor portion) to provide for research and development to produce the next-generation security cards for programs employing Global Positioning System (GPS) technology. Nine firms were solicited and eight proposals were received. Expected contract completion date is December 31, 2006. Solicitation issue date was April 10, 2005. Negotiation completion date was June 16, 2005. The Space and Missile Systems Center, Los Angeles Air Force Base, California, is the contracting activity.

Cost-Plus-Fixed-Fee

A cost-plus-fixed-fee (CPFF) contract may take one of two basic forms: (1) the completion form, or (2) the term form. The completion form describes the scope of work by stating a definite goal or target and specifying an end product. This form of contract normally requires the contractor to complete and deliver the specified end product (such as a final report of research accomplishing the goal or target) within the estimated cost.

The term form describes the scope of work in general terms and obligates the contractor to devote a specified level of effort for a stated time. Under this form, if the government considers the contractor's performance satisfactory, it pays the fixed fee at the expiration of the agreed-upon period, when the contractor states that the contracted level of effort has been expended in performing the contract work. The term form may be used only if the contractor is obligated by the contract to provide a specific level of effort within a definite time period. Both completion and term types permit contracting for efforts that might otherwise present too great a risk to contractors, but neither type gives the contractor incentive to control costs. Normally, the government prefers the completion form over the term form because of the differences in obligation assumed by the contractor.

Sample Completion Form

Suppose the government awarded First Aid, Inc., a CPFF contract to perform a study on AIDS. The contract requires First Aid, Inc., to submit a report detailing its findings when the study is complete. The contract has an estimated cost of $500,000 and a fixed fee of $50,000. Assuming that First Aid, Inc., had the following actual costs, it would be paid the following:

	Scenario #1	Scenario #2	Scenario #3
Actual costs	$ 450,000	$ 500,000	$ 550,000*
Fixed fee	$ 50,000	$ 50,000	$ 50,000
Total paid	**$ 500,000**	**$ 550,000**	**$ 600,000**

Notice that the fixed fee is not affected by the actual costs of contract performance.

* This example assumes that the contracting officer gave the contractor permission to exceed the estimated contract cost.

Sample Term Form

Suppose the government awarded Joe's Security, Inc., a CPFF contract for guard services. The contract is in the term form and requires Joe's Security, Inc., to provide 10,000 staff-hours at an estimated cost of $200,000. The contract has a fixed fee of $20,000.

Period of Performance	Level of Effort	Guard Rate	Actual Costs
01/01-12/31/98	10,000 staff-hours	$20.00/hr.	$ 200,000
			$20,000 Fixed Fee
			$220,000 Total Paid

continued

continued

In this case, the contractor certified that the level of effort specified in the contract was expended in performing the contract work. If a contractor is in jeopardy of exceeding the level of effort hours during the contract performance, the contracting officer may either amend the contract or issue a new contract or procurement for the remaining work. More than likely, the contracting officer will amend the contract before its expiration to avoid having to issue a new procurement, which tends to be more time-consuming and costly to the government.

CPFF contracts are the most commonly used cost-reimbursement contracts. With this contract type, the government pays all of the contractor's allowable costs, in addition to a fixed fee (or profit). The fixed fee does not vary with the costs of performing the contract, but may be adjusted as a result of changes (or modifications) in the work to be performed under the contract. The terms of the contract determine the allowability of costs.

This type of contract is used primarily when the contract price is significant, the work specifications cannot be precisely defined, and the uncertainties involved in performing the contract are significant. The problem with CPFF contracts is that they give the contractor little incentive to control costs because the fee remains the same regardless of the actual costs. The government assumes all the cost risk. However, a contractor's costs may not exceed the contract's estimated cost, unless the contracting officer approves the deviation.

CPFF Advantages

■ CPFF contracts offer little risk to the contractor.

■ Fee/profit is fixed, despite actual performance costs.

■ All allowable performance costs are reimbursed.

CPFF Disadvantages

■ Amount of profit or fee is limited (usually to 10%).

■ For the government, CPFF contracts give the contractor little incentive to control costs.

■ CPFF contracts are costly for the government to administer.

Cost-Plus-Incentive-Fee

A cost-plus-incentive-fee (CPIF) type of contract is a cost-reimbursement contract that allows for an initially negotiated fee that is adjusted by a formula based on the relationship of total allowable costs to total target costs. This contract type specifies a target cost, a target fee, minimum/maximum fees, and a fee adjustment formula. After contract performance, the fee payable to the contractor is determined in accordance with the formula. The formula provides, within limits, for increases above the target fee when total allowable costs are less than target costs and decreases below the target fee when total allowable costs exceed target costs.

This contract type bears the basic incentive-sharing features of an FPI contract in terms of an expressed sharing formula for the costs above and below an established target cost. A CPIF contract does not, however, contain a ceiling price. It does contain a provision for a minimum/maximum fee. At predetermined points above and below the target cost (the point of maximum or minimum fee), the contract converts into a CPFF contract. This means that a contractor is eligible for a minimum fee, no matter what its actual contract costs turn out to be; however, this minimum fee can be zero or even a negative number. The maximum fee is usually limited to 10% of the target cost. A CPIF contract is typically used when realistic incentives can be negotiated and the government can establish reasonable performance objectives.

Sample CPIF Contract

Suppose the Department of Agriculture awarded Pest Control, Inc., a contract to develop a pesticide for cornfields. Pest Control, Inc., negotiated the following contract cost projections:

Target cost	= $ 6,000,000
Target fee	= $ 500,000
Maximum fee	= $ 600,000
Minimum fee	= $ 400,000
Sharing formula	= 70/30 (government/contractor)

The contracting officer used a sharing formula of 70/30 to ensure that Pest Control, Inc., is not unfairly penalized for contract overruns. Therefore, if Pest Control, Inc., actually incurred $6,250,000 in contract costs, it would make the following profit on the contract:

Actual cost	$ 6,250,000 *
Less: target cost	$ 6,000,000
Contract overrun	($ 250,000)
Contractor sharing %	30%
Total overrun profit	($ 75,000)
ADD: target profit	$ 500,000
Total profit	**$ 425,000**
ADD: actual cost	$ 6,250,000
Total contract value	**$ 6,675,000**

* This example assumes the contracting officer gave Pest Control, Inc., permission to exceed the target cost.

continued

continued

If, on the other hand, Pest Control, Inc., had actually incurred $5,500,000 in contract costs, its profit on the contract would be the following:

Actual cost	$ 5,500,000
Less: target cost	$ 6,000,000
Contract underrun	$ 500,000
Contractor sharing %	30%
Total underrun profit	$ 100,000 *
ADD: target profit	$ 500,000
Total profit	**$ 600,000**
ADD: actual cost	$ 5,500,000
Total contract value	**$ 6,100,000**

* Pest Control, Inc., is not entitled to the complete contract underrun ($500,000 x 30% = $150,000) because the maximum fee is limited to $100,000.

CPIF contracts are more likely to be used in situations where the cost reduction can be identified (e.g., energy contracts) and where the government/contractor share in the reduction.

CPIF Advantages

■ If the contractor performs the job at less than the target cost, it accrues additional fee or profit (rewards for good management).

■ All allowable costs of performance are reimbursed.

CPIF Disadvantages

■ CPIF contracts are costly for the government to administer.

■ The amount of profit or fee is limited (usually to 10%).

Cost-Plus-Award-Fee

A cost-plus-award-fee (CPAF) contract is a cost-reimbursement contract that provides for a fee consisting of a base amount (which may be zero), fixed at the inception of the contract, and an award amount that the contractor may earn in whole or in part during the contract's performance. This award fluctuation is designed to motivate the contractor to achieve excellence in such areas as quality, timeliness, technical ingenuity, and cost-effective management.

The amount of the award fee to be paid is determined by the contracting officer's evaluation of the contractor's performance in terms of the criteria stated in the contract. The government makes this determination unilaterally and it cannot be appealed by the contractor. The contractor receives the base fee provided it satisfactorily completes the contract. Base fees are paid in the same manner as the fixed fee in a CPFF contract; they are independent of the award criteria. However, not all CPAF contracts have a base fee. Some firms, for example, forgo base fees as a demonstration of their commitment to lower costs and as a demonstration of their confidence that they will succeed and make it up on the award fee.

Sample CPAF Contract

Suppose Harvey's Moving Company was awarded a contract to move office furniture from the General Services Administration office in Washington, D.C., to the GSA office in Kansas City, Missouri. The contract states that the award fee paid to Harvey's Moving Company will be based on the following items:

- Estimated cost—the job should be completed at or below the estimated cost.

- Deadline—the job should be completed within two weeks.

continued

continued

■ Packaging requirements—the furniture should be properly packaged.

■ Proper distribution—the furniture should be delivered to the proper office locations in the new building.

This contract has the following features:

Estimated cost	$ 1,500,000
Base fee	$ 75,000
Award fee	$ 50,000

Let's assume that Harvey's Moving Company met most of these requirements, except that some furniture was delivered to the wrong locations in the office building. Harvey's Moving Company was paid the following:

Actual cost	$ 1,475,000
Base fee	$ 75,000*
Award fee	$ 45,000
Total paid	**$ 1,595,000**

* The base fee is not affected by the actual contract performance costs.

Evaluation summaries are typically given to the contractor to allow for comments and observations on the evaluator's findings. This gives the contractor an opportunity to appeal the award fee recommendation. The contractor must qualify or justify actions taken during the contract's performance.

After considering the contractor's comments, the contracting officer (or the evaluation official) makes a unilateral award fee decision. That decision is not subject to further discussions, and the contractor may not appeal the decision.

CPAF Advantages

■ The fee is made up of a fixed portion and an award fee portion. The fixed fee is guaranteed. The award fee is based on performance.

■ All allowable performance costs are reimbursed.

CPAF Disadvantages

■ The base fee is typically small (usually around 3% of the target cost).

■ The total fee (base fee plus award fee) cannot exceed 10%.

■ ■ ■

Cost-reimbursement contracts are the government's least favorite contracting method because they place all, or essentially all, of the cost risk on the government. The government is prohibited from using cost-reimbursement contracts unless the costs of performing the contract cannot be determined with reasonable accuracy at the time of contract signing. The government is also prohibited from using cost-reimbursement contracts for acquiring commercial items.

Once a cost-reimbursement contract is signed, the government must closely monitor the work to ensure that it is done in an effective and efficient manner. The government then reimburses the contractor for its allowable costs in performing the work.

■ ■ ■

16 Other Contract Types

Berry's World

SO BUSINESS IS REALLY GREAT, EH?

NOT REALLY! THAT'S MY PAY PACKAGE.

CEO

© 1996 by NEA, Inc

What's in this chapter?

- Indefinite-delivery contracts
- Time and materials contracts
- Labor-hour contracts
- Letter contracts
- Basic ordering agreements
- Performance-based contracting
- Multiyear contracts
- Options
- Life-cycle costing

The government uses many other contract types in addition to fixed-price and cost-reimbursement contracts. These other contract types, which are special modifications or variations of fixed-price or cost-reimbursement contracts, provide the government flexibility in a number of different situations.

INDEFINITE-DELIVERY CONTRACTS

Frequently, the government can specify accurately what it intends to purchase but cannot define the exact delivery dates and/or the quantity that will be required. Contracting activities use indefinite-delivery contracts to procure commonly used supplies and services when the exact time for delivery is unknown at contract award. The actual delivery of these supplies or performance of services is made when the contracting officer places an order. Indefinite-delivery contracts result in a fixed-price contract. One of the primary advantages of this contract type is that it permits contractors to maintain a limited stock of the supplies that are being purchased in storage depots. It also permits direct shipment by the contractor to federal agencies.

There are two types of indefinite-delivery contracts: requirements contracts and indefinite-quantity contracts.

Requirements Contracts

Requirements contracts are used to fill all actual purchase requirements of designated government activities for supplies or services during a specified contract period. This contract type typically is used for acquiring supplies or services when the government anticipates recurring requirements but cannot specify the precise quantities of supplies or services it will need during the contract period. The delivery or performance is scheduled when orders are placed with the contractor. These are also known as "call contracts."

The contracting officer determines a realistic estimate of the total quantity required in the solicitation and the resulting contract. This estimate is not, however, a representation to the contractor that the estimated quantity will be required or ordered, or that conditions affecting requirements will be stable or normal. The contracting officer may obtain the estimate from records of previous requirements and consumption or by other means.

The contract also may state the maximum limit of the contractor's obligation to deliver and the government's obligation to order. The contract may specify maximum or minimum quantities that the government may order under each individual order and the maximum that it may order during a specified period of time. Most requirements contracts do not guarantee that a contractor will receive any orders. The contract only guarantees that the government will purchase all its requirements for the supplies and services in the contract from the contractor during the contract term.

There are two types of requirements contracts: delivery order contracts and task order contracts. A delivery order contract is used to issue orders for delivery of supplies during the contract period, such as furniture and fixtures, but it does not specify a firm quantity of supplies (other than a minimum or maximum quantity). A task order contract is used to issue orders for the performance of tasks during the contract period, such as repairs and maintenance, but it does not specify a firm quantity of services (other than a minimum or maximum quantity).

Indefinite-Quantity Contracts

Indefinite-quantity contracts provide for an indefinite quantity, within stated limits, of supplies or services to be furnished during a fixed period of time. (These contracts are also referred to as indefinite-delivery/indefinite-quantity—ID/IQ contracts.) This contract type may be used when the government cannot predetermine, above a specified minimum, the precise quantities of supplies or services that it will require during the contract period. An indefinite-quantity contract should only be used when a recurring need is anticipated. Delivery or performance is scheduled on the basis of orders placed with the contractor.

This contract requires the government to purchase a minimum quantity of supplies or services during the contract period. It also states the maximum quantity of supplies and services the government can order from the contractor. The contracting officer may obtain the basis for the maximum from records of previous requirements and consumption or by other means.

The government encourages contracting officers to make multiple awards of indefinite-quantity contracts for the same or similar supplies or services. When multiple-award contracts are used, the contracting officer ensures that each awardee is given a fair opportunity to be considered for each order in excess of $2,500. Each federal agency also designates an ombudsman for task order contracts and delivery order contracts, who reviews contractor complaints and ensures that all contractors are afforded a fair opportunity to be considered, consistent with the procedures in the contract. The ombudsman must be a senior agency official who is independent of the contracting officer.

TIME AND MATERIALS CONTRACTS

The government uses time and materials (T&M) contracts to acquire supplies and services, such as financial or accounting services, on the basis of direct labor hours and materials. Direct labor is provided at specified fixed hourly rates that include wages, O/H expenses, G&A expenses, and profit. The direct labor rate is also referred to as a loaded labor rate. Materials are provided by the contractor at cost, including, if appropriate, material-handling costs as part of material costs; however, these material-handling costs must be clearly excluded from the labor-hour rate. Basically, a T&M contract combines the features of a cost-reimbursement contract and a fixed-price contract.

Sample T&M Contract

Suppose Joe Smith, a senior systems engineer, receives a T&M contract to provide technical assistance to the Department of the Navy. Joe's annual salary is $41,600; therefore, he has the following hourly rate:

Annual wage: $ 41,600/2,080 hours = $ 20.00
(52 weeks x 40 hrs./week = 2,080 hrs.*)

* The government often requires the contractor to use a figure much lower than 2,080 hours/year in order to break out holidays, vacation, and sick leave. The remaining hours are referred to as "productive hours." Productive hours are often figured at 1,920 hours/year.

Hourly Direct Rate	O/H Rate 40%	Subtotal	G&A Total 22%	Total Cost	Fee on Cost 10%	Total Billing Rate/ Hour
20.00	8.00	28.00	6.16	34.16	3.42	$ 37.58*

* This balance represents the loaded labor rate.

Joe's next step is to determine his total billing. If this job took 200 hours to complete and required the purchase of a new computer, the total bill would be calculated as follows:

	Total Hours	Loaded Labor Rate	Amount Billed
Senior Systems Engineer	200	$ 37.58	$ 7,516.00
Total labor			$ 7,516.00
Materials: Computer			$ 5,500.00*
Total billing			**$ 13,016.00**

* This computer was billed at actual cost.

T&M contracts are typically used when estimation of the costs or extent of the work with any degree of certainty is impossible at the time of contract award. T&M contracts are also used primarily for service procurements rather than product procurements. In general, contracting officers rarely use T&M contracts because they give contractors an incentive to increase costs to increase profit. Government monitoring of contractor performance is required to provide reasonable assurance that efficient methods and effective cost controls are being used.

Because of these limitations, T&M contracts should be used only when the contracting officer determines that no other contract is suitable and the contract includes a ceiling price that the contractor may exceed only at its own risk.

LABOR-HOUR CONTRACTS

A labor-hour contract is simply a variation of the T&M contract. The only difference is that the contractor does not supply materials.

LETTER CONTRACTS

A letter contract (or a letter-of-intent contract) is a written preliminary contractual instrument that authorizes a contractor to begin manufacturing supplies or performing services immediately. The government typically uses this contract type when its interests demand that the contractor be given a binding commitment so that work can start immediately, and negotiating a definitive contract is impossible because of the time restraints of the work requirements. For its convenience, the government issues letter contracts, which have no firm price but do contain standard contract clauses and a limitation on the government's liability.

For example, if there is a national emergency, such as an earthquake, the government will issue letter contracts to contractors to help provide immediate relief. The letter contract should be as complete and definite as possible under the circumstances. Each letter contract must contain a negotiated definitization schedule that includes:

■ Dates for submission of the contractor's price proposal, required cost or pricing data, and if required, make-or-buy and subcontracting plans

■ Start date for negotiations

■ Agreement between the government and the contractor on the date by which definitization is expected to be completed.

The target date for definitization should be within 180 days of the date the letter contract is issued or before completion of 40% of the work, whichever occurs first. The contracting officer may, in extreme cases and according to agency procedures, authorize an additional period. Contractors are reimbursed for only 80% of expenditures and receive no fee while under a letter contract, which gives the contractors a great incentive to get the contract definitized. If, after exhausting all reasonable efforts, the parties fail to reach an agreement on price and fee, the contracting officer may unilaterally establish a reasonable price and fee. This determination may be appealed by the contractor in accordance with the disputes clause (see Chapter 17).

Because of the uncertainties involved with letter contracts, they may be used only after the contracting officer determines in writing that no other contract is suitable. In addition, the contracting officer may not commit the government to a definitive contract in excess of the funds available at the time the letter contract is executed.

BASIC ORDERING AGREEMENTS

A basic ordering agreement (BOA) is not a contract. It is a written instrument of understanding, negotiated between the government and a contractor, that contains:

■ Terms and clauses applying to future contracts (orders) that might be awarded to the contractor

- Description of supplies or services

- Methods for pricing, issuing, and delivering future orders.

This agreement provides for uniform treatment of specific supplies or services under several contracts awarded to one contractor. The BOA also lists the contracting activities (or buying offices) that are authorized to place orders under the agreement. BOAs may be used with negotiated fixed-price or cost-reimbursement contracts; however, the contracting officer must still use competitive solicitations whenever possible.

A BOA allows the government to expedite the procurement of supplies or services when specific items, quantities, and prices are unknown at the time of the agreement. BOAs typically are used when past experience or future plans indicate that a substantial number of requirements for supplies and services will result in procurements from the contractor during the forthcoming year. For example, if the government purchases a high-resolution printer, it may establish a BOA for future toner purchases.

Each BOA specifies the point at which an order becomes a binding contract. For example, the agreement may state that the issuance of an order gives rise to an immediate contract. A contract may also be formed when the contractor accepts the order by signing and returning a copy of it.

BOAs have similar characteristics to basic agreements (BAs). See FAR 16.702 for a detailed explanation of BAs.

PERFORMANCE-BASED CONTRACTING

Performance-based contracting methods attempt to base the total amount paid to a contractor on the performance quality levels achieved and standards met on the contract (i.e., motivate the contractor to perform at optimal levels). Each performance-based contract should:

- Describe the work in terms of "what" is to be the required output, rather than "how" the work is to be accomplished

■ Use measurable performance standards, such as terms of quality, time-liness, and quantity

■ Specify procedures for reductions of fee or for reductions to the price of a fixed-price contract when services are not performed or do not meet contract requirements

■ Include performance incentives (where appropriate).

Contracting activities should also develop quality assurance surveillance plans when acquiring services. These plans should recognize the responsibility of the contractor to carry out its quality control obligations, and they should contain measurable inspection and acceptance criteria.

The contract type most likely to motivate the contractor to perform at optimal levels should be chosen. Fixed-price contracts, for example, are generally appropriate for services that can be objectively defined and for which the risk of performance is manageable.

MULTIYEAR CONTRACTS

In 1972, the Commission on Government Procurement recommended that Congress authorize all federal agencies to enter into multiyear contracts (or procurements) that are based on clearly specified requirements. A multiyear contract is for the purchase of supplies and services for more than one year, but not more than five years. This recommendation was based on the Commission's findings that the use of multiyear contracts would result in significant savings to the government because they enable contractors to offer better overall prices while maintaining a steady workload, reduced administrative costs, and a stabilized workforce.

Congress was reluctant to approve multiyear contracts because it has no authority to approve programs that future Congresses must fund. It was also reluctant to approve contracting arrangements that are difficult to change in subsequent years. Congress did recognize, however, that one- or two-year planning and funding horizons are generally too short for many of the government's larger procurement requirements. The Armed

Services Procurement Act of 1947 was amended to authorize the use of multiyear contracts for Department of Defense procurements. It wasn't until passage of the Federal Acquisition Streamlining Act of 1994 that Congress authorized all federal agencies to use multiyear contracts (see Chapter 2).

Because of the many uncertainties involved with multiyear contracting, Congress issued a number of restrictions on their use. For example, federal agencies that propose to use multiyear contracts must seek advance approval during the budget process for specific multiyear acquisition candidates. Furthermore, Congress limited the total contract amount. (This maximum amount is referred to as the cancellation ceiling.) The Department of Defense, National Aeronautics and Space Administration, and Coast Guard may not enter into multiyear contracts with a cancellation ceiling in excess of $100 million, without the agency head's written notification of the proposed contract and cancellation ceiling to Congress. The cancellation ceiling limitation is $10 million for all other federal agencies.

The FAR encourages the use of multiyear contracts to achieve:

- Lower costs

- Increased standardization

- Reduced administrative burdens

- Substantial continuity of production or performance and, thus, avoidance of annual start-up costs, preproduction testing costs, make-ready expenses, and phase-out costs

- Stabilization of contractor workforce

- Avoidance of the need to establish quality control techniques and procedures for a new contractor each year

- Broader competitive base, resulting from greater opportunity for participation by firms that might not otherwise be willing or able to compete for lesser quantities—particularly for contracts involving high start-up costs

■ Greater incentive for contractors to improve productivity through investment in capital facilities, equipment, and advanced technology.

Full-Funding Contracts

A contract has full funding when, at the time of award, it has sufficient funds to cover the total estimated costs to deliver a given quantity of complete end items or services.

The entire funding needs of the current year production quantity must be provided by the government and no part of the purchase can depend on future year appropriations. Full funding is common in fixed-price contracts and relatively small cost-reimbursement contracts.

The government's primary advantage in using full-funding contracts is that purchasing a larger quantity of products over several years typically results in lower unit prices for those items. The government's disadvantage in using this contract method is that prices for these items may drop in future years. Contractors submit a price proposal for both current one-year and multiyear program requirements. The government awards the contract to the proposal that offers the lowest unit prices.

Multiyear Basis Contracts

If the government awards the contract on a multiyear basis, it only obligates the contract funds for the first-year requirement, with succeeding years' requirements funded annually. If the funds do not become available to support the succeeding years' requirements, the federal agency must cancel the contract, including the total requirements of all remaining program years.

Because of this cancellation risk, the contract often contains a contract provision that allows for reimbursement of unrecovered nonrecurring costs included in the price of the canceled items to protect the contractor against losses resulting from the cancellation. These nonrecurring costs might include special tooling and test equipment, preproduction engineering, initial rework, initial spoilage, and costs incurred for the assembly, training, and transportation to and from the job site of a specialized workforce.

For each program year subject to cancellation, the contracting officer establishes a cancellation ceiling price for these unrecovered nonrecurring costs. In determining the cancellation ceiling, the contracting officer estimates the reasonable preproduction or start-up, training, and other nonrecurring costs. The cancellation ceiling is applicable to, and normally amortized over, the items or services to be furnished under the multiyear contract requirements.

The cancellation ceiling price is reduced each program year in direct proportion to the remaining requirements subject to cancellation. For example, suppose a contracting officer in the General Services Administration awarded a multiyear contract to Security Experts, Inc., to install a new security system in its Washington, D.C., office. The contract is for three years and the contracting officer estimated the cancellation ceiling price to be 10% of the total multiyear contract price:

Total multiyear contract price	$ 5,000,000
	10%
Cancellation ceiling price	$ 500,000

The cancellation ceiling price is then reduced by the contracting officer over the three-year contract period:

Cancellation ceiling price	$ 500,000
Year 1: 30% x 500,000	($ 150,000)
	$ 350,000
Year 2: 30% x 500,000	($ 150,000)
	$ 200,000
Year 3: 40% x 500,000	($ 200,000)
	_____

The contracting officer also establishes cancellation dates for each program year's requirements.

Although multiyear contract requirements are budgeted and financed only for the first program year, the contracting officer solicits prices for both the current-year program requirement alone and the total multiyear program requirements. The primary purpose of obtaining these dual proposals is to determine the better contracting period. Typically, a 10% savings in favor of multiyear contracting has been used as an evaluation benchmark for most evaluations, although lower savings have justified multiyear contracting in some situations.

Multiyear contracts typically are used when the need for the supplies or services is reasonably firm and continuing over the contract's period. In addition, these contracts are used when the design for the supplies being acquired is stable and the technical risks associated with such supplies are not excessive. The contracting officer can use sealed bidding or negotiated procurement procedures when soliciting for multiyear contracts. Multiyear contracts typically result in a fixed-price contract. In any multiyear contract, the government must indicate the evaluation period, which typically ranges from five to ten years.

OPTIONS

Suppose Computer Learning Center was awarded an option contract to provide computer training services to the Department of Commerce. The contract has a one-year base period and four option periods:

	Beginning Date	Ending Date	Maximum Contract Labor Costs	Exercised
Base year	01/01/05	12/31/05	$1,800,000	Yes
Option I	01/01/06	12/31/06	$1,900,000	Yes
Option II	01/01/07	12/31/07	$2,000,000	Yes
Option III	01/01/08	12/31/08	$2,000,000	Yes
Option IV	01/01/09	12/31/09	$2,100,000	Pending
Total Contract Value			**$9,800,000**	

When multiple option periods are identified in the solicitation, Option I (or the first option period) is frequently exercised simultaneously with the base year (or the initial contract award).

An option gives the government a unilateral right to purchase additional supplies or services called for by the contract or to extend the term of the contract. Option contracts are not the same as multiyear contracts, which require the government to purchase the entire multiyear procurement quantity, unless the requirement is canceled or the funds for the items are made unavailable. To exercise an option, a contracting officer must determine that funds are available and the need for the option exists. The presence of an option is no guarantee that the government will exercise the option and purchase the additional supplies and services.

The contracting officer considers price and other related factors when determining whether to exercise the option. For example, a contracting officer would exercise an option if a new solicitation fails to produce a better price or more advantageous offer than that offered by the option. An option contract does not allow the contracting officer to use anticipated market conditions as a basis for deciding whether or not to buy any year's requirements. The solicitation states the basis on which the options will be evaluated. To exercise an option, the contracting officer must provide a written notice to the contractor within the period specified in the contract.

If the contracting officer decides to exercise the option, he or she must certify that all administrative and regulatory requirements have been met by the contractor for the base year. This certification is filed with the original contract. The contract is then modified to incorporate the option, citing the appropriate contract clause as the authority.

Generally, the government avoids option contracts because they tend to affect competition negatively. Option contracts typically are used only when supplies or services are readily available on the open market or when indefinite quantity or requirements contracts are not appropriate. The contracting officer can use sealed bidding or negotiated procurement procedures when soliciting for option contracts. In addition, the contracting officer can use either fixed-price or cost-reimbursement type contracts.

LIFE-CYCLE COSTING

Suppose a contracting officer in the Department of Transportation is acquiring a satellite dish, the life of which is determined to be four years. Because satellite dishes tend to have high support costs, the contracting officer seeks costs that apply to the:

■ Outright purchase of the satellite dish

■ Total leased price/costs

■ Total leased price/costs with an option to purchase.

Now let's assume that Satellites "R" Us submits the following prices/cost estimates to the government:

Total purchase price: $ 500,000

Estimated maintenance costs (by year):
2005	$ 15,000
2006	$ 18,000
2007	$ 21,000
2008	$ 24,000

Leased price/costs (by year):
2005 ($10,000 per month)	$ 120,000
2006 ($12,000 per month)	$ 144,000
2007 ($14,000 per month)	$ 168,000
2008 ($16,000 per month)	$ 192,000

Purchase option: The government has the option of purchasing the satellite dish for $375,000 at the beginning of 2007.

This satellite dish will also incur the following operating costs:

Electricity: $ 3,000 ($250 a month)
Rent: $ 12,000 ($1,000 a month)

The next step is to calculate the total cost of each purchase option.

1. Outright purchase of the satellite dish:

	2005	2006	2007	2008	Totals
Purchase price	$ 500,000	—	—	—	$ 500,000
Maintenance costs	15,000	18,000	21,000	24,000	78,000
Electricity costs	3,000	3,000	3,000	3,000	12,000
Rent	12,000	12,000	12,000	12,000	48,000
Totals	530,000	33,000	36,000	39,000	$ 638,000

2. Lease price/costs of the satellite dish:

	2005	2006	2007	2008	Totals
Lease costs	$ 120,000	144,000	168,000	192,000	$ 624,000
Maintenance costs	—	—	—	—	—
Electricity costs	3,000	3,000	3,000	3,000	12,000
Rent	12,000	12,000	12,000	12,000	48,000
Totals	135,000	159,000	183,000	207,000	$ 684,000

3. Total cost when the purchase option is exercised:

	2005	2006	2007	2008	Totals
Lease costs	$ 120,000	144,000	—	—	$ 264,000
Purchase option	—	—	375,000	—	375,000
Maintenance costs	—	—	—	—	—
Electricity costs	3,000	3,000	3,000	3,000	12,000
Rent	12,000	12,000	12,000	12,000	48,000
Totals	135,000	159,000	390,000	15,000	$ 699,000

In this example, the contracting officer would purchase the satellite dish outright because that option offers the lowest overall cost to the government. This illustration is designed to provide a basic understanding of life-cycle costing (LCC). Many other costs and factors could apply to the acquisition and operation of a satellite dish.

LCC is the estimation and analysis of the total cost of acquiring, developing, operating, supporting, and (if applicable) disposing of an item or system being acquired. Both direct and indirect costs make up the total LCC of the system. LCC enhances the decision-making process in system acquisitions and is used as a management tool and decision criterion throughout the acquisition process.

The government is concerned about a system's LCC because of the rapidly increasing cost of supporting the system once it is placed into operation. In fact, for many system acquisitions, the cost of operating and supporting the system over its useful life is greater than the acquisition cost. The LCC program is designed to reduce these operating and support costs by analyzing the operating and support implications of design alternatives. When a federal agency determines that LCC could be an important aspect of a particular program, it decides on the degree and method of implementation. The solicitation states the requirements as they relate to the proposal and the source-selection process.

An LCC model comprises one or more systematically arranged mathematical calculations that formulate a cost methodology to arrive at reliable cost estimates. The input to the formula comes from descriptions of the equipment, organizational structures, processes, and procedures. LCC models always reflect later costs, which result directly from the contemplated decision or action, rather than merely the initial costs. Most federal agencies have computer software to assist with LCC evaluations. The General Services Administration even makes its LCC program, called BARS, available to agencies at no charge and to vendors for a nominal cost. Various commercial packages are also in widespread government and commercial use.

To get more detailed information on LCC, contact:

National Technical Information Service (NTIS)
Technology Administration
U.S. Department of Commerce
Springfield, VA 22161
Phone (800) 553-6847

WWW.NTIS.GOV

■ ■ ■

Selecting the contract type should not be based on either the government's or the contractor's individual prejudices. Rather, the selection should be based on an objective analysis of all factors involved and of the contract type that fits the particular procurement.

■ ■ ■

Contract
Administration

"Our billing system was perfect until the boss put in his two-cents worth. Now all of our figures are off by two cents."

What's in this chapter?

- Contract administration office
- Contract financing
- Getting paid
- Changes clause
- Contract modifications
- Constructive changes
- Government-furnished property
- Inspection and acceptance
- Contractor data rights
- Records retention
- Audits/examination of records
- Contract Disputes Act
- Alternative dispute resolution
- Termination for convenience
- Termination for default
- Contract closeout

Once the federal procurement process of solicitation, source selection, negotiation, and contract formation is complete, a contractor must be prepared to deal with the responsibilities associated with the contract's performance. So what happens after the contract is awarded?

Both the government and the contractor are responsible for the contract's administration. The government acts through its agent, typically the administrative contracting officer (ACO), who performs or oversees contract-related functions, such as monitoring, inspection and acceptance, contract changes, disputes, and payment claims. The ACO's degree of involvement depends on the type and nature of the contract. A contractor, on the other hand, performs the contract's requirements in accordance with its terms and conditions. In addition, the contractor must comply with the applicable labor laws, prepare required reports, seek contract modifications when unforeseen circumstances arise, perform inspections, prepare invoices, and retain contractual records.

CONTRACT ADMINISTRATION OFFICE

Many federal agencies use a contract administration office (CAO) to administer contract functions. Federal agencies throughout the country establish CAOs to service contracts within their geographic boundaries. Each CAO assists in such areas as correcting administrative errors, explaining special clauses and requirements, processing requests for progress payments, ensuring on-time performance, inspecting/accepting final products, and ensuring payment. The CAO also advises the contracting activity and other interested parties of all pertinent matters under its purview relating to the contracts. FAR 42.3 details the CAO's functions.

CONTRACT FINANCING

Government financing is available to contractors under certain circumstances. For example, a contractor with a large fixed-price contract that has a long lead time would be eligible for contract financing. The government cannot treat the need for financing as a handicap during the source-selection process. The government typically uses three methods to finance a contract: progress payments, guaranteed loans, and advance payments.

Progress Payments

The contractor receives progress payments as work progresses on the contract. Payments are typically based on the costs incurred by the contractor during contract performance; however, they do not relate to any contract milestones or completion stages. Contracting activities customarily apply a standard progress payment rate to the contract performance costs. This standard rate ranges from 75% to 85% of the incurred costs for large businesses and 80% to 95% for small businesses. Progress payments are only used with fixed-price contracts.

For example, assume Office Store receives a firm-fixed price contract for the production of 400 executive desks for the General Services Administration on January 1, 2006. The contract's value is $400,000, and it is expected to be completed over a one-year period. The contracting officer determines that this contract is eligible for progress payments, which will be made on a quarterly basis:

QTR	Costs Incurred Y-T-D	Standard Rate	Payment
1st	100,000	90%	$ 90,000
2nd	90,000	90%	$ 81,000
3rd	80,000	90%	$ 72,000
4th	80,000	90%	$ 72,000
Total Payments			**$ 315,000**

Office Store receives the remaining balance of $85,000 upon contract completion.

Before a contracting officer authorizes progress payments, he or she determines whether or not the contractor's accounting system can reliably segregate and accumulate contract costs and properly administer the progress payments. Partial payments that are based on percentage (or stage) of completion are generally treated as a method of payment and not a method of contract financing.

Guaranteed Loans

Guaranteed loans are essentially the same as conventional loans made by private financial institutions; the only difference is that the government shares in any losses up to its guaranteed percentage (usually 90% or less). The private lending institution handles all administrative aspects of the loan. The contractor makes the principal and interest payments to the lending institution and pays a fee to the government for the privilege of the guarantee.

Guaranteed loans may be made by the following federal agencies:

- Department of Defense

- Department of Energy

- Department of Commerce

- Department of Interior

- Department of Agriculture

- General Services Administration

- National Aeronautics and Space Administration

- Small Business Administration.

For more information on guaranteed loans, see FAR 32.3.

Advance Payments

Suppose the Department of Agriculture (DOA) awarded a firm-fixed-price contract on July 1, 2006, to The Sky's the Limit, Inc., to design and build a satellite. The contract's total value is $6,000,000 and the estimated contract period is three years. Because of the satellite's high cost, the contracting officer agrees to advance the contractor $1,500,000 each year of the contract:

Advance Payment	Amount
Year 1	1,500,000
Year 2	1,500,000
Year 3	1,500,000
Total advance payments	**4,500,000**

The Sky's the Limit, Inc., completes the satellite on August 15, 2009, at which time DOA pays the contract balance:

Total advance payments	4,500,000
Total contract value	6,000,000
Final payment	**1,500,000**

Advance payments are government money advances made to a contractor prior to, in anticipation of, and for the purpose of complete performance under one or more contracts. These payments are then liquidated (or applied) against the contract amount owed the contractor upon the delivery of the contracted supplies or the performance of the contracted services. Because these payments are not measured by contract performance, they differ from partial, progress, or other payments based on contract performance. Prime contractors also may obtain advance payments to use in making advance payments to subcontractors.

For a contractor to obtain advance payments, the contracting officer must determine that the advance payment is in the government's best interests and the contractor must post adequate security (bank accounts or other significant assets). See FAR Part 32.4 for information on advance payments.

GETTING PAID

Every contract or purchase order has specific instructions for preparing and submitting invoices. Information on where to send the invoice (or bill), number of copies to send, and required government codes is generally included on the contract's cover page. If the instructions are incomplete or unclear, call the contracting officer immediately. If you want to be paid in a timely manner, you must prepare your invoice according to the contract's instructions.

Each invoice submitted to the government must contain:

- Contractor's name and address

- Invoice date (as close as possible to the mailing date)

- Contract number or other authorization for supplies delivered or services performed (including order number and contract line item number)

- Price of supplies delivered or services performed

- Shipping and payment terms (e.g., shipment number and date, prompt-payment discount terms); bill of lading number and shipment weight appear on government bills of lading

- Name and address of contractor official to whom payment is sent (must be the same as that in the contract or in a proper assignment notice)

- Name, title, phone number, and mailing address of the person to be notified in the event of a defective invoice

- Any other information or documentation required by the contract (such as evidence of shipment).

Contractors are strongly encouraged to assign an identification number to each invoice.

The contractor must support all of its invoices with an approved receiving report or any other government documentation authorizing payment. The Department of Defense, for example, uses DD Form 250, Material Inspection and Receiving Report, to demonstrate government inspection and acceptance. Any receiving report or other government documentation authorizing payment must, at a minimum, include:

■ Contract number or other authorization for supplies delivered or services performed

■ Description of supplies delivered or services performed

■ Quantities of supplies received and accepted or services performed

■ Date supplies were delivered or services performed

■ Date supplies or services were accepted by the designated government official

■ Signature or electronic equivalent (when permitted by agency regulations), and printed name, title, mailing address, and telephone number of the designated government official responsible for acceptance or approval.

The agency receiving official should forward the receiving report or other government documentation to the designated payment office by the fifth working day after government acceptance or approval, unless other arrangements have been made.

Payments will depend on the contract type, its terms and conditions, and the allowability of those costs (see Chapter 15). Under fixed-price contracts, final payment is due when the government accepts the completed contract; however, the contractor may be entitled to partial (or progress) payments. The contractor obtains final payment by submitting a proper voucher or invoice, with the appropriate backup, such as form DD 250.

For cost-reimbursement contracts, the normal payment procedure is to invoice the government for allowable costs and fees incurred as contract

MATERIAL INSPECTION AND RECEIVING REPORT

Form Approved
OBM No. 0704-0248

The public reporting burden for this collection of information is estimated to average 30 minutes per response, including the time for reviewing instructions, searching existing data sources, gathering and maintaining the data needed, and completing and reviewing the collection of information. Send comments regarding this burden estimate or any other aspect of this collection of information, including suggestions for reducing this burden, to Department of Defense, Washington Headquarters Services, Directorate for Information Operations and Reports, (0704-0248), 1215 Jefferson Davis Highway, Suite 1204, Arlington, VA 22202-4302. Respondents should be aware that notwithstanding any other provision of law, or person shall be subject to any penalty for failing to comply with a collection of information it does not display a currently valid OMB control number.

PLEASE DO NOT RETURN YOUR COMPLETED FORM TO EITHER OF THESE ADDRESSES.
SEND THIS FORM IN ACCORDANCE WITH THE INSTRUCTIONS CONTAINED IN THE DFARS, APPENDIX F-401.

1. PROCUREMENT INSTRUMENT IDENTIFICATION (ORDER) NO.	6. INVOICE NO./DATE	7. PAGE OF	8. ACCEPTANCE POINT
(CONTRACT) NO. SP0600-YY-D-0000 AB01		1 1	D

2. SHIPMENT NO.	3. DATE SHIPPED	4. B/L	5. DISCOUNT TERMS
ABC-0001	10/30/06	Prepaid Rail Road Company	Net 30 Days
		TCN	

9. PRIME CONTRACTOR CODE	10. ADMINISTERED BY CODE
Coal Diggers, Inc. 490 West Point Street Columbus, OH 43216-5000	DESC-AC Defense Fuel Supply Center 8725 John J. Kingman Rd., Ste 2941 Ft. Belvoir, VA 22060-6222
11. SHIPPED FROM (If other than 9) CODE	12. PAYMENT WILL BE MADE BY CODE
Coal Diggers, Inc. 490 West Point Street Columbus, OH 43216-5000	DESC-AC Defense Fuel Supply Center 8725 John J. Kingman Rd., Ste 2941 Ft. Belvoir. VA 22060-6222
13. SHIPPED TO CODE	14. MARKED FOR CODE
DLA Stream Plant 700 Robbins Ave. Philadelphia, PA 19111-5096	

15. ITEM NO.	16. STOCK/PART NO. DESCRIPTION (Indicate number of shipping container -type of container – container number)	17. QUANTITY SHIP/REC'D*	18. UNIT	19. UNIT PRICE	20. AMOUNT
0001	" x " Bituminous Coal Total Cars Shipped 12	1,000	TONS	$ 500	500,000

21. CONTRACT QUALITY ASSURANCE		22. RECEIVER'S USE
a. ORIGIN ■ CQA ☐ ACCEPTANCE of listed items Has been made by me or under my supervision and they conform to contract, except as noticed herein or on supporting documents.	b. DESTINATION ☐ CQA ☐ ACCEPTANCE of listed items Has been made by me or under my supervision and they conform to contract, except as noticed herein or on supporting documents.	Quantities shown in column 17 were received in apparent good condition except as noted.
		DATE RECEIVED SIGNATURE OF AUTHORIZED GOVERNMENT REPRESENTATIVE
DATE SIGNATURE OF AUTHORIZED GOVERNMENT REPRESENTATIVE	DATE SIGNATURE OF AUTHORIZED GOVERNMENT REPRESENTATIVE	TYPED NAME:
TYPED NAME:	TYPED NAME: TITLE:	TITLE: MAILING ADDRESS:
TITLE: MAILING ADDRESS:	MAILING ADDRESS:	COMMERCIAL TELEPHONE NUMBER:
COMMERCIAL TELEPHONE NUMBER:	COMMERCIAL TELEPHONE NUMBER:	* If quantity received by the Government is the same as quantity shipped, indicate by (X) mark, if different, enter actual quantity received below quantity shipped and encircle.

23. CONTRACTOR USE ONLY

I certify that on October 30, 2006, Coal Diggers, Inc. shipped the materials called for by contract SP0600-YY-D-0000 CLIN0001 via Railway Inc. in railcars on 12 bills of lading in accordance with the applicable requirements for shipment. I further certify that the supplies are of the quality specified and are in all respects in conformance with the contract requirements, including specifications, size consist, item description, and in the quantity shown on this acceptance document and the attached mine analysis.

Date: October 30, 2006   Title: Joe Smith, President   Signature:

DD FORM 250, AUG 2000   PREVIOUS EDITION IS OBSOLETE.

Sample DD Form 250

work progresses. Most contracting activities allow contractors to submit invoices either monthly or semimonthly. Contractors typically use SF 1034, Public Voucher, to bill the government. If you need additional space to detail the supplies or services being invoiced, you should use SF 1035, the continuation sheet. The voucher should be accompanied by the appropriate backup documentation, such as the number of labor hours expended by labor category.

Use SF 33, Solicitation, Offer, and Award (Block 13), for any other requests for payment if a prompt-payment discount is offered.

PROMPT PAYMENT ACT

In 1982, Congress passed the Prompt Payment Act to require federal agencies to pay interest on contractor invoices that are not paid in a timely manner. The bill was enacted because contracting activities were chronically tardy in making payments, which caused many contractors to have cash flow problems, even putting some out of business. Contracting activities, therefore, pay contractors interest, at a rate periodically set by the Treasury Department, on amounts owed to the contractor and not paid within 30 days of receipt of a properly prepared invoice. The interest penalty begins the day after the required payment date and ends on the date when payment is made. The temporary unavailability of funds needed to make timely payments does not excuse the contracting activity from obligations to pay interest penalties.

The contracting activity must notify the contractor within seven days of receiving an erroneous invoice to explain any defects or improprieties. This act also prohibits contracting activities from taking prompt-payment discounts after the discount period has expired. Therefore, the burden of completing formal acceptance and making payments on time to qualify for the discount falls on the government. For more information on prompt payment, see FAR 32.9.

Standard Form 1034 Revised October 1967 Department of the Treasury 1 TFM 4-2000 1034-122	**PUBLIC VOUCHER FOR PURCHASES AND SERVICES OTHER THAN PERSONAL**	VOUCHER NO. 0005

U.S.DEPARTMENT, BUREAU, OR ESTABLISHMENT AND LOCATION	DATE VOUCHER PREPARED 10/31/05	SCHEDULE NO.
U.S. Department of Energy 1000 Independence Ave., SW Washington, DC 20585	CONTRACT NUMBER AND DATE DE-AC05-98AD63275	PAID BY
	REQUISITION NUMBER AND DATE 01-99PP00323.000 06/15/05	

PAYEE'S NAME AND ADDRESS

Safety Shuttle, Inc.

450 Sharp Street
Albuquerque, NM 87103

DATE INVOICE RECEIVED

DISCOUNT TERMS

PAYEE'S ACCOUNT NUMBER

GOVERNMENT B/L NUMBER

SHIPPED FROM   TO   WEIGHT

NUMBER AND DATE OF ORDER	DATE OF DELIVERY OR SERVICE	ARTICLES OR SERVICES (Enter description, item number of contract or Federal supply schedule, and other information deemed necessary)	QUAN-TITY	UNIT PRICE COST	PER	AMOUNT (¹)
0001AB	10/16/05 To 10/31/05	Shuttle bus service For detail, See SF1035 – total amount of claim transferred from page 1 of 1 SF 1035 Cost-Reimbursement – Provisional Payment				6,000.00

(Use continuation sheets if necessary)   **(Payee must NOT use the space below)**   TOTAL   6,000.00

PAYMENT: ☐ PROVISIONAL ☐ COMPLETE ■ PARTIAL ☐ FINAL ☐ PROGRESS ☐ ADVANCE	APPROVED FOR Provisional Pmt =$ Subject to Audit BY² Joel J. Hunt, Auditor Defense Contract Audit Agency (DCAA) TITLE 123 Anyplace, Any City, State 00000 (703) 555-1111	EXCHANGE RATE =$1.00	DIFFERENCES

Amount verified; correct for

(Signature or initials)

Pursuant to authority vested in me, I certify that this voucher is correct and proper for payment.

_____   _____   _____
(Date)   (Authorized Certifying Officer)³   (Title)

ACCOUNTING CLASSIFICATION

CHECK NUMBER	ON ACCOUNT OF U.S. TREASURY	CHECK NUMBER	ON (Name of bank)
CASH $	DATE	PAYEE³	

¹ When stated in foreign currently, insert name of currency.
² If the ability to certify and authority to approve are combined in one person, one signature only is necessary; otherwise the approving officer will sign in the space provided, over his official title.
³ When a voucher is receipted in the name of a company or corporation, the name of the person writing the company or corporate name, as well as the capacity in which he signs, must appear. For example: "John Doe Company, per John Smith, Secretary" or "Treasurer", as the case may be.

Previous edition usable

PER

TITLE

NSN 7650-00-634-4206

PRIVACY ACT STATEMENT
The information requested on this form is required under the provisions of 31 U.S.C. 82b and 82c, for the purpose of disbursing Federal money. The information requested is to identify the particular creditor and the amounts to be paid. Failure to furnish this information will hinder discharge of the payment obligation.

Sample SF 1034

CHANGES CLAUSE

The changes clause allows the contracting officer to make unilateral changes to a contract in one or more of the following areas:

■ Drawings, designs, or specifications

■ Descriptions of services

■ Shipment or packing methods

■ Place of inspection, delivery, or acceptance

■ Performance location.

The changes clause does not apply to government purchases for commercial items.

A unilateral change occurs when the government orders the contractor to change the performance requirements without prior contractor approval. The changes, however, must be within the scope of the original contract. For example, the contracting officer cannot direct a construction contractor to perform research and development services. The changes clause used by the contracting officer depends on the contract type.

The contracting officer is the only individual authorized to make these changes. The document used to implement a unilateral change is a change order (SF 30, Amendment of Solicitation/Modification of Contract). If the change order requires the contractor to incur additional costs, the contracting officer must equitably adjust the contract to compensate the contractor. An equitable adjustment may include changes to:

■ Contract price

■ Delivery or performance schedules

■ Inspection requirements.

If the change order reduces the overall cost to the contractor, the contracting officer adjusts the contract accordingly. Failure to agree on an equitable adjustment may become a dispute under the disputes clause. For more information on change orders, see FAR 43.2.

CONTRACT MODIFICATIONS

Contract modifications are written changes in the specification, delivery point, delivery rate, contract period, price, quantity, or other contract provisions of an existing contract. These changes may be accomplished by unilateral action under a contract provision or by bilateral (or mutual) action of the contracting parties. Bilateral changes must be in writing and signed by both parties. A unilateral modification is signed only by the contracting officer. (The contractor must proceed as directed even if it doesn't agree with the changes because the government "promises" the contractor that it can submit a request for equitable adjustment.)

Unilateral modifications are typically used to:

■ Make administrative changes

■ Issue change orders

■ Make changes authorized by clauses other than a changes clause (such as property clause, options clause, suspension of work clause)

■ Issue termination notices.

Bilateral modifications, also called "supplemental agreements," are contract modifications that both the contractor and the contracting officer sign. Bilateral modifications are used to:

■ Make negotiated equitable adjustments, resulting from a change order

■ Definitize letter contracts

■ Reflect other party agreements that modify the contract terms.

Only contracting officers, acting within the scope of their authority, can execute modifications on the government's behalf. Contracting officers use SF 30, Amendment of Solicitation/Modification of Contract, for contract modifications. A contract will not be modified solely for the contractor's benefit. Furthermore, modifications for mutual consideration must show net benefits to the government.

Modifications to contracts, including those issued unilaterally, are priced before they are executed, if that can be done without adversely affecting the government's interest. If the modification could result in a significant cost increase, either a final price or a ceiling price is negotiated. For more information on modifications, see FAR 43.

CONSTRUCTIVE CHANGES

Constructive changes, also known as *de facto* changes, are actions (or failures to act) by the government that cause the contractor to perform additional or different responsibilities from those expressed in the contract. These changes are not accompanied by a formal change order. The following constitute constructive changes:

■ Defective specifications

■ Requirements to adhere to delivery schedules when a contractor is entitled to an extension (e.g., for an excusable delay due to an act of God)

■ Excessive inspection requirements

■ Unwarranted rejection of supplies following inspection

■ Acceleration of the contract's performance requirements

■ Interference with the contractor's performance by government personnel.

The contractor should notify the contracting officer in writing when a government action affects the contract terms and conditions. This notifi-

cation or claim should be sent as soon as the change is identified. Upon
claim receipt, the contracting officer investigates the circumstances of
the alleged change. If the contracting officer agrees with the claim, the
alleged government action is confirmed as a legitimate change and
appropriate written directions are issued. Contractors should be certain
they receive written authorization before proceeding with a constructive
change.

If, on the other hand, the contracting officer feels the action is "within
the scope of the contract," he or she may reject the claim. In that case,
the contractor files a claim under the disputes clause.

GOVERNMENT-FURNISHED PROPERTY

For most government contracts, the contractor will furnish all property
or equipment necessary to perform the requirements. However, the government allows contractors to use government property for the purpose
of significant savings, standardization, or expedited contract production—or if the government benefits. Some common types of government-furnished property include facilities, materials, special tooling, and
special test equipment.

Contractors must segregate the government-furnished property or equipment from their own. In addition, contractors must maintain adequate
control records, such as receipt documents and maintenance records.
The government identifies all government-furnished property in the
solicitation and resulting contract. See FAR 45 for more information on
government-furnished property.

INSPECTION AND ACCEPTANCE

Inspection and acceptance requirements protect the government's interests. For purchases at or below the simplified acquisition threshold (and
for the purchase of commercial items), the government typically relies on
the contractor to test whether the items conform to the contract quality

requirements. The contractor must keep complete records of its inspection work and make them available to the government.

For noncommercial purchases that exceed the simplified acquisition threshold, the contractor has the following inspection requirements:

■ The contractor must maintain an acceptable system for the inspection of supplies or services.

■ The contractor must maintain records that completely document the inspections it conducts during contract performance.

■ The government may inspect and test all supplies and services at any time prior to acceptance. The government also can inspect the subcontractors' plants.

■ The government may require replacement or correction of supplies and services that fail to meet contract requirements. If the contractor fails to replace or fix the rejected supplies or services, the government can have another contractor provide them and charge any additional costs to the defaulting contractor. The government also can terminate the contract.

If the government fails to conduct inspections or tests, the contractor still must furnish supplies as specified by the contract.

Acceptance is the government's acknowledgment that the supplies or services meet the contractual requirements, as evidenced by the signature of the government's authorized representative (typically, the contracting officer). The government typically uses three forms for inspection and receiving documentation:

■ DD Form 250, Material Inspection and Receiving Report

■ DD Form 1155, Order for Supplies and Services

■ SF 44, Purchase Order-Invoice-Voucher.

Each contract specifies the point of acceptance for the supplies and services. Title to the supplies and services passes to the government upon acceptance.

Under the inspection clause for FFP contracts, acceptance is conclusive unless there is fraud, latent defect, gross mistake amounting to fraud, or as otherwise provided in the contract.

FIRST ARTICLE APPROVAL

First article testing is a specialized type of government inspection required for some contracts. A first article is a preproduction sample or lot of items prepared for the contract. This inspection procedure ensures that the contractor can furnish a product that conforms to the contract requirements. The contract may require the government, the contractor, or both to perform first article testing; upon successful completion, the contractor may begin production.

First article testing may be appropriate when:

- The contractor has not previously furnished the product to the government.

- The government requires assurance that the product is appropriate for its intended use.

- An approved first article will serve as a manufacturing standard.

First article testing is usually inappropriate for:

- Research and development contracts

- Products requiring qualification before award (such as when an applicable qualified product list exists)

- Products normally sold in the commercial market

- Products covered by complete and detailed technical specifications.

continued

continued

A first article should not be confused with a bid sample. Bid samples are used by bidders or offerors to demonstrate their products' characteristics. First articles, in contrast, are samples of the items required by the contract. See FAR 9.3 for more information on first articles.

CONTRACTOR DATA RIGHTS

One of the most complex and misunderstood areas in federal contracting is determining the owner of data produced or used under a contract. Do the data rights belong to the government or the contractor? Both have valid and specific interests in data.

The government has extensive needs for technical data, such as research results, engineering drawings, and manuals. Therefore, in most contracts, the government exerts its authority to acquire data rights. Contractors, on the other hand, have an economic interest in the data components or processes that they have developed at their own expense. Public disclosure of these data could jeopardize their competitive advantage.

Each contract arrangement includes provisions to balance the government's need for data rights against the contractor's interest in protecting proprietary data. The government uses three types of data rights to protect its interests:

■ *Unlimited rights.* The government's right to use, duplicate, or disclose data for any purpose (and to have or permit others to do so).

■ *Limited rights.* Limited data rights may include restrictions on the data being (1) released or disclosed outside the government, (2) used by the government for manufacture, or (3) in the case of computer software documentation, used for preparing the same or similar computer software.

■ *Government purpose license rights.* Rights to use, duplicate, or disclose data, in whole or in part and in any manner, for government purposes only, or to permit others to do so for government purposes only (such as for competitive procurements).

The source of funds used in developing data dictates the type of data rights clause in a contract. If the data were developed at the government's expense (i.e., the government paid the contractor for developing the product), the government holds unlimited rights. When the contractor develops the data wholly at its private expense and the information has not been made available to the public without restrictions, the government holds limited rights. The limited rights protection is effective only if the contractor suitably identifies and marks the data to which the government asserts limited rights. Government purpose license rights typically apply to partially funded contracts (or contracts for which the contractor has contributed more than 50% of the development costs).

RECORDS RETENTION

Contractors and subcontractors must retain and make available to the government certain books, records, documents, and other supporting evidence, if the contract exceeds the simplified acquisition threshold. Generally, contractors must retain these records for three years after final contract payment. Most accounting or financial records, however, have a retention period of four years. In addition, many contractual arrangements have a retention policy that is unique to the contract.

The retention period is calculated from the end of the fiscal year during which the contractor entered a charge or allocated a cost to a government contract or subcontract. For example, assume Urban Crisis, Inc., researched highway congestion in urban areas for the Department of Transportation and received the final contract payment on November 15, 2005. Urban Crisis, Inc., operates on a calendar-year basis (January 1 through December 31) and the contract requires a four-year retention period. Therefore, the contractor must maintain the contract records until December 31, 2009:

Final payment date	November 15, 2005
Retention period	4 years
End of retention period	December 31, 2009

If the contractor operated on a fiscal-year basis (October 1 through September 30), the end of the retention period would be September 30, 2010:

Final payment date	November 15, 2005
Retention period	4 years
End of retention period	September 30, 2010

AUDITS/EXAMINATION OF RECORDS

The government can examine and audit books, records, documents, and other data relating to claimed performance costs; cost and pricing data used to support contract pricing; and any cost, funding, or performance reports required under the contract. This audit requirement applies to virtually all contracts; however, because audits require significant time and expense to perform, they are typically not used for small purchases (under $100,000) or contracts awarded under sealed bidding procedures.

The government's right of examination includes its right to inspect the contractor's plants that are engaged in performing the government contracts at all reasonable times. This right begins at the start of the contract and continues until the retention period expires (usually four years for financial records), following the final contract payment. These audit rights appear in 10 U.S.C. 254 (b) and (c).

Auditors act as the contracting officer's principal financial advisors on matters relating to contract cost/price. They express opinions on the allowability, allocability, and reasonableness of contract costs claimed by contractors for reimbursement. Auditors use applicable public laws, procurement regulations (the FAR), and cost accounting standards to determine contractor compliance.

CONTRACT DISPUTES ACT

The Contract Disputes Act of 1978 established procedures and requirements for asserting and resolving claims by (or against) contractors. This act allows contractors with a dispute to seek redress outside the judiciary system, thereby saving the government and contractor time and money. The main provisions of this act include:

■ Strengthening the authority and capabilities of the Board of Contract Appeals

■ Giving contractors the option of direct appeal to the U.S. Claims Court, bypassing the Board of Contract Appeals

■ Providing the government with the right to seek judicial review of adverse Board of Contract Appeals decisions

■ Providing contracting activities with more flexibility in negotiating and settling contract disputes

■ Establishing new Board of Contract Appeals procedures for handling small claims

■ Establishing a statutory requirement for interest on claims

■ Establishing a requirement for certification of contractor claims.

The disputes clause (at FAR 52.233-1) applies to all government contracts, either expressed or implied. This clause requires the contractor to pursue resolution of its claims through the administrative procedures delineated in the Contract Disputes Act. In addition, the clause requires the contractor to continue contract performance pending resolution of a dispute, unless the dispute arises outside the contract or in breach of the contract.

Claims and Disputes

Many times during contract performance, the government and the contractor differ on contractual issues. If the differences persist, the contractor should submit a written claim to the contracting officer. A claim is a written demand or written assertion by one of the contracting parties seeking, as a matter of right, payment, an adjustment or interpretation of contract terms, or other relief arising under or relating to the contract. All disputes under government contracts begin with a claim submitted by a contractor.

For a claim to be valid, it must:

■ Be in writing. A voucher, invoice, or other routine request for payment does not, in itself, constitute a claim.

■ Seek the payment of a specific sum, adjustment of the contract terms, or other relief.

■ Be certified by the contractor, if the claim seeks relief in excess of $100,000. For example:

> I certify that the claim is made in good faith; that the supporting data are accurate and complete to the best of my knowledge and belief; that the amount requested accurately reflects the contract adjustment for which the contractor believes the government is liable; and that I am duly authorized to certify the claim on behalf of the contractor.

The government tries to resolve all claims by mutual agreement at the contracting officer's level and to avoid litigation if at all possible. Normally, the contracting officer reviews the pertinent facts of the claim and, after discussions or negotiations with the contractor, reaches agreement and modifies the contract. The contracting officer may obtain advice and assistance from legal and other advisors, but it is ultimately his or her responsibility to make the final decision.

The contracting officer must issue a decision on any claim of less than $100,000 within 60 days from receipt of the contractor's written request for that decision. If the claim exceeds $100,000, the contracting officer must, within 60 days from receipt of a written request, either issue a decision or notify the contractor when a decision will be issued. The contract-

ing officer furnishes the final decision in writing. This decision statement, at a minimum, includes:

■ Description of the claim or dispute

■ References to pertinent contract provisions

■ Statements of the factual areas of agreement/disagreement

■ Statement of the contracting officer's decision, with supporting rationale.

If the contractor disagrees with the contracting officer's determination or
assessment, he or she may appeal the decision to the Board of Contract
Appeals within 90 days from receipt of the decision. The notice should
indicate that an appeal is planned, reference the decision, and identify the
contract by number.

Board of Contract Appeals

The Board of Contract Appeals hears and decides contract disputes. In
performing its functions, the Board of Contract Appeals may issue sub-
poenas that are enforceable by the U.S. District Courts. In addition, the
board can seek related facts and data through the discovery process and
take depositions, as necessary.

Many federal agencies have established boards, such as the General
Services Administration Board of Contract Appeals and the Department
of Transportation Board of Contract Appeals. The Armed Services Board
of Contract Appeals handles all DOD contract disputes. Some small agencies use GSA's Board of Contract Appeals.

For a claim of $50,000 or less, small claim or expedited procedures pro-
vide a decision within 120 days. Claims that are $100,000 or less come
under accelerated procedures, which require a decision within 180 days,
whenever possible. If the claim is for more than $100,000, the Board will
conduct a formal hearing with no time limit on the decision.

Either the contractor or the government may appeal the Board's decision within 120 days with the U.S. Court of Appeals. If either party disagrees with the Court of Appeals decision, it must file an appeal with the Supreme Court within 60 days. Supreme Court decisions are final.

The Contract Disputes Act allows contractors to appeal a contracting officer's decision directly to the U.S. Claims Court, bypassing the Board of Contract Appeals. If a contractor chooses this route, it must file the appeal within one year of the contracting officer's final decision. There are no time limits on the court to make a decision. Most contractors favor using the Board of Contract Appeals because it tends to be less costly and time-consuming.

Either party may appeal the decision of the Claims Court to the Court of Appeals within 60 days of the decision, and the Court of Appeals decision may be appealed to the Supreme Court. The Equal Access to Justice Act permits small businesses and individuals to recover attorney or agent fees if they prevail in administrative or court actions brought against the government, if the agency's position was not substantially justified. The contractor has 30 days from the decision date to submit an application for reimbursement to the government (or the agency involved in the dispute).

ALTERNATIVE DISPUTE RESOLUTION

Federal courts are swamped with cases, causing the average dispute to take more than a year to resolve. If a contractor wants an accelerated decision, it might consider alternative dispute resolution (ADR). The Administrative Disputes Act of 1990 authorizes the use of ADR to settle disputes brought to the Board of Contract Appeals or the Claims Court. Each ADR must have:

■ An issue in controversy

■ A voluntary election by both parties to participate in the ADR process

■ An agreement on alternative procedures and terms to be used in lieu of formal litigation

■ Process participation by officials of both parties who have authority to resolve the issue.

Requests to use ADR must be made jointly by the government and the contractor to the board or court that is responsible for hearing the dispute. The board will then examine the issues involved with the dispute and determine whether ADR would be appropriate. If a contracting officer rejects a contractor's request for ADR, the contractor must be given a written explanation citing the reasons why the procedures are inappropriate for the dispute resolution. Contractors that reject an ADR request must inform the agency of their objections in writing.

Alternative dispute resolution procedures may include, but are not limited to, conciliation, facilitation, mediation, fact-finding, minitrials, arbitration, and use of ombudsmen. Federal agencies are encouraged to use ADR procedures to the maximum extent practicable.

TERMINATION FOR CONVENIENCE

Each government contract contains a provision not found in commercial contracts—the ability to terminate the contract for any reason. The "termination for convenience" provision exists because of the government's need to end contracts when its requirements are eliminated, such as when a war ends or when Congress eliminates a program. The government may terminate the entire contract or just part of it. Partial terminations can actually occur several times during the life of a contract. The contracting officer makes those decisions.

When a contracting officer terminates a contract for the government's convenience, he or she provides the contractor with a written "notice of termination" stating:

■ That the contract is being terminated for the convenience of the government

■ The effective date of termination

■ The extent of termination

■ Any special instructions

■ The steps the contractor should take to minimize the impact on personnel, if the termination, together with all other outstanding terminations, will result in a significant reduction in the contractor's work force.

If the government terminates a contract for convenience, it must pay the costs incurred by the contractor up to the termination date, plus a reasonable profit. The government uses several different termination clauses depending on the kind of contract. See FAR 52.249-1 though 52.249-5.

TERMINATION FOR DEFAULT

The government holds the contractual right to terminate a contract in whole or in part if a contractor fails to perform its obligations under the contract. The government may exercise its right to terminate a contract if the contractor fails to:

■ Deliver supplies or perform services within the time specified in the contract

■ Perform other contract provisions

■ Make progress, endangering performance of the contract.

Human nature being what it is, contracting officers try very hard not to let conditions deteriorate to the point where they must terminate a contract for default. First, it shows poor contract management. Second, it brands a contractor as a "non-performer" and endangers future business. Most contracting officers much prefer to terminate a contract using termination for convenience procedures, which enables them to negotiate the remaining contract requirements with another contractor.

When a contract is terminated for default, the contracting officer provides the contractor with a written notice of termination. The written notice of termination for default must be unequivocally clear and must state:

■ The contract number and date

■ The acts or omissions constituting the default

■ That the contractor's right to proceed with further performance of the contract has been terminated

■ That the supplies and services under the terminated contract are subject to reprocurement against the contractor's account and that the contractor is liable for any excess costs

■ That the notice constitutes a decision of the contracting officer that the contractor is in default as specified and the contractor can appeal according to the procedures stated in the disputes clause.

If the government terminates a contract for default, the contractor becomes liable for expenditures on undelivered work and must repay any advance or progress payments applicable to the undelivered work. The contracting officer may direct the contractor to transfer title and deliver all completed or partially completed (but not yet accepted) supplies and manufactured materials to the government. The government will then pay the contractor the contract price for any completed supplies that were delivered and accepted. The contracting officer and the contractor will negotiate the value for the partially completed supplies and the manufacturing materials provided.

Termination for default is serious business. Not only does a contractor lose its contract, but the contractor must also pay the government for any excess reprocurement costs. Reprocurement costs are those incurred by the government in procuring other sources, supplies, and services similar to those terminated for default. In addition, reprocurement costs include any other damages the government incurs as a result of the terminated contract. Therefore, the contractor is responsible for the costs the government pays to an alternate source that exceed the price payable under the contract.

The following example illustrates how the reprocurement process works. Suppose a contractor defaulted on a contract to build five executive desks for $250,000. The contractor completed two of the desks but was behind schedule on the others. The government requested that the contractor deliver the two completed desks and stop work on the other three desks:

5 executive desks	$ 250,000
Payment for 2 completed desks	$ 100,000
Balance of contract	$ 150,000

Next, the government decided to purchase the remaining desks from an alternate source for $175,000. The contractor that defaulted must pay the difference:

Alternate source price	$ 175,000
Original contract price (3 desks)	$ 150,000
Balance owed by default contractor	$ 25,000

If a contract was terminated for default and it is subsequently determined that the contractor's delay was excusable, the termination for default may be converted to a termination for convenience. For example, if the contractor can establish that the failure was due to the following circumstances, it would be considered excusable:

■ Defective specifications

■ Late or defective government-furnished property

■ Suspensions of work and stop-work orders received

■ Strikes

■ Floods or fires

■ Freight embargoes.

If the contractor believes that the termination for default was improper because its failure to perform the contract was excusable, it may file a claim under the disputes clause. The government uses several different termination clauses for various kinds of contracts. See FAR 52.249-6 though 52.249-10.

CONTRACT CLOSEOUT

Contract closeout is the action that occurs when a contractor completes a contract. The primary purpose of a contract closeout is to ensure that the contractor has complied with all the contractual requirements and that the government has fulfilled its obligations. A contract is considered fully completed when:

■ The contractor has completed the required deliveries and the government has inspected and accepted the supplies

■ The contractor has performed all services and the government has accepted these services

■ All option provisions, if any, have expired

■ The government has given the contractor a notice of complete contract termination.

A contract is fully closed when it is both physically and administratively complete.

■　■　■

Contract performance is just the tip of the iceberg when it comes to fulfilling your contractual obligations. Contractors also must comply with applicable labor laws, prepare required reports (such as monthly status reports), seek contract changes/modifications, perform inspections, prepare invoices, retain contractual records, and carry out other administrative duties. All requirements that apply to your contract are spelled out in the contract document.

■　■　■

> ## Closing Remarks
>
> To quote a famous tennis phrase, "the ball is now in your court." This book gives you information that will help you break into and succeed in the federal government marketplace. If you learn the system and are patient and persistent, you can make good money, even big money, doing business with the federal government.

Acronyms

APPENDIX

"I knew it was time to simplify our organization when we started creating acronyms for our acronyms."

This business is filled with acronyms. To be successful doing business with the government, you need to be familiar with a multitude of acronyms.

ACO	Administrative Contracting Officer
ADR	Alternative Dispute Resolution
AF	Air Force
AGAR	Department of Agriculture Acquisition Regulation
AID	Agency for International Development
AIDAR	Agency for International Development FAR Supplement
AMS	Acquisition Management System
B&P	Bid and Proposal
BA	Basic Agreement
BIC	Business Information Center
BOA	Basic Ordering Agreement
BPA	Blanket Purchase Agreement

BSC   Business Service Center

CAGE   Commercial and Government Entity

CAO   Contract Administration Office

CAR   Department of Commerce Acquisition Regulation

CAS   Cost Accounting Standards

CASB   Cost Accounting Standards Board

CBD   Commerce Business Daily

CCR   Central Contractor Registration

CDRL   Contract Data Requirements List

CFR   Code of Federal Regulations

CICA   Competition in Contracting Act (1984)

CLIN   Contract Line Item Number

CO   Contracting Officer

COC   Certificate of Competency

COR   Contracting Officer's Representative

COTR   Contracting Officer's Technical Representative

CPAF   Cost Plus Award Fee

CPFF   Cost Plus Fixed Fee

CPIF   Cost Plus Incentive Fee

D&B   Dun & Bradstreet

DAASC   Defense Automatic Addressing System Center

DARPA   Defense Advanced Research Projects Agency

DCAA   Defense Contract Audit Agency

DCMC   Defense Contract Management Command

DEAR   Department of Energy Acquisition Regulation

DFARS   Department of Defense FAR Supplement

DFAS	Defense Finance and Accounting Service
DLA	Defense Logistics Agency
DLIS	Defense Logistics Information Service
DOA	Department of Agriculture
DOC	Department of Commerce
DOD	Department of Defense
DOE	Department of Energy
DOJ	Department of Justice
DOT	Department of Transportation
DRL	Data Requirements List
DUNS	Data Universal Numbering System
EC	Electronic Commerce
EDI	Electronic Data Interchange
EFT	Electronic Fund Transfer
EPA	Environmental Protection Agency
EPS	Electronic Posting System
ESB	Emerging Small Business
FAA	Federal Aviation Administration
FAC	Federal Acquisition Circular
FAR	Federal Acquisition Regulation
FARA	Federal Acquisition Reform Act (1996)
FASA	Federal Acquisition Streamlining Act (1994)
FBO	FedBizOpps
FIC	Federal Information Center
FFP	Firm-Fixed Price
FOB	Free on Board

FOIA	Freedom of Information Act
FPDS-NG	Federal Procurement Data System-Next Generation
FP/EPA	Fixed-Price with Economic Price Adjustment
FPI	Fixed-Price Incentive
FR	*Federal Register*
FSC	Federal Supply Classification
FSG	Federal Supply Group
FSS	Federal Supply Schedule
FY	Fiscal Year
G&A	General and Administrative
GAAP	Generally Accepted Accounting Principles
GAO	General Accounting Office
GFP	Government-Furnished Property
GPO	Government Printing Office
GSA	General Services Administration
GSAR	General Services Administration Acquisition Regulation
GWAC	Government-wide Acquisition Contract
HCA	Head of Contracting Activity
HHS	Health and Human Services
HHSAR	Department of Health and Human Services Acquisition Regulation
HUBZone	Historically Underutilized Business Zone
ID/IQ	Indefinite Delivery/Indefinite Quantity
IFB	Invitation for Bid
IFSS	International Federal Supply Schedule
IR&D	Independent Research and Development

LCC	Life-Cycle Costing
LH	Labor Hour
MAS	Multiple Award Schedule
NAICS	North American Industry Classification System
NASA	National Aeronautics and Space Administration
NAVSEA	Naval Sea Systems Command
NCMA	National Contract Management Association
NIIS	New Item Introductory Schedule
NIST	National Institute of Standards and Technology
NOA	Notice of Award
NSF	National Science Foundation
NSN	National Stock Number
NTIS	National Technical Information Service
ODC	Other Direct Cost
OFPP	Office of Federal Procurement Policy
O/H	Overhead
OMB	Office of Management and Budget
OSDBU	Office of Small and Disadvantaged Business Utilization
PCO	Procurement Contracting Officer
PIIN	Procurement Instrument Identification Number
PO	Purchase Order
POC	Point of Contact
PR	Purchase Request
PSA	Presolicitation Announcement
PSC	Product and Service Code
R&D	Research and Development

RFI	Request for Information
RFP	Request for Proposal
RFQ	Request for Quotation
RFTP	Request for Technical Proposal
SADBUS	Small and Disadvantaged Business Utilization Specialist
SAP	Simplified Acquisition Procedures
SAS	Single Award Schedule
SAT	Simplified Acquisition Threshold
SBA	Small Business Administration
SBDC	Small Business Development Center
SBIR	Small Business Innovation Research
SCA	Service Contract Act
SCF	Simplified Contract Format
SCORE	Service Corps of Retired Executives
SDB	Small Disadvantaged Business
SEC	Securities and Exchange Commission
SF	Standard Form
SIC	Standard Industrial Classification
SIP	Schedule Input Program
SML	Solicitation Mailing List
SOW	Statement of Work
SSA	Source Selection Authority
STTR	Small Business Technology Transfer Research Program
T&M	Time and Materials
TAR	Department of Transportation Acquisition Regulation
TCO	Termination Contracting Officer

TINA	Truth in Negotiations Act
UCF	Uniform Contract Format
USC	United States Code
USCG	United States Coast Guard
USDA	United States Department of Agriculture
VA	Department of Veterans Affairs
VAAR	Veterans Administration FAR Supplement
VBOP	Veterans Business Outreach Program
VSB	Very Small Business
WBC	Women's Business Center
WBS	Work Breakdown Structure
WOB	Woman-Owned Business
WOSB	Woman-Owned Small Business

Federal Agencies and Departments

© 1999 Randy Glasbergen.   www.glasbergen.com

GLASBERGEN

"I heard on TV that everyone is getting rich on the Internet. Is this little slot where the money comes out?"

The federal government is huge. There are so many federal agencies and departments that it would take more then 50 pages of this book to list them all. The best way to locate information on these is to visit the following web address:

WWW.LIB.LSU.EDU/gov/fedgov.html

This website provides a listing or directory of most government agencies and departments (including links to their web pages).

Glossary

Copyright 2001 by Randy Glasbergen.   www.glasbergen.com

"Yes, I have some management experience.
When I was ten, I ran a lemonade stand.
I had 40 lemons working for me."

> The glossary terms that are enclosed in a box represent a little government contracting humor (which may or may not be more accurate than the term's formal definition).

Acceptance
The act of an authorized government representative, by which the government assumes ownership of existing identified supplies tendered or approves specific services rendered as partial or complete performance of the contract.

Accumulating Costs
The collecting of cost data in an organized manner, such as through a system of accounts.

Administrative Contracting Officer (ACO)
A contracting officer who is responsible for administrative functions after a contract is awarded.

Advance Payments
Advances of money by the government to a contractor, prior to contract performance.

Affiliates
Business concerns, organizations, or individuals related, directly or indirectly, when (1) either one controls or has the power to control the other, or (2) a third party controls or has the power to control both. Some examples of control include (but are not limited to) interlocking management or ownership, identity of interests among family members, shared facilities and equipment, common use of employees, or a business entity organized following the debarment, suspension, or proposed debarment of a contractor that has the same or similar management, ownership, or principal employees as the contractor that was debarred, suspended, or proposed for debarment.

Agency
One party, known as the principal, appoints another party, known as the agent, to enter into a business or contractual relationship with a third party.

Agency Supplements
Regulations issued by individual federal agencies for the purpose of supplementing the basic Federal Acquisition Regulation (FAR).

Allocable Cost
A cost that is assignable or chargeable to one or more cost objectives in accordance with the relative benefits received.

Allowable Cost
A cost that meets the tests of reasonableness and allocability and complies with generally accepted accounting principles and cost accounting standards, specific limitations or exclusions set forth in FAR 31, and agreed-to terms between contractual parties.

Amendment
A change (correction, deletion, or addition) to a solicitation before it is due. The amendment becomes part of the resulting contract.

Appropriation
Authority to obligate public funds that will result in immediate or future outlays.

AUDITORS—People who go in after the war is lost and bayonet the wounded.

Basic Ordering Agreement (BOA)
A written instrument of understanding, negotiated between a contractor and an agency, contracting activity, or contracting office, that contains (1) terms and clauses applying to future contracts (orders) between the parties during its term, (2) a description, as specific as practicable, of supplies or services to be provided, and (3) methods for pricing, issuing, and delivering future orders under the basic ordering agreement. A basic ordering agreement is not a contract.

Bid
An offer in response to an invitation for bid (IFB).

BID—A wild guess carried out to two decimal places.

Bid and Proposal (B&P) Costs
Costs incurred in preparing, submitting, or supporting any bid or proposal, which are neither sponsored by a grant nor required in the performance of a contract.

BID OPENING—A poker game in which the losing hand wins.

Bidder
An offeror who submits a bid in response to an IFB.

Bidders List
A register maintained by a contracting activity that lists contractors who have expressed an interest in furnishing a particular supply or service.

Certificate of Competency (COC)
A certificate issued by the Small Business Administration stating that the holder is responsible (with respect to all elements of responsibility,

360 Federal Contracting Made Easy

including but not limited to, capability, competency, capacity, credit, integrity, perseverance, and tenacity) for the purpose of receiving and performing a specific government contract.

Closeout
The process for closing out the contract file following contract completion.

Commercial Items
Supplies or services that are sold competitively to the general public.

Competitive Range
All proposals that the contracting officer determines to have a reasonable chance of being selected for award based on cost or price and other factors stated in the solicitation.

COMPLETION DATE—The point at which liquidated damages begin.

Contingent Fee
Any commission, percentage, brokerage, or other fee that is contingent upon the success that a person or concern has in securing a government contract.

Contract
A mutually binding legal relationship, obligating the seller to furnish supplies or services and the buyer to pay for them.

Contracting Officer (CO)
A government agent with the authority to enter into, administer, or terminate contracts and make related determinations and findings.

Contracting Officer's Technical Representative (COTR)
A federal employee to whom a contracting officer has delegated limited authority (in writing) to make specific contract-related decisions.

CONTRACTOR—A gambler who never gets to shuffle, cut, or deal.

Cost Accounting Standards (CAS)
Standards designed to achieve uniformity and consistency in the cost accounting principles followed by government contractors and subcontractors on selected large-dollar-value contracts (see Part 30 of the FAR).

Cost and Pricing Data
All facts, as of the date of price agreement, that prudent buyers and sellers would reasonably expect to affect price negotiations.

Cost-Reimbursement Contracts
Contracts that provide for payment of allowable incurred costs to the extent prescribed in the contract. These contracts establish an estimate of total cost for the purpose of obligating funds and establishing a ceiling that the contractor may not exceed (except at its own risk) without the contracting officer's approval.

CRITICAL PATH METHOD—A management technique for losing your shirt under perfect control.

Debriefing
Informing unsuccessful offerors of the basis for the selection decision and contract award. This information includes the government's evaluation of the significant weak or deficient factors in the offeror's proposal.

DELAYED PAYMENT—A tourniquet applied at the pockets.

Delivery Order
A written order for supplies under an indefinite-delivery contract.

Direct Costs
Any cost that is specifically identified with a particular final cost objective.

Emerging Small Businesses
Firms that are no larger than 50% of the applicable small business size standard.

ENGINEER'S ESTIMATE—The cost of construction in heaven.

Evaluation Factors
Factors in selecting an offer for award.

FedBizOpps
The single government point-of-entry on the Internet for federal government procurement opportunities over $25,000.

Federal Acquisition Regulation (FAR)
The body of regulations that is the primary source of authority over the government procurement process.

Federal Register
A daily publication that informs the public of proposed rules, final rules, and other legal notices issued by federal agencies.

Federal Specifications (Specs)
Specifications and standards that have been implemented for use by all federal agencies.

Federal Supply Schedules
Indefinite-delivery contracts established by the General Services Administration with commercial contractors. These schedules provide federal agencies with a simplified process for obtaining commonly used supplies and services at prices associated with volume buying.

Fee (or Profit)
Money paid to a contractor over and above total reimbursements for allowable costs.

Fixed-Price Contract
A contract type that establishes a firm price regardless of the actual cost of contract performance or, in appropriate cases, an adjustable price up to a ceiling amount.

General Accounting Office (GAO)
The audit agency of the U.S. Congress. GAO has broad authority to conduct investigations on behalf of Congress and to review certain contract

decisions, including contract award protests and contracting officers' decisions.

Government-Furnished Property
Property in the possession of, or directly acquired by, the government and subsequently made available to the contractor.

Indefinite-Delivery Contract
A type of contract used when the exact times and/or quantities of future deliveries are unknown at the time of contract award. There are three variations of indefinite-delivery contracts: definite-quantity, requirements, and indefinite-quantity.

Independent Research and Development (IR&D) Cost
The cost effort that is neither sponsored by a grant nor required in performing a contract, and that falls within any of four areas: (1) basic research, (2) applied research, (3) development, and (4) systems and other concept formulation studies.

Invitation for Bid (IFB)
The solicitation document used in sealed bidding.

LAWYERS—People who go in after the auditors and strip the bodies.

Letter Contract
A written preliminary contractual instrument that authorizes the contractor to begin manufacturing supplies or performing services immediately.

LIQUIDATED DAMAGES—A penalty for failing to achieve the impossible.

LOW BIDDERS—Contractors who are wondering what they left out of their bids.

Micropurchases
Purchases that are $2,500 or less.

Modifications
Written changes to a solicitation/contract. If the modification is for a solicitation (request for proposal), it must be made after discussions between the offerors and the contracting officer. On the other hand, contract modifications are written changes in the specification, delivery point, delivery rate, contract period, price, quantity, or other provisions of an existing contract.

Option
A unilateral right in a contract by which, for a specified time, the government may elect to purchase additional supplies or services called for by the contract or may elect to extend the term of the contract.

Order of Precedence
A provision that establishes priority among various parts of a solicitation.

Pre-award Survey
An evaluation by a surveying activity of a prospective contractor's capability to perform a proposed contract.

Pre-bid/Preproposal Conference
A meeting held with prospective offerors before bid opening or before the closing date for proposal submission. The purpose of this conference is to brief the offerors and explain complicated specifications and requirements.

Progress Payments
Payments made under a fixed-price contract on the basis of either (1) costs incurred by the contractor as work progresses under the contract, or (2) physical progress in accomplishing the work.

PROJECT MANAGER—The conductor of an orchestra in which every musician is in a different union.

Protest
A written objection by an interested party to a solicitation, proposed award, or contract award.

Request for Proposal (RFP)
The solicitation document used in negotiated acquisitions.

Request for Quotation (RFQ)
A document used in soliciting quotations. RFQs are used when the government does not intend to award a contract on the basis of the solicitation, but wishes to obtain price, delivery, or other market information to be used in preparing a purchase order or for planning purposes.

Sealed Bidding
Method of procurement (prescribed in Part 14 of the FAR) in which the government publicly opens bids and awards the contract to the lowest responsive, responsible bidder.

Set-Aside
An acquisition reserved exclusively for offerors who fit into a specified category. For example, set-asides are commonly established for small businesses and businesses in labor surplus areas.

Simplified Acquisition Procedures (SAP)
Procurement procedures used for obtaining supplies and services that are under $100,000 (including purchase orders, blanket purchase agreements, and imprest funds).

Simplified Acquisition Threshold (SAT)
The $100,000 ceiling (or limit) on purchases of supplies and services using simplified acquisition procedures.

Size Standards
Measures established by the Small Business Administration to determine whether a business qualifies as a small business for purposes of implementing the socioeconomic programs enumerated in Part 19 of the FAR.

Small Business Concern
A concern (including its affiliates) that is independently owned and operated, not dominant in the field of operation in which it is bidding on government contracts, and qualifies as a small business under the criteria and size standards in 13 CFR Part 121.

Small Disadvantaged Business
A small business that is at least 51% owned by one or more individuals who are both socially and economically disadvantaged, or a publicly owned business that has at least 51% of its stock owned by one or more socially and economically disadvantaged individuals and that has management and daily business controlled by one or more such individuals.

Sole Source Acquisition
A contract for supplies and services that is entered into with only one source.

Source Selection
The process of soliciting and evaluating offers for award.

Specification
A document prepared by the government that describes the technical requirements of the supplies and services being acquired, including the criteria for determining whether these requirements are met.

Standard
A document that establishes engineering and technical limitations and applications of items, materials, processes, methods, designs, and engineering practices. It includes any related criteria deemed essential to achieve the highest practical degree of uniformity in materials or products, or interchangeability of parts used in those products.

Statute
A law enacted by the legislative branch of the government and signed by the President.

Task Order
A written order for services under an indefinite-delivery contract.

Time and Materials (T&M) Contract
A type of contract that provides for acquiring supplies and services on the basis of (1) direct labor hours at specified fixed hourly rates that include wages, overhead, general and administrative expenses, and profits, and (2) material handling costs as part of material costs.

Unallowable Costs
Any costs that, under the provisions of any pertinent law, regulation, or contract, cannot be included in prices, cost reimbursements, or settlements under a government contract.

Uniform Contract Format (UCF)
The solicitation/contract format used in most Invitations for Bid and Requests for Proposal.

Unsolicited Proposal
A written proposal that is submitted to an agency on the offeror's initiative for the purpose of obtaining a government contract. It is not in response to a formal or informal request.

Index

Defense Advanced Research Projects
Agency (DARPA), 58
Defense Contract Audit Agency
(DCAA), 35
Defense Contract Management
Command (DCMC), 201–202
Defense Finance and Accounting
Service (DFAS), 24
Defense Logistics Agency (DLA), 11,
24, 167–168, 201
Defense Logistics Information Service
(DLIS), 25
Deliveries or Performance (Section F),
239
delivery order, 301
delivery schedule, bid preparation,
197
Department of Agriculture
Acquisition Regulation (AGAR), 32
Department of Agriculture (DOA), 11,
99, 104, 320
Department of Commerce Acquisition
Regulation (CAR), 32
Department of Commerce (DOC),
104, 320
Department of Defense (DOD)
compared to other federal agencies,
7
Federal Acquisition Regulation, 26
guaranteed loans, 320
Mentor-Protégé Program, 113–115
small businesses, 57, 99, 104
Supplies or Services and
Prices/Costs (Section B),
236–237
Department of Defense FAR
Supplement (DFARS), 31–32
Department of Education, 104
Department of Energy Acquisition
Regulation (DEAR), 32
Department of Energy (DOE), 11, 99,
104, 320

Department of Health and Human
Services Acquisition Regulation
(HHSAR), 32
Department of Health and Human
Services (HHS), 11, 99, 104
Department of Interior (DOI), 11, 99,
320
Department of Justice (DOJ), 11, 270
Department of Labor, 43–44
Department of Transportation
Acquisition Regulation (TAR), 32
Department of Transportation (DOT),
11, 91–92, 99, 104
Department of Treasury (USTREAS),
11
Department of Veterans Affairs (VA),
11, 99
Description/Specifications/Statement
of Work (Section C), 238
designated industry group, 84
DFARS. See Department of Defense
FAR Supplement
DFAS. See Defense Finance and
Accounting Service
direct costs, 277
direct labor, 302
disabled veteran-owned business, 66
disadvantages of government
contracting, 15–17
dispute clause, 328
disputes, 336–338
Division of Program Certification and
Eligibility (DPCE), 90
DLA. See Defense Logistics Agency
DLIS. See Defense Logistics
Information Service
DOA. See Department of Agriculture
DOC. See Department of Commerce
DOD. See Department of Defense
DOE. See Department of Energy
DOI. See Department of Interior
Doing Business With GSA, 169

Need Answers to Your Questions about Federal Contracting?

These other resources from Management Concepts can help!

Federal Contracting Answer Book, by Terrence M. O'Connor and Mary Ann P. Wangemann
Using a Q&A format, *Federal Contracting Answer Book* provides clear, succinct answers to questions on all aspects of federal government contracting, particularly in the areas of new procedures and regulations. ISBN 1-56726-105-1, Product code B051, 528 pages, $99.

Winning Government Business: Gaining the Competitive Advantage, by Steve R. Osborne, Ph.D.
Focusing on how to win business from the federal government, *Winning Government Business* provides comprehensive treatment of the business development life cycle, equipping readers with the skills and knowledge they need to consistently win government contracts. ISBN 1-56726-106-X, Product code B06X, 320 pages, $62.

Government Proposals: Cutting through the Chaos, by Rebecca L. Shannon
This book makes the process of writing government proposals easier, smoother, and more effective than ever before. Checklists and sample materials are included. ISBN 1-56726-126-4, Product code B264, 240 pages, $49.

Guide to Contract Pricing: Cost and Price Analysis for Contractors, Subcontractors, and Government Agencies,
4th edition, by John Edward Murphy, CPCM
This brand new 4th edition takes the worry and guesswork out of contracting. From basic policy to analysis of various direct

and indirect costs, this book is a master reference for all your contract pricing questions. ISBN 1-56726-153-1, Product code B531, 250 pages, $99.

Past Performance Handbook, by Peter S. Cole and Joseph W. Beausoleil
Past Performance Handbook provides a comprehensive step-by-step approach to the use of past performance in government contracting. It addresses the two key aspects of past performance: evaluating an offeror's past performance as a factor for source selection, and evaluating the quality of a contractor's work upon completion of contract performance. ISBN 1-56726-103-5, Product code B035, 336 pages, $125.

How to Write a Statement of Work, 5th edition, by Peter S. Cole. ISBN 1-56726-148-5, Product code B485, 360 pages, $99 hardcover; 1-56726-149-3, Product code B493, $69 softcover.

The COR/COTR Answer Book, by Bob Boyd, CFCM. ISBN 1-56726-119-1, Product code B191, 440 pages, $79.

Pricing and Cost Accounting: A Handbook for Government Contractors by Darrell J. Oyer, CPA. ISBN 1-56726-089-6, Product code B896, 265 pages, $62.

The Work Breakdown Structure in Government Contracting by Gregory T. Haugan, Ph.D., PMP. ISBN 1-56726-120-5, Product code B205, 144 pages, $59

Order today for a 30-day risk free trial!
Visit www.managementconcepts.com or call (703) 790-9595.